Hooverville and the Unemployed

Seattle during the Great Depression

Randal Gravelle

Hooverville and the Unemployed

Dedication

For Jamie, because I can't sing.

Contents

Timeline

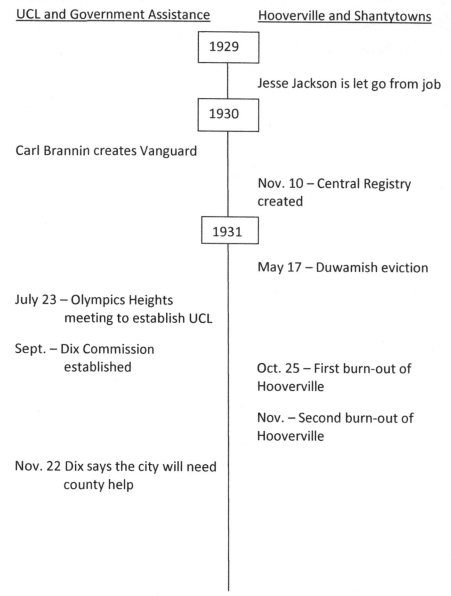

UCL and Government Assistance   Hooverville and Shantytowns

1929

Jesse Jackson is let go from job

1930

Carl Brannin creates Vanguard

Nov. 10 – Central Registry created

1931

May 17 – Duwamish eviction

July 23 – Olympics Heights meeting to establish UCL

Sept. – Dix Commission established

Oct. 25 – First burn-out of Hooverville

Nov. – Second burn-out of Hooverville

Nov. 22 Dix says the city will need county help

Hooverville and the Unemployed

UCL and Government Assistance	Hooverville and Shantytowns
	1932
Mar 8 – Dore elected Mayor	
July 4 – March on Olympia stopped	
	July 5 – Seattle Indians ballpark, Dugdale Park, is burned in arson
Aug. – Self-Help movement reaches peak	
	Aug. 21 – Union gospel Mission opens its doors
Sept. 8 – Georgetown commissary strike	
Nov. – UCL membership peaks at 12,000	
	1933
Jan. 17 – Second hunger march on Olympia	
Jan. 23 – WERA created	
Feb. 14 – Protesters take over County-City building	
Feb. 27 Commissary system abolished	

Hooverville and the Unemployed

UCL and Government Assistance	Hooverville and Shantytowns
Mar. 1 – Third march on Olympia blocked	
June 1 – FERA begins direct relief for states	
Nov. 8 – CWA created for winter work	

1934

Feb. – CWA work ends	Feb. – Mar. – Roy visits Hooverville
Mar. – UCL membership declines to 1,000	
June – WPA begins	
	July – Hooverville College is planned

1935

	Jan. 16 – Otto Johhanson is killed on the Duwamish
Apr. 5 – Congress sets aside $4 billion for WPA	May 3 – Robert Driscoll is captured
Dec. 1 – WPA employs 28,789 in Washington State	

Hooverville and the Unemployed

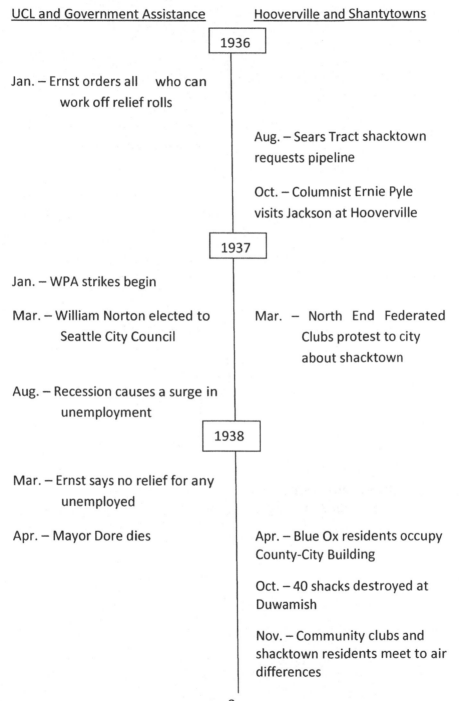

UCL and Government Assistance		Hooverville and Shantytowns
	1936	
Jan. – Ernst orders all who can work off relief rolls		
		Aug. – Sears Tract shacktown requests pipeline
		Oct. – Columnist Ernie Pyle visits Jackson at Hooverville
	1937	
Jan. – WPA strikes begin		
Mar. – William Norton elected to Seattle City Council		Mar. – North End Federated Clubs protest to city about shacktown
Aug. – Recession causes a surge in unemployment		
	1938	
Mar. – Ernst says no relief for any unemployed		
Apr. – Mayor Dore dies		Apr. – Blue Ox residents occupy County-City Building
		Oct. – 40 shacks destroyed at Duwamish
		Nov. – Community clubs and shacktown residents meet to air differences

Hooverville and the Unemployed

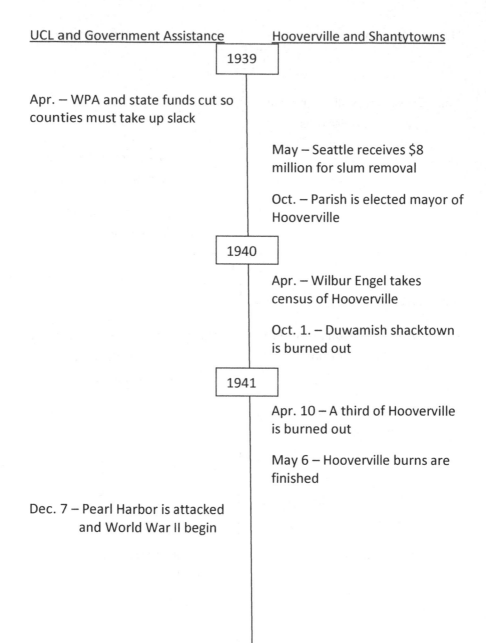

UCL and Government Assistance   **Hooverville and Shantytowns**

1939

Apr. – WPA and state funds cut so
counties must take up slack

May – Seattle receives $8
million for slum removal

Oct. – Parish is elected mayor of
Hooverville

1940

Apr. – Wilbur Engel takes
census of Hooverville

Oct. 1. – Duwamish shacktown
is burned out

1941

Apr. 10 – A third of Hooverville
is burned out

May 6 – Hooverville burns are
finished

Dec. 7 – Pearl Harbor is attacked
and World War II begin

Names

Barrett, Lawrence E. – President of the North End Federated Clubs; President of the Consolidated Clubs

Brannin, Carl– Co-editor of The Vanguard; Co-creator of the Unemployed Citizens League

Cronin, John F. – First President of the UCL

Dennett, Eugene– Agitprop for the Communists in Seattle

Dix, Irving F. – Chairman of Seattle's Commission for Improved Employment, better known as the Dix Commission.

Dobbins, Bill– Fourth President of the UCL

Dore, John– Mayor of Seattle 1932-1934, 1936-1938

Engel, Wilbur– Census-taker for Hooverville

Ernst, Charles F. – General Manager of Seattle's Local District Relief Organization; Director of WERA

Evans, Don H. – King County Commissioner

Harlin, Robert– Appointed Mayor of Seattle 1931

Hartley, Roland– Governor of Washington State 1925-1933

Hopkins, Harry– In charge of federal relief efforts under Franklin Roosevelt

Jackson, Jesse– First Mayor of Hooverville

Langlie, Arthur– Mayor of Seattle 1938-1941

Martin, Clarence Martin – Governor of Washington State 1933-1941

Murray, William H. – Communist and second President of the UCL; Reinstated President becoming the fifth and last President of the UCL

Nash, Louis– King County commissioner

Norton, William L. – Seattle City Councilman

Parish, George– Second Mayor of Hooverville

Pearl, Phil– Third President of the UCL

Roy, Donald Francis– Temporary Hooverville resident

Shannon, W. D. – In charge of King County relief

Stevenson, John– King County Commissioner

Wells, Hulet - Co-editor of The Vanguard; Co-creator of the Unemployed Citizens League

Williams, Pierce– Responsible for federal loans to Washington State

Zioncheck, Marion– West Seattle lawyer; member of the UCL; Congressman from Washington State First Congressional District

Abbreviations and Programs
CWA – Civil Works Administration
Dix Commission – Seattle's Commission for Improved Employment
FERA – Federal Emergency Relief Administration
IWW – International Workers of the World
Mass Action – Communist attempts to create support through strikes, marches and other protests
Self-Help – The UCL's attempt to provide supplies and assistance for their membership
TSW – Transient Services for Washington
UCL – Unemployed Citizens League
United Producers – UCL and other allied organizations
WERA – Washington Emergency Relief Administration
Workers Alliance – Communist unemployed organization
WPA –Works Progress Administration

Prologue

The smell of kerosene rose thick in the air as cans sloshed empty. Men who for ten years had called this place home stood by and watched. The assortment of sheds, cardboard and tin shanties and ramshackle homes built with cast away wood and nail were wetted down with the last drops of the combustible liquid. New needs dictated that this land be rededicated for a new purpose. It would no longer be a city for those with no job, no prospects and little hope. Instead it would become part of Franklin Roosevelt's Arsenal of Democracy for a war that lurked on the horizon.

The last of the kerosene was poured. Two-Name Dave Green, ex-car washer Wayne King, Hooverville Mayor George Parish and a handful of men in dirty clothes and battered hats stood on a berm. With a quiet whoosh the fire began. Smoke rose and dogs barked as a caterpillar tractor roared to life. King, a 34 year old, one-armed black man watched as his home burned and the clanking machine ripped into the shacks. "Going to be sleeping on a dock," he said. "Look at that rig busting down George's house. Just like nothing! Look at that. Sure is powerful. Right up into the fire."[1]

Meanwhile, Two-Name cranked up his player piano, one that had been bringing in nickels from his neighbors since he had brought the contraption down to the waterfront. This time, Green decided, it would be free. No one seemed to know how or where Two-Name picked up the nickelodeon, but today a jumpy, ragtime beat, St. Louis Blues, became the background to the snap and pop of the fire and the growling and shuddering of the bulldozer as it ripped through the wood and tin. On occasion, a roof held down by large stones or cement blocks crashed as it fell. The men watched, called out a warning to the tractor driver or made a joke to the man standing next to them.

Mayor Parish, red mustache neatly trimmed and pipe clenched in his teeth, looked on calmly. He recognized that it was almost the end of his reign. The slum town over which he held sway would soon be gone - not today but soon. He watched as the bulldozer cut his empire by a third. Next month the machinery and fire would return to finish the job. The shacks and sheds where he had sat and talked, where he had commiserated and laughed, where he made friends and kept the rougher element under-control were ripped to pieces and consumed by flame. Even as his world was being torn to pieces, he told reporters other property was already being claimed by those whose homes were felled that day. Building had commenced, he said, on a forty acre tract on West Marginal Way. Another shacktown sat on land at the base of Queen Anne Hill at Interbay. Perhaps he would join them there. Either way, though, this was the beginning of the end of his Hooverville Empire.

The last of the shacks on the waterfront would be plowed and burned in May. Some of the inhabitants would move on for a time, finally get a streak of luck and live in cozy apartments or clean, decent houses. Others would live on Skid Road panhandling even thirty years later. But the most famous Hooverville, the one whose picture came to symbolize the desperation and destitution of a generation; the one which at its height was home to 1,100 men, that Hooverville would end starting today. April 10, 1941. And, many said, good riddance.[2]

If you were a hobo or a drifter during the Great Depression, Seattle stood at the end of the line. There was no western option from here. As a result, the city absorbed those who realized that "better times" couldn't be found over the ridge, that moving from Boston to St. Louis, from Ogden to Eugene, from Spokane to Seattle took you nowhere but down the road. California had turned back the Okies and Arkies who had come there seeking the Promised Land. The young could take another lap around the nation looking for work or adventure or change of scenery. For the old, though, Seattle's Hooverville became the shore upon which the flotsam and jetsam washed up in an economic crash called the Great Depression.

While traditionally the Depression is said to have begun in 1929, for the people of the time, the start of the Depression commenced at different times for different people. For most, the Depression hit when they lost their jobs, houses and feeling of security. Generally, the Depression progressed from east to west, thus allowing the West Coast a couple of months warning to plan and prepare for the coming storm.

In 1930, months after the stock market crash, only 11% of Seattle workers were unemployed. By the time the most serious economic conditions began to invade Seattle, the people would be ready, or so many thought. Besides, this wasn't New York or Boston or Chicago. Westerners were used to dealing with hardship. Seattle had always been where the independent moved, those who could struggle on despite adversity. With neighborly help and individual initiative, they would persevere, just as their parents and grandparents had.

Little did they realize that this wasn't like any problem with which their parents had dealt. It wasn't a tornado or earthquake or other force of nature. As destructive as those things were, hard-work and determination could fix the damage and rebuild, at least materially, what was lost. There was no way to work harder to find jobs that simply didn't exist. By 1935, that 11% unemployment rate had climbed to over 25%.[3] And worse, it seemed as though rising unemployment might never stop. No one had faced a disaster this persistent and pervasive. This was a crumbling society in which there was no work and nowhere to move to find work. Determination was futile and optimism a lie.

Too often the story of the Great Depression is told from the airy heights of policy and big business. That story tells of how the convoluted machinations of bankers, politicians and intellectuals maneuvered to exploit or put right the catastrophe that caused the world to totter. That story follows the economic threads and high level political maneuverings that created a different political reality and

15

economic society. That story is important, but it is important only because of the effect it had on the people of the time. The real significance of the Great Depression lies in the damage, disillusionment and final rescue of individuals in a society facing economic collapse. In other words, the Depression is essentially a story of how those who paid the price for the easy credit and stock market gambles of the twenties, the unemployed, survived. And that is the story of this book.

For most people of the time, the Great Depression concerned one issue, unemployment. Reading about the lives of the common people of the time, one theme is repeated with amazing consistency. They lived in perpetual fear. There is a reason that when Franklin Roosevelt's said, "We have nothing to fear but fear itself," he struck such a strong chord in the people. He called it a "nameless, faceless" fear, but that wasn't quite true. They knew very well that the fear had a name – unemployment - and it had a face. It was the face of an uncle or friend or neighbor or, sometimes, the man or woman in the mirror. That face is shown in the photograph by Dorothea Lange in which a desperately thin woman holds her child and stares off into space as she contemplates where the next meal is coming from. It was captured in the flickering images on film as the Bonus Marchers, veterans of World War One, were burned out of their camps in an America they had fought to defend. And it is in a photograph of the Seattle waterfront in which hundreds of shack houses represented those who lost the employment lottery and ended up where no one ever imagined themselves.

That is the story this book attempts to tell. Statistics and dollar figures can't reproduce the individual lives and struggles of those hardest hit by the effects of the Depression. In order to understand the Depression, it is essential to understand those who faced the prevailing fear of the time, unemployment. How did they cope? How did the policies and politicians shape their lives? What did they do to try to "pull themselves up by their own bootstraps?"

While it's important to realize that each story of unemployment and desperation is unique in its details, it is possible to divide those who lost their jobs into two distinct groups. There were those who had been through unemployment and homelessness before, even during the supposed "good times," and there were the newly unemployed who believed the loss of a job was a serious but not devastating bump in the road.

The long-term unemployed castaways had already experienced the bewilderment and overwhelming anxiety that comes with job loss. Many had resorted to panhandling, prowling the back alley garbage cans and sleeping in the hobo jungles that dotted the entrances to most major cities. They were soon joined by foreigners with little or no support who had become stranded in America with no way home. The chronic unemployed and foreigners joined during the Depression to create the shacktowns that sprouted up around this country. They walked a dusty road of makeshift shanties and lived on the charity and the offal of society. They shuffled into shantytowns and slept in flea-infested shelters. They were different from the newly unemployed.

For those experiencing serious unemployment for the first time, this was a sobering challenge that metastasized into a life-altering experience that caused an uncertainty which never lost its grip, even decades later. They began by fighting since they assumed they could win. They read the want ads, applied for work well-below their level of education or experience and even organized with other recently unemployed men to form unions and cooperatives. But they ended up lost in ennui, realizing that the control they thought they had over their own life was an illusion.

This book follows the parallel paths these two groups of unemployed trod. It seeks to enter the shacks and shanties of the most destitute of the Great Depression and shine a light on their lives. At the same time, it looks at the more optimistic, recently unemployed as they attempted to cobble together a union and later fight for individual survival. Understanding these paths illuminates the dark realities of the time and gives us a more complete view of the tragedy that was the Great   Depression.

1

Shacktown: Eviction

Jesse Jackson, called "Jack" by friends, was a logger working north of Seattle near Bellingham, Washington. Jackson was a skinny man. He was once described as "small, brown-eyed, thin-lipped, gopher-toothed [with] a big smile [and] penetrating eyes [which] scintillated and sparkled."[1] Out in the forests of northwest Washington, Jackson worked a machine called the "donkey." After a tree was brought down, a line was attached to the tree. That line was connected to the donkey which was essentially a steam-powered winch. Jackson's job was to skid the tree down to a pick-up site using the machine. It was while working this machine that the Depression came home to him.

Jackson was originally from Texas where he was either a teacher, ranch hand or a professional baseball player, depending on his mood and the person to whom he was talking. At one point, he had been married but she died. When and how isn't recorded, but Jackson never remarried. Instead, he moved to Washington and set up hauling lumber.

The timber industry was hard hit by the depression, though. With people making less money, fewer houses were being built, and fewer houses meant less wood. The Washington lumber industry, a major employer in the state, was devastated by the bad economy. Roughly half of those involved in the trade lost their job between 1929 and 1931, the first two years of the Depression.[2] Hundreds of unemployed lumbermen soon found themselves standing in line next to Jackson waiting for that last paycheck.

For lumberjacks unemployment didn't just mean lost jobs. Since many lived onsite at lumber camps, it also meant lost housing. Therefore, there was nothing holding the men to any one place. As a result, many gave up trying to find jobs doing what they had been trained to do and filtered into the larger towns and cities. There they began looking for any work they could find, but competition for the few jobs was tight. Many of the unemployed lumberjacks figured that the larger the city, the greater the opportunities for work. After realizing that there were no jobs around Bellingham, especially for a man in his mid-forties, Jackson lit out for Seattle. Widowed, without children to support him, Jackson was truly on his own.[34]

A few men like Jackson, old and unemployed, had already found a miserable piece of property in Seattle to claim as their own. The land lay next to the Duwamish River between downtown and West Seattle on a manmade spot called Harbor Island. It was, at the time, the largest artificial island in the world. It was, also, a swampy, fetid field which had attracted no builders and was bordered on one side by a city dump. About fifty men had seen this as the perfect balance of undesirable enough to keep builders away but not so bad that tough men couldn't make it habitable. It was soon littered with their shacks and shanties. Here lived the despised, the transients, the unemployed and unemployable. Most citizens of Seattle accepted the fact that everyone needed a place to live, even the dispossessed. Still, no one wanted them to invade family oriented neighborhoods, nor did they believe bums should claim land that could be otherwise productive. In other words, both sides agreed that the Harbor Island shacktown was in a location that was an acceptable compromise.

It's not known exactly when the dispossessed began to move into this bug-and rat-infested place; before the present depression, certainly, and most probably even before the 1920s. Nevertheless, they had been there long enough to organize a rough community. This was their town-within-a-town. Rules had developed and houses, of a sort, were constructed. The men felt at home, or at least they had a shelter, which was the next best thing. Unfortunately, by 1930 City Fathers began to eye their swampland anew. Perhaps the property wasn't useless after all, Seattle's representatives figured. A new waterway down the Duwamish might be just the thing to rejuvenate the area. Of course, this waterway would cut right where the unwanted were living. The shacks had to come down; the shack-dwellers had to move on.

It was easy to find the laws to facilitate the removal of the men once the decision to take the land was made. It had been done before back in 1926. Then, the city had demanded that sixty squatter-houseboats be removed from the waterway adjacent to the shacktown to make for an easier passageway for ships.[5] The houseboats were moved or destroyed and the path cleared.

This removal would require a new justification, but it didn't take long to find it. Quoting the sanitary code, the city said that the squalid conditions were unacceptable. The proximity of the dump and the unhealthy conditions of the swampy ground made the area unsafe for human habitation. Clearly, this was not a new discovery; the land had always been unsafe. Now, though, the city wanted the land. Suddenly, Seattle officials became concerned about the health of the men living there, and it was for their own good that they were being pushed on. Where would they go, the displaced wanted to know. The city's concern for their well-being extended only as far as getting them out of the unsanitary conditions that blocked progress. Where the squatters went after that was no business of the city.

21

So on May 12, 1931, eleven days after the Empire State Building, the tallest, most advanced building in the world, opened, the residents at the Duwamish shacktown were given five days to clear out of the dilapidated shacks in which they resided. Fortunately it was late spring, leaving them plenty of time to plan for winter. The men packed their few belongings and headed down the road. They joined the others on Skid Road, under bridges and any other temporary hiding place they could find. There weren't many men. The city could simply absorb these downtrodden few. For now anyway.[6]

2

The City: Birth of an Idea

Most of the newly unemployed were not forced to live in shantytowns or sleep in parks. They were a vital part of the city. They still paid on mortgages or rented apartments and had been, until recently, hard-working men. They were the ones who rose at the crack of dawn and went to work no matter the weather or personal ailment. They climbed into their cars, waved goodbye to their children and motored to work. Or they architects and carpenters, worked in the bank and paved the streets. They didn't ask for help and they knew that their family relied on them.

At first, it was a surprise when they lost their jobs. They were momentarily stunned, certainly, but then they took a deep breath and proceeded forward. They knew that if they just persevered and went out every day, they would find something. Sure, they might have to take a pay cut or accept work outside their chosen field. These were hard times, after all. But they were from independent people and difficulty was nothing new. They checked the newspapers, talked to anyone who might know of an opening and pounded the pavement. But as the search for work extended from days to weeks to months, the initial surprise turned to shock. Many of the newly unemployed had always believed that the only people who didn't work were those who didn't really want to. Bums, they called them. Bums were lazy and shiftless with no ambition and even less sense of responsibility. Bums refused to work. Bums were looking for a hand out. Now, though, the guilty suspicion that they might be reduced to the very bums they disparaged began to eat at their

23

confidence. A man that couldn't support his own family was no man at all. They knew the talk because they had, just a short while before, spouted it and believed it. Shock turned to shame.

There is no average when talking about these men and women. They were Bill and Harriet or Tim down the street in the little brown house. For what it was worth, though, a 1934 survey gave a statistical view of the newly unemployed in Washington State. He was no new-comer to the state having lived there for over twenty years. A white male, forty-two years of age, he was married with 2.34 persons as dependents. He was an unskilled worker who had watched his life slowly dissemble. After having worked in his chosen field for fifteen years, he had been let go. He was able to find a job for a couple of years but it was in an unfamiliar field and it too petered out. Since then, he had spent the past ten months looking for work but had come up empty.[1]

Even for those who were still employed, the specter of that sad talk with the boss haunted their nights. Fear was ever present, even if they weren't a casualty yet. Bluff and confidence only lasted so long until the realization came that survival depended on a business that was on a precarious edge. Pay cuts and sweaty palms were the reality of the day.

Not everyone was down and out, though. Some had been in wars, both figurative and literal, and they understood that there was no room for surrender. A few tough, independent men decided to meet this thing head on. There were old International Workers of the World (IWW) members who had shut down Seattle during the General Strike of 1919. Hardcore communists, both old and new, sprung from the fertile ground of the Depression. Admirers of fascist Benito Mussolini and anarchists thought this might be their time. Among those who were searching for an alternative to the present distress were two Seattle socialists. Carl Brannin and Hulet Wells were part of the Seattle labor movement. They had fought bosses and politicians in the past, and they knew that fighting for a way forward was the only solution now.

Carl Brannin, born in 1888 and originally from Cisco, Texas, was skinny with jutting ears. He knew what it was to work hard, having sold subscriptions and hustled fruit at the local train station to raise tuition money for college. Brannin attended the Agricultural and Mechanical College of Texas where he worked on the student newspaper and went on strike against the college president. After graduation, he floated from job to job, selling insurance and real estate, working in a mill and doing home repair. He was a reader, though, and he thought deeply. He was influenced by the "single-tax" theory and was soon to come under the spell of a brand of active Christianity that advocated for the physical well-being of the individual as well as the spiritual. This guided him into a job at a YMCA in Dallas helping other men find work. There he began to understand the desperation that comes from being jobless. This educated his move to socialism where he campaigned for the Socialist Party candidate for President and called for public ownership of electricity. When World War I broke out, pacifist Brannin registered for the draft "under protest." He was so thin, though, that the draft board gave him a 4-F classification. Instead of being sent to Europe to fight, he was sent to Washington, D. C. to investigate conflicts between labor and management in war industries. By 1918 and the end of the War, Brannin knew something about hard work, desperate men and labor problems. Seattle would give him an advanced degree in these subjects.

In 1920, Seattle's reputation as a radical city drew Brannin. He had heard about the General Strike of 1919 which shut down the city and sent tremors through the nation. This was a place he could call home. Throughout his life, Brannin had written pieces for various labor newspapers and journals, so upon arriving in Seattle he contacted the local labor organization and continued writing. Unfortunately this provided him no income to speak of. Unable to find any work to provide for himself and Laura, his wife, the couple ended up in a shacktown that originally had been organized as an anarchist cooperative. The cooperative part of the town predictably fell apart, but the shacks remained and there the two lived.

Then, in 1922, he received good news from Texas. He had been given land there ten years prior by an aunt. As they were drilling some exploratory wells, oil oozed up. There was enough oil to allow Brannin and Laura to forget about work, move into more suitable housing and live comfortably, but he refused to let the new luxury spoil him. True, he used the influx of cash to travel but only so he might further his education. He also used his modest wealth to advocate for social justice and to help a local cause that was close to his heart. The Seattle Labor College, an institution started in 1920, educated those interested in unions and socialism. Brannin was now free to lecture and help with correspondence courses for workers. Eventually he became Director. While at the Labor College, Brannin met a like-minded man, Hulet Wells.

Coinciding with the beginning of the Depression, Brannin began his own labor newspaper in January 1930. It advocated for the unemployed and the poor. Calling it the Vanguard, Brannin brought in his close friend Wells to co-edit.[23]

Wells had his own eclectic history. He had traveled to the Klondike to make his fortune in the gold fields during the 1898 Alaskan gold rush. With gold hard to find and prices on supplies sky high, Wells headed back to Seattle broke. On the trip back,

Wells suffered from a case of typhoid fever. By the time he arrived in Seattle, he was delirious and, since he had no money, was taken to a charity hospital.

Hulet Wells (above) along with Carl Brannin was co-editor of the Vanguard and co-founder of the Unemployed Citizens League. *Wikipedia.*

After recovery, he found work in logging camps for a time. But Wells didn't enjoy country life or working in the wilderness. His life-long dream was to live and work in the city. In 1904, Wells finally achieved his goal and found a job at the Seattle Post Office, but there he quickly became disillusioned. Working in a dank basement up to fourteen hours a day, six and sometimes seven days a week, Wells questioned the economic system.

Eventually, Wells became a confirmed socialist. At one point, he was briefly jailed for distributing The Socialist newspaper on Seattle streets. When he escorted Socialist Presidential candidate Eugene Debs during his 1908 trip to Seattle, Wells returned to work to find his pay had been cut by 10% for engaging in political activities as a government employee. A year later he was fired for "insubordination" when he refused to give up supporting political causes.

Soon after, he found a job with publically owned City Light where he joined the union. In 1912, Wells was nominated as the Socialist candidate for mayor of Seattle, a campaign in which he placed fourth capturing an impressive fifteen percent of the vote. Part of the reason he was able to garner so many votes was that Wells was known for being able to work with people of differing beliefs. This ability was noted by those in the unions, so in August, 1915, he was elected President of the Seattle Central Labor Council.

During World War I, Wells refused to be quiet about his opposition to United States' involvement. President Wilson, though, had pushed through legislation making it illegal to speak out against the war effort. As a result, Wells was imprisoned for sedition during the war. At McNeil Penitentiary, believing himself to be a political prisoner, he refused to do what he termed, "slave labor," and so was put in solitary confinement. While there, he was handcuffed to a bar which forced him to keep his hand raised above his head for eight hours a day.

After the war, he traveled to the Soviet Union, met Lenin and Trotsky and learned of Soviet life. Upon returning to America, Wells had a difficult time finding work because of his prison record. When he did find a job he was inevitably fired for labor activities. Later, he started his own business building houses but was unable to make a go of it. When he finally found work on a road crew in 1929, a company shill turned him in as a labor agitator, and he was fired yet again. He was 50 years old, unemployed and struggling.

Four years prior, back in 1925, Wells had found time to volunteer to work at the Seattle Labor College. There he met a kindred spirit in Carl Brannin. Wells and Brannin were both practical socialists rather than ideologues and soon became friends. So when Brannin created The Vanguard, a monthly newspaper, with support from the Seattle Labor College, it was natural that Wells would be his co-editor.

Besides working together, the two lived near each other in the Olympic Heights area of West Seattle.[4] They walked the same streets and saw the same ragged unemployed in their neighborhood asking for change and seeking whatever shelter they could find in the rain. Many appeared on the verge of starvation. Brannin and Wells had always fought for those who were down and out. They had no problem opposing powerful factions, but what could they do?

The answer came one summer evening in 1931. Wells and his wife Nesta were visiting with Brannin and Laura and the conversation drifted to the plight of the unemployed. Brannin and Wells were once again discussing the inability of local communists to organize the jobless. Nesta, who apparently tired of this tread-worn debate, said, "Well, then, why don't you organize them?"[5] Why not, they agreed.

Brannin and Wells discussed options. Finally, they decided to call a meeting of those unemployed in their immediate neighborhood. They chose Friday, July 23, 1931, at the Olympic Heights Community Club as the time and place for the first meeting. Brannin printed up cards and posted them in grocery stores and other spots around the neighborhood. Using their newspaper, The Vanguard, the two men published an article calling for all unemployed to gather together in their own locales. "Canvas your neighborhood and get the unemployed to agree to meet at some central place, perhaps your home to talk things over," it said. "Call the Seattle Labor College for a speaker for such meetings. The situation may be bad but it is not hopeless. Action can get results. Inactivity breeds defeat and death. Act now."[6]

They didn't know it yet, but Brannin and Wells were about to start a movement that would challenge Seattle politics and inspire a national trend.

Forty people attended that first meeting at Olympic Heights. Instead of simply complaining about the situation and lack of opportunity, discussion centered on how they, the unemployed, might help themselves. They talked of charity and work. They weren't bums, they reiterated. They wanted to work and had no desire to be given charity. Unfortunately, most knew through weeks of searching for jobs that didn't exist, that an alternative was needed. Who had money to hire more men? Many independent businesses were going under themselves, and those that were able to survive did so by laying off workers, not hiring more. The only place that seemed to have any money was the government, but these men despised the dole. They didn't want to be handed money; they wanted to work for it. At some point the conversation drifted to areas of the city that could use improvements. Weren't there plenty of roads that needed repairing, streets that needed cleaning, bridges that needed mending? This was far from a new idea. Others surely had the same thoughts. In fact, Wells and Brannin anticipated this debate and had come equipped with specific goals for the group. Work not dole became the central theme for their fledgling organization. They would not ask for relief, but for jobs on public projects. Before they broke up that night, they agreed to call themselves the Unemployed Citizens' League, and they decided to find out if other neighborhoods wanted to join them. As part of that effort, the newly formed organization would conduct a survey of other locations in the city to determine the extent of unemployment in Seattle.[7]

It was rapidly determined that desperate men infused most every neighborhood in the city. The Unemployed Citizens' League (UCL) was met with enthusiasm by the jobless. Within a couple of weeks, a second UCL was formed in West Seattle headed by Charles W. Gilbreath, another Labor College volunteer. This sparked more interest. Quickly, the idea of local UCL clubs spread. A third UCL was formed at "The Junction," also in West Seattle. Fortuitously, a lawyer, Marion Zioncheck, attended the meeting at The Junction. He would provide legal assistance and later political legitimacy as Congressman from Washington's First District. By the end of August there were seven UCLs in West Seattle alone. Quickly, other neighborhoods throughout the city heard what was happening and the idea crossed from one district to another. Pulling themselves up by their bootstraps instead of taking a hand-out appealed to the newly unemployed.[8][9]

As the size of the organization expanded, Brannin decided the local clubs needed to coordinate information and action. He organized a committee comprised of representatives from each of the locals to swap ideas. This became the Central Federation. Immediately, the Central Federation began the work of defining specific objectives for the UCL. After discussion among the representatives, the new group had its goals and direction. In sum, the UCL was dedicated to providing food relief in the short-term, meaningful work for the unemployed as soon as possible, and unemployment insurance for the long-term.[10] The enthusiasm and pride of people refusing to allow the circumstances to dictate events became contagious. More locals were organized. The unemployed were not going to be catatonic victims.

By September 1931, less than three months after the initial meeting at Olympic Heights, there were twenty newly-minted local UCL affiliates. Each sent five members to the Central Federation meeting on September 25 at the Eagles' Auditorium. Here they discussed the need for immediate support from the city. The top priority was to convince Seattle to create a million dollar fund to employ the unemployed on public works. In order to foster a sense of self-respect and so as not to conflict with organized labor, the UCL also resolved to maintain a minimum pay scale of $4.50 a day for general labor. This was the going rate for manual work, and they refused to be reduced to beggars.

They realized that the number of unemployed was rapidly rising, though, and understood that no one man or small group of men should dominate the limited amount of work that the city could provide. To prevent political favoritism, anyone who was unemployed would be allowed to register for the jobs. Therefore, they would have to share the available work and each individual might only end up working two or three days a week. That $4.50 would have to stretch between work days. This made it even more imperative that the wage stay at scale. At the same meeting, other issues were raised, including a call for the cessation of evictions for those unemployed who were unable to pay back taxes or rent.

That night, elections for committee offices were held as well. John F. Cronin was elected President of the Central

Federation with Brannin as Executive Secretary. Three additional Executive Committee members rounded out the leadership. Unfortunately, neither the President nor the Executive Committee was given any real authority. This, combined with the independent nature of the local UCLs, would come back to haunt the organization. In essence, the Central Federation, the coordinating brain of the UCL, had no control over the local limbs.

While this was not supposed to be a political meeting, John Dore, candidate for Seattle Mayor, was allowed to address the crowd. He called for a special session of the state legislature to take up the unemployment crisis. At the same time, he warned the audience that he didn't think a special session was likely since Governor Roland Hartley "as a lumberman [was] interested in low wages and low taxes [and] he [was] afraid of a move to put taxes where they belong, on the rich." Dore continued to win the hearts of the gathering by declaring, "I'm in favor of taking the huge fortunes away from those who stole them from the workers of America."[11] Dore's speech would pay dividends in the coming election.

The meeting also sparked a door-to-door canvas by many of the locals to boost their membership. While numbers slowly climbed from this drive, the initial exponential growth was never matched. As one UCL leader remarked, "It was hard to get the people to come out. The unemployed shared the traditional American idea of individual responsibility in time of unemployment." Still, as the UCL gained recognition and respect, some neighbors did join and local UCLs benefitted from new membership.

For many, joining UCL became a way to gain a semblance of control in a confusing new world. These men and women may not have been natural joiners, but the UCL allowed them to

33

commiserate with others in the same situation and to feel as if they were doing something besides hoping. Many were voters who believed that a large enough UCL could influence public work in Seattle, and most were desperate enough to accept any job, even if it only meant $4.50 twice a week. The UCL provided comfort, camaraderie and cash.

The UCL also fostered a sense of pride. Members knew that the UCL constitution was clear: "In the absence of [unemployment] insurance legislation, we condemn unreservedly all forms of private charity for this purpose." The UCL, many reasoned, would not beg for a hand-out but instead fight for work. There was honor in that. So by October, Nesta's simple suggestion had taken root and blossomed to a full-fledged organization with twenty-two locals, a coordinating Central Federation and a completed constitution.[12]

Meanwhile, Seattle City Council was aware of the rising UCL. The Council discussed and debated and finally approved UCL's million dollar request for public improvements. The money was earmarked primarily to improved streets and parks. And even if less than half that amount was readily available, the Seattle Council demonstrated a firm commitment to helping the unemployed. This is the way government was supposed to work, most agreed: Citizens saw a need, organized a committee, identified a solution, and petitioned the elected officials who responded to a legitimate request.

The Council then established a commission to organize the relief work under Irving F. Dix, a well-respected businessman and the president of the Seattle Community Fund, a charitable association established to help the poor. Dix was an engineer, having graduated from Pratt Technical Institute in New York City. From there, he worked for Bell Telephone and Telegraph and rose to the position of plant manager in Los Angles. In 1929, he was transferred to Seattle and immediately immersed himself in local affairs by becoming chairman of both the Community Chest and American Red Cross drives. As chairman of the new commission, Dix was given a hefty charge: he would be responsible for coordinating public and private relief. On top of which, he was also to encourage job growth in both of these sectors. His new organization was officially called Commission for Improved Employment but was better known as the Dix Commission. Dix clearly had his work cut out for him.[13]

The two most important priorities were immediate emergency relief until the jobs could begin and a method of registering those in need of work. Dix jumped quickly into the breach. The Commission began by dividing the city into five districts and collecting food and clothing to be distributed in each of those districts. The hungry and those in need of clothes could receive the necessities immediately. At the same time, sign-ups sheets went out for those unemployed who wanted a job. By September 21, 4,100 unemployed had registered for relief work. The hope was that charity at the distribution centers would rapidly be replaced by jobs.

While there was much more to be done, it appeared that things were going smoothly. Then the City Council met. Discussion centered on the daily wage for general labor. Wasn't $4.50 too much to pay for unskilled workers? Many of the workers had no training in the jobs they would receive. They would be slow and need to learn as they went. Why should they be paid as much as others with more experience? Besides, these were meant to be temporary jobs. No one was expecting to have to live off these wages for very long. Also, the work, while not exactly make-work, wasn't essential either. The city was only creating these jobs to provide emergency employment for the unemployed. If these tasks were never done, it wouldn't really matter. Should unnecessary work be paid at the same rate as truly vital work? Then, too, what incentive was there for those who received top salaries to seek other employment? Finally, the available city capital would need to stretch. Therefore, in order to spread the money around and to keep the workers from getting too comfortable with the relief employment, the City Council decided to set the wage on a sliding scale of between $1.50 and $3.00 a day.

Here organized labor brought down its heavy foot. Uneven wages meant unfair competition. Unions refused to support public work if this lower wage was implemented. How could unions demand livable wages when the unemployed could be hired for so much less? This was believed to be an attempt to underbid union work and undercut those who still had jobs.

The UCL, too, steadfastly refused to work for less than $4.50 a day. They would not come, hat in hand, to beg for work from the city. They were workers who only needed a temporary leg up. It was $4.50 per day or nothing.

After three contentious weeks, and with the opposition clear, firm and well-organized, the City Council relented. Relief work would begin at $4.50 a day for registered unemployed men.[14]

While the plans for work relief were being developed and running through the government mill, the UCL went forward on another initiative to help its members. This initiative began when unemployed UCL member Fred Runce took his two sons south of Seattle to a vacant lot. There they chopped down trees and cut it up for firewood to prepare for the coming winter. In August, while Runce was at a UCL meeting in Columbia City, he mentioned his firewood gathering. Runce then suggested that the local should do the same but on a more grand scale. Many agreed with Runce, and soon there were sixteen camps set up to supply firewood to UCL members.[15] At the same time groups of men, some affiliated with UCL and others not, began to cooperate with local farmers exchanging work for food. They agreed to pick strawberries for the farmer for a portion of the crop. Eastern Washington became literally fertile ground for UCL members. The unemployed trucked excess wood from the makeshift lumber camps across the Cascades to places like Yakima to trade for fruit which the farmer couldn't afford to get to market anyway. Charitable farmers in the east allowed the city folk to dig up potatoes that would otherwise rot in the ground. This was the modest beginning of what was called "Self-Help." In Self-Help, the unemployed would combine their skills and materials to form a mutually supportive society. The most important needs were obvious: food, shelter and warmth, and child welfare.[16]

Much of the food the UCL collected from Self-Help was grown on unclaimed land. Near Seattle there were plenty of fields that lay abandoned or unused. Gardens began to spring up north of the city at Alderwood Manor and in the south at Rainier Valley. Vegetable gardens growing potatoes, carrots, squash and tomatoes sprang up from donated land and seed throughout the area. At the Seattle docks, fish that went unsold was given to the UCL. The Fisherman's Union even loaned boats to UCL members so they could catch their own on Puget Sound. Left-over fruits and vegetables were gathered from sympathetic grocers, and the food was given directly to members or cooked at the UCL commissaries.

The Self-Help movement spread to other arenas besides food and firewood. Those members who had special skills contributed as well. Barber shops and beauty parlors provided free haircuts and styling to UCL members. Shoe repairs were able to extend the life of worn footwear - 40,000 pair in the first five months of 1932 alone. Tailors helped repair, patch and mend UCL members' clothes. There was even a garage to keep cars limping along. One local group ran its own cabinet shop, while another revived a coal mine.

While not strictly a UCL enterprise, a separate Women's Division was created by the former Seattle Mayor Bertha Landes. Under the Dix Commission, Landes worked hand-in-glove with the League. Beginning in November, 1931, women registered to work in two sewing rooms. The machines were donated by the Singer Company while the Textile Tower and Metropolitan Building contributed space. Businesswomen and the University of Washington chipped in financing, and the women were given two days of work a week for which they were paid $2.50 a day, significantly less than the $4.50 paid to men, but welcomed nonetheless. The finished product was sold to the Firland Sanitarium, child welfare offices and Goodwill. The money collected from the sales provided more work for the women, and the cycle continued.[17]

From firewood to food to clothes, the UCL looked after its own. A health clinic was even opened to provide free dental and emergency care. This idea of Self-Help by and for the unemployed spread across the nation and was featured in newspapers and magazines. Colliers, Business Week, Atlantic Monthly and Nation published articles on the Self-Help movement begun in Seattle. The New York Times wrote stories and the Department of Labor even printed a pamphlet entitled, "Cooperative self-help activities among the unemployed," to help new groups get started.[18]

Certainly, America was suffering but with the right determination, we could pull ourselves out, or so said the experiment in Seattle. This wasn't yet the Great Depression; it was only a depression. It was 1931 and Hoover was still in the

White House. As President, he felt that the government had no responsibility to help the individual worker. He had reluctantly involved the federal government by creating an employment service for those seeking work. The Emergency Relief Organization was given the responsibility of creating a central location in each state to list job openings. This was as far as Hoover was willing to go, but he wasn't alone. Few people believed the national government was primarily responsible for fixing this economy. Businesses failed because the owners couldn't stay competitive. The unemployed were either too lazy or unwilling to adapt. The UCL Self-Help was a beautiful example of how to deal with even the most extreme situations.

By December 18, 1931, UCL commissaries were open and feeding the membership; jobs were on their way. The depression could be tamed with firm determination and willingness to do the hard work. Or so they thought.[19][20]

3

Shacktown: Relocation

David E. Skinner and John W. Eddy had combined forces in January 1916 to create the Skinner and Eddy Corporation, "Builder of Steel Steamships." To construct their ships they had purchased prime waterfront real estate in Seattle, one of the busiest ports on the West Coast. During World War I, the Skinner and Eddy shipyard had produced more vessels than any other port in America, and at one point, over 13,000 people made a living working at this plant. But the war ended in 1918 and the call for new ships slowed. By 1923, Skinner and Eddy didn't have enough orders to stay afloat. They realized they had no choice but to call it quits. Skinner and Eddy laid off their workers and shut their doors. The equipment was taken out and sold or salvaged. The buildings were removed. About all that remained of a company that had once broken records for quickest ship construction in the world were a few cement platforms scattered across an abandoned lot.[1]

That left nine acres open right at the base of downtown in the shadow of the Smith Tower, the tallest building in the city. Some of the old-timers might have even been familiar with this spot from before the Skinner and Eddy days. Until 1908, a shacktown had occupied this very place. About 1,200 shacks housing 3,500 men had occupied a swath of waterfront property sweeping from the Skinner and Eddy property at the foot of Spokane Avenue and winding for three miles. Eventually, though, the Health Commissioner became concerned when the pack of rats scuttering throughout the area had become so massive that he feared an outbreak of the Bubonic Plague. To prevent this, the shackville had been burned out.[2] Almost certainly some of the Duwamish castaways had heard of the history of this spot and decided to check it out.

Even though the Skinner and Eddy land lined a busy port, most other people found this spot undesirable. It was within blocks of shelters and flophouses and illegal bars. Prostitutes wandered just north of here and speakeasies and the less reputable bars, blind pigs, poured their poison within easy staggering distance. Puget Sound lapped up against the shore contributing an oily, fishy stench. There were no "good people" living near here to complain, at least not loudly. Besides, the men who had been booted out of their Duwamish shantytown had spent the last five months drifting from place to place, but with winter coming they knew they had to find more permanent shelter.

On top of everything else, within a couple blocks, at Railroad and Washington, the Volunteers of America ran a busy soup kitchen which served meals twice a day. At night a man might even get "a bowl of Salvation Army stew-soup." Everyone, regardless of age, race, newly unemployed or in tatters from years of joblessness, stood in two parallel lines at the soup kitchen. Once in the large dining hall, they sat at the long tables, side-by-side, and ate.[3] This abandoned dock was ideal. A man could look for a job, stand in the soup line or buy a drink, all within walking distance of his shack.

Jesse Jackson, the unemployed lumberjack, was among the forlorn wanderers who ended up here, but not before a few detours. Jackson had put some money away for a rainy day, so when he was first let go in the logging industry in 1929, he lived on the emergency funds and looked for work. Unfortunately, jobs were few and life expensive. Two years had leached away most of his excess cash. Then his niece and nephew needed a boost to help them through college, so Jackson donated the last few hundred that he had and was busted flat.[4] So in October, 1931, with his reserves drained, he signed up at the Central Registry in Seattle.

The Central Registry for Homeless Men had been established by the Seattle Community Fund on November 10, 1930 as a way of organizing help for the poor. This fund originally united the services of the Compass-Siloah Mission, Jewish Welfare Society, Goodwill Industries, Saint Vincent de Paul Society, Salvation Army, Seattle Seamen's Mission and the Volunteers of America. Prior to that, each charity provided its own tracking and assistance. This allowed the savvy beggar to take advantage of the lack of communication between groups. Experienced panhandlers could get extra helpings of food at various soup kitchens, a rotating wardrobe at donation centers and multiple nights in shelters spread throughout downtown. The Central Registry prevented that. At the Central Registry the homeless came in and signed up at one of three windows. There they were given a booklet of tickets which allowed them to get meals, housing and necessary supplies without receiving duplicate services. At first, there was reluctance by some of the charities to turn over the evaluation of the needy to an outside agency, but once the system had proven its worth, the Central Registry became a welcome collaborator, and other organizations began to join these founding agencies. By 1932, the Central Registry would be credited with helping some homeless job-seekers find not just food and shelter, but clothes, shoes, a haircut, laundry and bathing facilities. In fact, the Travelers' Aid Society teamed up with the Central Registry to provide assistance for "homeless and friendless" boys up to age 20. Besides given the same assistance the men received, some of the older boys were placed in free or cheap housing and given jobs when possible.[5678]

The Central Registry, then, is where those on their uppers went. It was charity and nothing but. As a homeless man without a family, Jackson had nowhere else to turn. He went up to the window and was asked some questions. Name, legal residence, occupation, age, and length of unemployment were all recorded. After answering the questions, he was given a booklet of tickets which could be exchanged for a single nightly meal at the soup kitchen. Jackson went down the street and found a soup kitchen where he submitted a ticket. What he received in exchange was, to quote Jackson, "pig swill." His next step was to find a place to sack down. Using his Central Registry tickets he found a shelter that would accept him. There was no bed, no blanket, only a hard floor and a few newspapers he had collected that day to cushion and cover him. The night passed slowly. The next morning, hungry from the small portions of lousy food and tired from sleeping on the bare ground, Jackson knew he couldn't last long on this "charity." In fact, "[o]ne week of this abuse was enough," said Jackson. He took the little he had and hit the streets. Here he wasn't alone.[9]

Twenty men including Jackson found themselves at the old Skinner and Eddy property. They were joining the eventual two million across the nation who would end up homeless in shantytowns, back alleys, park benches, and urban and rural jungles.[10] Judging the quality of the place and the options available, they decided here was as good as any and better than most. They began the process of prowling the area for junk boards, cast away linoleum and tin scraps. Shanties slowly rose in no particular order and dictated by the materials found or stolen by each man. A few, lacking any materials, dug into the dirt to create an underground den.

Shortly after, other men joined those first pioneers, and within a few days fifty shacks and shelters rose on the once abandoned land. The busy construction and availability of land attracted even more homeless. Unfortunately, as the numbers grew, it became increasingly difficult for the city to turn a blind eye to the burgeoning village. Soon, the situation at the waterfront came to the official attention of city health inspectors. Precedent had been established, and once again just as at Duwamish, the residents were told that their shacks' lack of running water or appropriate toilets created unsanitary conditions. A notice was tacked on the door or at the entrance of each hovel telling the inhabitant he had three days in which to find new housing. The men discussed their options. They also talked about how much work they had put in constructing the shacktown. Too much time and effort had been put in creating these shanties. Besides, they reasoned, where else could they go? The city had to know that men needed some sort of shelter, especially with winter coming on. It had to be a bluff.

So it was at five in the morning on Sunday, October 25, 1931, under a pouring sky, a hundred tired men were rousted out of their makeshift shacks and burrows. Soaked through, they watched as police moved in and dumped kerosene over the camp and lit the match. The men grabbed what little they had and watched as their work turned to smoke and headed skyward. The police did a thorough job and left the drenched men shivering in the rain.

Neither the police nor the Health Department realized, though, that the Depression was creating a new type of desperation. These weren't the same people that had been so easily chased out of Duwamish a few months before. The competition from growing numbers of homeless and an increased desperation had hardened them. The men waited until the police wiped their hands and headed off and immediately began to rebuild. Unburned or slightly scorched wood was salvaged and new material was pillaged. Slowly, with the rain continuing to pound, the men raised a second village on the ashes of the first. Where else could they go? Not through violence, but through persistence they would stake their claim. Within a short time, their Phoenix-slum rose again[11][12]

Hooverville resident. October 27, 1931. *Courtesy of Paul Dorpat.*

Seattle Mayor Robert H. Harlin had not been told of the purposed destruction of the waterfront shacks and his reaction was swift. "I am amazed and astounded! What in the world did they do that for?" he barked.

Harlin, a labor-endorsed mayor, had known about the waterfront inhabitants. In fact, he had sent his own driver down to do an informal inspection of the grounds. The report that came back said the men on the waterfront were doing their best to collect scrap metal and make a life for themselves. Harlin said, "I had no idea that the health department planned to throw them out and cut them adrift in times like these. I'll call Hanley down about this."

E. T. Hanley, the City Health Commissioner had teamed up with the Chief of Police William B. Kent to clean up this Skinner and Eddy health hazard. The two men assumed it was simply another unpleasant part of their job. Instead, they were called in to explain to an irate mayor why they would destroy the only shelter broken men had and send them into the terrible rainstorm. Kent, at first surprised by the mayor's reaction, pleaded, "We're not trying to burn people out of their homes. The burning of the shacks was done on orders of the health department and three days notice was given the squatters to get out. There were no women or children there – just men, drifters from out of town. Officers found frightfully unsanitary conditions there breeding spots of disease that constituted a menace to the city's health. And business houses complained that the squatters resorted to petty thievery, stealing everything that wasn't nailed down."[13]

There was theft. An ex-hobo summed it up best, "Hell, yes. Everybody was a criminal. You stole, you cheated through. You were getting by, survival. Stole clothes off lines, stole milk off back porches, you stole bread."[14] These men stole but only in a limited way and only what was necessary, they would claim. Kent was the law, though, and he didn't feel he could turn away from theft for whatever reason.

The meeting between Mayor Harlin, Health Commissioner Hanley and Police Chief Kent and three additional councilmen helped calm the Mayor. The next day he tempered his statement to say that he was "amazed and astounded" that the police didn't take into account the weather and the fact that the men had no other place to go with winter coming. The inference was that the ousted men should have been given alternative housing before the property was put to the torch. The Mayor's wavering encouraged Kent's assertiveness. Kent claimed that the men who were burned out were the type who would decline help anyway. "These men absolutely refuse to patronize soup kitchens and Salvation Army flophouses but would rather exist as they do, stealing what they can't acquire honestly and living under the most impossible sanitary conditions."

Health Commissioner Hanley supported Kent saying, "We've had this same condition for the past 10 years, even in the best of times. Infection breeds rapidly and you'd be surprised, for example how fast a rat from one of these places could travel out to Laurelhurst." Laurelhurst was a well-known enclave of the well-to-do, and the comment clearly insinuated more than rodents might invade these places of comfort.

Mayor Harlin, having calmed down, decided the situation needed a more objective evaluation. Therefore, he told three councilmen to investigate the evictions and come to some conclusion on how to house the destitute men. Hanley, clearly not in agreement with the Mayor, had only one non-comment, a sarcastic huff.[15]

Regardless, even the conservative Seattle Times recognized the quandary. In an editorial entitled "Must Have Shelter," the Times agreed with Police Chief Kent saying that the men burned out weren't even from Seattle. But, the article continued, the reason so many people had come from all over to settle in Seattle was because the city had "widely advertised" the relief available here. Therefore, the newspaper believed the men had been lured to the city. Also, the editors expressed an admiration for those who were burned out, since they had only come to

Seattle to better their situation. This was what ambitious and independent men did. As a result, the newspaper supported Mayor Harlin and advocated for a replacement shelter for those whose shacks had been destroyed.[16]

The investigation into the burning of the shacks was held. Despite Mayor Harlin's doubts and the pressure from the Times, Councilman James Scavotto, chairman of the investigating committee, determined that the residents had been given adequate warning. The committee sided with the Police Chief and the Health Commissioner. In fact, the burning was in complete alignment with precedent. The Duwamish burning was only one example of a policy that according to Scavotto's commission had been "pursued for several years." Scavotto agreed with the rest of the committee that the city should try to help the needy, but he stood firmly against Seattle becoming a "hoboes' heaven."[17][18]

Less than a month later, after the men on the waterfront had rebuilt, the police returned. With the permission of the Scavotto Commission and the acknowledgement of the Mayor, the police trekked down to the shantytown. Once again the destitute men were turned out, once again the police moved in, once again the village was put to the torch.

And once again the work of rebuilding began as soon as the police were out of sight.

There was one difference, though. This time the men learned their lesson. Simply rebuilding as they had done before would get them nowhere. The police would return and the whole scene would be replayed unless the men came up with a new plan. So, instead of rebuilding their shacks the same as they had done previously, they dug in. Instead of easily combustible shanties, they built torch-proof caves. They removed the sand from around the cement emplacements that

Skinner and Eddy had used to fill in holes before abandoning the land. They used tin and linoleum to cover the burrows and slipped down into the dirt. There was little light and only claustrophobic grave-like conditions, but with few options, they learned to adapt. They sat on the mounds of dirt from their caves and talked for a bit. When tired they headed into the damp, musty holes. If the officials were going to send them packing this time, it would have to be a hole-by-hole eviction.[19]

4

The City: An Idea Grows

Most of the unemployed in Seattle had been able to maintain their housing despite lost jobs. The newly unemployed who had formed the Unemployed Citizens League were struggling but had different concerns than those who were battling city officials on the waterfront.

It was 1931 and Christmas was coming. The Bon Marche department store at Third and Pine in downtown Seattle had its decorations up. The more upscale Frederick and Nelson, two blocks away, was for the first time selling new mint chocolate treats this holiday season called Frango's. Meanwhile, two brothers had opened a store on Second Avenue. They remodeled it, and decided to change the name their father had given the business. They settled on their own last name, "Nordstrom." All were busy despite hard times. In the toy department you could pick up Fisher Price's "Doctor Doodle," a duck on a string for toddlers which quacked when pulled or a Lionel Blue Comet Train Set for a boy or a Raggedy Ann doll for a girl. Christmas carols played on the radio and Christmas trees adorned most Seattle houses. But not all celebrated the holiday season that Depression year. For many unemployed parents, the trees and toys and window displays only reminded them that they were failures.

In South Seattle at the White Center Unemployed Citizens' League, members began to realize that Christmas wouldn't come for their sons and daughters. Broke and barely able to feed and shelter their families, the men got together to talk about the upcoming holiday. A few had already planned on building hand-made toys for the children. Four men decided to pitch in by going door-to-door around the neighborhood to see what they could collect. For three days these men went knocking on their neighbors' doors asking for used toys and toys that other children had outgrown. Other men decided to contact local stores. Some even solicited the busy department stores downtown for donations. Through all of these efforts, fourteen department stores agreed to help out. After all the collections were complete, a pile of gifts were prepared. Two hundred youngsters showed up for the UCL Christmas party. Children tore open packages. The adults ate and looked on. For just a moment, it seemed, hard times were forgotten.[1]

Meanwhile, the Self-Help movement was booming. Every night between four and five tons of pears, peaches and apples were being hauled in from Yakima Valley to the commissaries created by the UCLs. Eighteen separate commissary locations spread throughout Seattle provided food for the families of members.[2] That fall and winter of 1931, one hundred twenty thousand pounds of fish found its way to the tables of the unemployed. At the same time, ten thousand cords of firewood heated their homes. Success bred optimism. Other ideas were being kicked around. Some in the UCL suggested that the organization should consider starting its own bakery or running its own dairy. By that December, hope hadn't trumped fear, but most saw a dim light at the end of the tunnel.[3]

One of the greatest worries of the unemployed was eviction. With no money to pay rent or mortgage, a month without a paycheck meant a knot in the stomach. Two months without a paycheck meant dry-mouth fear. No one wanted to return home to find a padlock on their door and their belongings stacked on the sidewalk. For those married men, this was a sign that they had failed as providers. For those with children, this proved they were no longer men at all.

It became imperative, then, that the UCL find a way to help those about to be evicted. Unfortunately, there was no way the funds could be raised to provide for everyone threatened with loss of housing. But, even if money wasn't available, labor was abundant, and free time rested heavily on the unemployed. Perhaps lack of rent money and restlessness could be intertwined to solve both problems. Maybe a deal could be struck with the property owners. With that in mind, whenever a UCL brother was unable to pay rent, the leadership would contact the landlord. A roof might be repaired or stairs rebuilt or a plumbing problem fixed for forgiving a delinquent bill. After all, the residence was just going to sit vacant anyway, UCL representatives suggested. It wasn't like people were lining up with cash to rent out the room. Why not take advantage of a bad situation to get skilled labor and improve the value of a home or apartment? Everybody wins.[4] While this was never a permanent solution and only worked occasionally, it provided a friendly alternative for kindly landlords and terrified parents.

With Self-Help like this, many felt they had found a solution to the worst humiliations of the Depression, even if only temporarily. There was even time for UCL sponsored dances and clubs. In the depths of despair, they created a community that was a life-raft for drowning men and women. And they had done it all with their own sweat and with only a minimal influx of cash. Yet, underlying the surface optimism, there was a looming sense that it could all come crashing down. Yes, they had food, clothes, shelter and unity for now, but everyone knew they were all living close to the cliff. Every solution was temporary in nature. Too much of what they received depended on the kindness of others. There were many problems left unaddressed.

One such problem was gasoline. There was no way to barter or exchange for gas, and gas was essential to get the donated food from Eastern Washington. "Chiseling" was the only way they could afford the gas to retrieve the food from Eastern Washington and move produce from the various gardens to the commissaries. Chiseling in UCL lingo was defined as begging and finagling. The person donating the gas might have a cousin who was part of UCL or suggestions could be made about remembering the owner when the men found employment again. This was all part of chiseling. Unfortunately, this meant the amount of fuel was limited by the skill of the negotiator and the patience of the supplier. And everybody knew that the supplier's patience was not unlimited.

A second problem that was left unaddressed was that all UCL labor was donated by the membership on a voluntary basis. A core group was out nearly every day finding some way to contribute. Others reluctantly spent a few hours here and there, while some could only be seen when it was time to eat at the commissary. Regardless, no one kept formal track of the hours worked, just as no one checked to see if members were donating goods. There was a pride in this lack of recordkeeping. No one was paid a penny for their work and everyone understood the importance of sticking together. If they kept track of who did or didn't help, it would no longer be voluntary and so would only cheapen the endeavor. That was the thought, anyway.

Nature was another problem. Winter meant less fruits and vegetables were available from Eastern Washington and their community gardens. No one seemed to have any good alternatives. So, while the commissaries were organized and ready to provide a handout, the reality was there wasn't always much to distribute.

To top it off, the city which had at first seemed like an amenable rich uncle, became increasingly desperate and reluctant. The Dix Committee, formed in September, had realized by November that they had bit off more than they could chew. On November 22, 1931 Dix admitted, "Those who think the situation is well in hand and that the needs of the destitute citizens have been provided for until the return of prosperity through measures already taken, are living in a fool's paradise." After only two months, Dix began to understand the magnitude of the unemployment problem and realize that staunching the bleeding would take more than a few band-aids.

In fact, the city which had rushed to pledge a million dollars for relief, had allocated only half a million. Worse, in December Seattle found that it could only spare $10,000 to pay for work relief for the entire month. With unemployment possibly running as high as 50,000 people, the problem was self-evident; the job was too big for the city alone to handle.

Commissioner Dix had to patch together a rescue plan. He would use the infrastructure of the UCL. They had commissaries and labor. They were already established and trusted by the unemployed. Plus it was free. Since the commissary workers, clerks and leadership of the UCL were unemployed themselves, they would best know how to implement relief and placate the restless. Dix also called on the county to help finance a major portion of the relief. By diving into the deeper pockets of the county and combining the efforts with that of the city, it was thought that additional resources would get to the needy.[5] Dix hoped by creating a team comprised of the City of Seattle, King County and the Unemployed Citizens' League, enough money and resources could be gathered to weather the storm. Unfortunately, this trio created a political gale of its own.

5

Shacktown: Hooverville

The caves had worked. Burning down the shacks and hovels was one thing, but having to drag men out and fill in the holes which had become their homes was too much. The shacktown residents and the City had clearly reached an impasse. Seattle could not tolerate the unsanitary and dangerous conditions down on the waterfront. The men who had built there had nowhere else to go and weren't leaving no matter how many times they were tossed out. It was time for a truce.

A meeting was held in which the city laid down the conditions for allowing the men to continue to live in the shacktown. Hanley, the Health Commissioner, first insisted that if the men were to be tolerated, they would have to quit their rat holes. From this point forward all housing had to be built above ground. Second, some basic rules of sanitation must be adhered to. The police and fire made a few requests regarding safety and security of their own. Some city authority insisted women and children must be actively discouraged from residing in the camp. There was nothing in the agreement that the homeless men couldn't abide, so a deal was struck. The city would tolerate the shanties as long as the economic emergency remained and as long as the men followed the agreement.

To keep order and make sure no one at the shacktown got out of control and spoiled the deal, the men figured they should elect a committee of its own. Because of the diversity of races packed so tightly in such a small space, it was decided the committee would consist of two whites, two blacks and two Filipinos. The residents were called out and elections were held. Only a disappointing one-fifth of the entire shacktown opted to participate.[1] But among the newly elected committeemen was a skinny, ex-lumberjack. Jesse Jackson was soon dubbed the "Mayor" of the rat-infested village. Reuben Washington, a black man, was chosen as "police chief." Both titles were unofficial and carried no weight, other than the weight of consensus. The new committee, though, did give a conduit through which the city and the shacktown could communicate.

Hooverville Mayor Jesse Jackson with Reuben Washington. January 13, 1935. *Seattle Times.*

Jackson would later claim that around this time the name "Hooverville" was created "one evening [sitting] around an open campfire."[2] But in fact, the name Hooverville can be traced back to Charles Michelson, Publicity Chief for the Democratic National Committee. In an attempt to lash the depression securely to Hoover, Michelson tied the President's name to the worst visual reminders of the desperate times. The term "Hooverville" for the congregations of pieced together shanties that sprouted in all major cities in America, stuck. It was soon joined by "Hoover blankets," newspapers used to cover those sleeping outside in the cold, and "Hoover flags," pockets turned inside out to indicate how broke the man flying the flags was. "Hoover cars" were mules pulling gasless automobiles and "Hoover hogs" were rabbits. The term Hooverville first saw the printed page in 1930 when the New York Times used it to describe a shacktown in Chicago.[3] That was over a year prior to the conversation Jackson remembered. Perhaps one of the men had heard or read of a "Hooverville" without recollecting it. Whatever the origin, the men sitting around that Seattle campfire decided "Hooverville" would properly honor the man they thought most responsible for their situation.

While the name Hooverville was chosen in a humorous vein, the men found little funny about the President's attitude regarding the unemployed. At the same time the men were being burned out of their houses the first time, Hoover had said that the depression would be over quickly and "the number who are threatened with privation is a minor percentage."[4] In that one phrase Hoover wrote off the men sitting at the Seattle Waterfront along with the hundreds of thousands across the country who were building their own makeshift houses. There was deep resentment against the nation's Chief Executive in Hooverville and across the nation.

Still, life went on. The men rebuilt under the new guidelines. This time they had the approval of the city and even some help from local businesses. Scrap lumber, discarded metal, and recycled glass was rapidly transformed into livable shanties. Trucks of food were distributed by some of the area businessmen, and within a few weeks over a hundred shacks replaced the holes that had once pocked the old shipyards.

From 1931 to 1941, the mud pathways of Hooverville would remain, winding past every type of ramshackle housing that a creative mind with no money could imagine. One house might be covered in tin from oil cans pounded flat and nailed onto the frame. Another was a square wooden box no more than eight feet a side with a slant roof and no visible window. Still another neatly built house had a flagpole sitting in the front yard with an outstretched flag snapping on windy days.

Most of the roofs were simple tin or tarpaper. Some used nails to keep the roofing on but many just used broken cement or large rocks to weigh down whatever roofing material was available. Still, there were more than a few covered in composite shingles, tacked in and secure, as professional a job as anyone might see walking down the best streets of Seattle.

The majority of houses were extremely small. They ranged between six by nine feet and twelve by fifteen feet. The largest house was fifteen by twenty-five feet, containing 375 square feet of living space. One unlucky or lazy resident only had enough material to construct a claustrophobic shack that measured out at three by eight feet. In order to keep the heat in and to reduce the amount of scavenging for wood or coal to a minimum, ceilings crouched between six and eight feet. Most shacks consisted of a single room which served as bedroom, kitchen, dining room and front parlor.

Hooverville, Seattle, Washington. June 10, 1937. *University of Washington Libraries, Special Collections, Lee 250.*

The stability of the house varied from the questionable to the dangerous to the rock-solid. One carpenter built a four room house with two bedrooms, a kitchen and a tiny dining room. He even encircled the whole estate with a white picket fence and provided a stone walkway to his door. More common, though, were slapdash affairs where the wind whistled through cracks and crevices and the rain dripped on the residents inside. A small handful of men stuck poles under canvas coverings to create makeshift tents. Only a single house was two-stories tall. The second story was described as having "a 4' by 6' piano-crate-like structure [which] loom[ed] above the surrounding ecological insanity like a minaret in Cairo..."5 Almost all the structures demonstrated ingenuity since the amount of money available to supplement found materials was extremely limited. One man did admit to spending $52 on construction, but that was a rare exception, and when he later sold his shack he could only get $15 from his original investment.

At first, houses had their floors directly touching the ground, but in 1933 the city required they be elevated by at least a foot. This was done to give the cats a fighting chance against the rats which had taken over the place. Unfortunately, a mysterious illness spread through the cat population and the majority died, frequently trapped under hovels or in other hard to reach spots. The smell was said to be horrific, and the rats were unaffected by the whole experiment.

A few men refused to entirely abandon the caves they had dug during their battle with the city. Instead, they attached a half-sized wood facing. Since the floor was lower than ground level, the men didn't have to scavenge so much building material. On top of that, the dirt kept the heat down in the summer and cold from overwhelming in the winter. The downside was the frequent Seattle rain meant that the inside was often damp and humid.

Inside the above-ground houses, conditions ran the gamut from neat as a pin to truly unlivable. Interior walls were usually cardboard or paper which acted as rudimentary insulation. Some covered their walls with wrapping paper to add a more festive air. Others used actual scavenged wallpaper, but this was found to be less than ideal since bedbugs seemed to be attracted to it, perhaps feasting on the old glue. Others used paints from the remnants of several near-empty cans, which led to some oddly colorful walls. Nearly every house had at least one window. These ranged from small slits of glass to one shack which had constructed half of an entire wall out of window pane and added a four by six foot skylight. The glass itself was kept clean by many but was totally obscured by filth by others. Flowerboxes proudly adorned a few of the windows.

Almost every residence had some source of heat which usually consisted of a fire built in old kerosene cans, oil drums, or tin cans. A few had built brick fireplace-like structures. All were vented by jerry-rigged stovepipes which were often faulty causing the inside to be nearly as smoky as the outside. Mostly the fuel for the fire was driftwood, scrap or a few bits of pilfered coal. The haze of smoke was thick throughout the camp particularly on cold days, but even on warm days the smoke lingered as the heaters doubled as cooking stoves.

Many kept small woodpiles outside their shacks. Occasionally, someone would steal from another's woodpile. This led to the practice of boring holes into a stick or two and working a shotgun shell into the gap. An explosive bang never seemed to hurt anyone, but it identified the thief and did substantial damage to their makeshift stove. It also discouraged the crook from trying it again.

The primary furniture was a bed. All were secondhand or homemade. Bunk beds were used in two man hovels. Almost no one slept on a cot. Mattresses, quilts or even straw were laid down. To keep the lice from overwhelming the sleeper, mattresses were hung outside on clear days. One man slept on artificial grass, another used overcoats, and a third with more morbid tastes awoke each morning in a coffin. Blankets, quilts, canvas bags, torn and sewed together or threadbare kept the sleeper warm at night. Newspapers were used by the less fortunate.

The rest of the interior was as individual as the occupant. Mirrors were hung in one; framed photographs tacked up in another one. Newspaper and magazine cut outs were popular if they had brash girls with nice legs. Men who would never wear them were particularly interested in lingerie, it seemed, by the ads pasted on the walls. But also magazine covers and postcards adorned the interior. Floors were bare wood or covered in castaway rugs or scraps of linoleum, shaped to fit.

Since most had little room, places to sit were limited. Hand crafted stools and makeshift benches were popular as were wooden boxes, but resourceful residents even found a few office chairs that swiveled. Tables, dressers, cabinets, and shelves were present in varying degrees of repair.

Poking around inside the shacks, one found kerosene cans to carry water, eating utensils, a pot or pan, a spare shirt or pair of pants, a can converted into a kerosene lamp, and a tool or two. In a few of the hovels there were magazines, books or a crystal radio which required no electricity but whose reception was spotty at best.[6] What was missing was also interesting: there was no running water, no electricity, no tub, no place to relieve oneself, no closets, no ovens, no iceboxes, no telephones, no children, almost no women and very little litter on the pathways.

As well as thick smoke, the air was noxious with the smell of unwashed men since there was no bathhouse, although most tried to bathe at least once a week. Urine permeated the air as only two outhouses were available and in the nearly all-male environment, it was acceptable to relieve oneself anywhere along the path. While very little greenery survived the constant trod of the men, a hardy bush often shaped into trees, was the prevalent vegetation. A tangle of clotheslines dripped with freshly washed clothes for those who hadn't given up on all remnants of respectability.

East of Hooverville ran Railroad Avenue with a rumble and howl of passing trains. The primary entertainment of the men was chewing the fat, and the buzz of voices could be heard alongside the hammering and repair work that was frequently needed due to the haphazard construction. Nearer to the waterfront one could hear the lapping of the waves and occasional blast of a horn from a ferry.

Fresh water was piped into two locations, one inside the village and the second near the dock. Some brought their kerosene cans to fill each day. Two men wheeled a barrel over, filled it and wheeled it back. These two attached the barrels to hoses and fashioned a spigot to have running water in their shacks.

The two privies were difficult and sometimes dangerous to get to. They sat at the end of narrow wooden catwalks with a sizable drop onto a rock landing. During the day, a line formed and at night, especially if drunk, the perilous trail was avoided unless it was an extreme situation. Once successfully navigated, the effluence was deposited straight into Puget Sound.

For those who wanted it, religion was available. One church consisted of nothing more than a canvas covering open on three sides with rows of boards placed over wood boxes for pews. An altar sat at the front on a raised platform. But it was well-used and not the only church in the village. Individuals, too, expressed their religious leanings. On at least one house there were several religious exhortations including: "The wages of sin is death."

A major benefit, at least it was thought to be so by many of the men, was the proximity of shelters, flophouses, speakeasies and cheap prostitutes. Within a few blocks a man with little money could get drunk, laid and sleep it off, without having to worry about how to get back home the next day.

Healthy entertainment was more difficult to find. During the winter months the city did provide a Recreation Center at 212 Occidental Avenue. Late in the afternoon until early in the evening, the homeless could walk up the hill to the Center and read, play chess, checkers or dominos or just talk. And those who had been on the vaudeville circuit but were now among the jobless masses, performed for their homeless brethren once a week. The Recreation Center was popular enough that over the winter of 1932-1933 nearly 600,000 visits were recorded.[7]

Just as Hooverville wasn't the first shacktown in Seattle, it wasn't the only one either. There were reports of a dozen such places under the names of Marysville, Hoovertown, Churchill, Angel City, and Tipperary.[8] Indian Town was on the Duwamish mudflats. Hollywood was at 6th Avenue south of Lander. Reno was north of Lander. Louisville was considered upper-class as it sat under the Magnolia Bridge; the Magnolia district being a well-known neighborhood of the wealthy.[9] Shacktowns were spread around Seattle from the industrial center to West Seattle to Airport Way to Interbay. Two shacktowns were located by Beacon Hill, and another was near lower Queen Anne Hill.[10] Hooverville was only the largest and best known shacktown, but whatever the conditions were like there were replicated to some degree in all the other shantytowns in Seattle.

6

The City: An Idea Hijacked

The job was too big for Dix and his Commission. Dix had admitted as much in November and so brought in King County to help pay for relief and the Unemployed Citizens League to provide structure. He called the newly combined organization the Local District Relief Organization and it opened in January 1932. Dix had already established five districts for distribution. The twenty-two UCL locals would use the services of the district where they were located. In charge of the whole operation was general manager Charles F. Ernst.

Ernst, a graduate of Harvard, had been a social worker in Boston and for eight years worked at the South End House, a settlement house established to help the poor advance educationally, financially and spiritually. Afterwards, he had gone on to private industry working for the Hood Rubber Company of Massachusetts. In 1927, the company transferred him to Seattle to be the local sales manager.[1] With a top-notch education, experience in helping the impoverished and a background in private business, Ernst was thought a well-rounded choice. That was not to be, however. Ernst would prove to be a thorn in the side of all those seeking relief for nearly the whole of the Depression. He appeared to have little sympathy for those he was charged with helping. In fact, he seemed to take self-righteous satisfaction in cutting both the amount of relief offered and the number of people receiving assistance. None of that was evident at first, however, and so Ernst was appointed Director of the Local District Relief Organization.

Out of financial necessity the UCL had teamed up with the city. The city, too, had partnered with the county out of financial necessity. The hazards of pairing a homegrown self-help group with two local governments became clear quickly. This marriage of necessity required political savvy and infighting. These were skills few of the unemployed were adept at. It wouldn't take long before the UCL realized it was outmatched and in a battle for its soul.[2]

As the UCL became more intertwined with government, the need for stricter accountability became more evident. Regardless of the UCL's pride over their volunteer spirit, they would need to rein in their lax recordkeeping if they wanted government money. Ernst began by advocating for professional managers to track the resources for the city and county. This would, he explained, make sure relief was being properly distributed. It would be these professionals who would eliminate favoritism and prevent theft. Since the managers had to be of high quality, they needed to be salaried rather than volunteers. They required offices and staff and all the equipment necessary to monitor the program. All of this, of course, would cost money. Ernst's budget began to swell. UCL members realized that for every dollar spent on administration, a dollar would be taken away from relief. They had a system using volunteers that worked fine and didn't cost a cent, they complained. But, they were told, if they wanted government money, the UCL was bound by the inherent red tape.

By the time Ernst's system was running at full speed, the cost would rise to $6,417.50 per month, a sum the volunteer workers in the UCL found unconscionable and wasteful. This was food out of the mouths of the hungry just to make certain that food didn't get into the mouths of the undeserving. Surely, the amount saved couldn't equal the potential amount lost.[3]

Next, the professionals were sent out to ensure that no one was receiving relief unjustly. Each recipient was visited and interviewed. They were forced to reply to what were deemed intrusive and suggestive questions. Instead of the assumption that the unemployed were trying their hardest to find work and survive, they felt they were being accused of scamming the system. Why else would they need to be visited in their own homes and questioned so thoroughly?

At first, Ernst appeared sympathetic to the complaint. In fact, he established a school to train the unemployed themselves in interviewing and determining eligibility. Those who were trained were even sent out in lieu of the professionals for a time. Unfortunately, this turned out to have its own difficulties. The newly coined social workers were of inconsistent quality. Some ended up being too harsh in their evaluations; others refused to pry deeply enough. Whether that was due to poor training or the fact the interviewers were too intimately connected to the interviewees can never be known. Either way, Ernst scrapped the experiment and returned to hiring professional interviewers.

All the government intrusion made it clear that the men were no longer in control of their own League. Many felt under the Local District Relief Organization they had reverted to charity cases. The attempt to pull themselves up by their bootstraps had crumbled. They were no longer independent men working together and relying on their own strength and ingenuity. The feeling began to develop that they were becoming relief cases dependent on the government dole.

The fact that the number of unemployed continued to grow only added to UCL members' sense of frustration. The January 18, 1932 report to the Dix Commission listed 6,153 families registered on UCL relief rolls, and of those only 55 percent were able to get any assistance. By February the number of families grew to 9,864. The best Dix was able to do that month was to give sporadic work to 4,750 men. In other words, the numbers of unemployed continued to increase dramatically while the percentage of those helped decreased by 7 percent in a single month. The unemployed hadn't totally given up, but yielding so much control to the government and seeing their numbers continue to swell was a serious blow to their confidence.[4]

Still, the UCL had one ace left up their sleeve. During the 1931 election for mayor of Seattle, they had thrown their support to John Dore early. During the September meeting at the Eagle's Auditorium, he had gained the approval of the UCL by loudly and publically announcing his support of taxing the rich to help the unemployed. He had declared his staunch belief in a standard wage for relief work and limiting the fortunes of the extremely wealthy. He spoke for the poor, unemployed and weak. In so doing, he had won the hearts and votes of the UCL.[5][6]

Dore, though, had a questionable reputation. Some believed he was an opportunist and a populist. Earlier Dore had run for county prosecutor, and in that campaign he gave the voters an added incentive to vote for him. If elected, he said, he would decline any payment for his services. This had led to disbarment hearings, one of two such hearings in his career, before the State Supreme Court. His opponents charged that this tactic was simply veiled bribery aimed at the citizenry. Dore's supporters claimed that the disbarment attempt was a politically motivated attack on their generous candidate.[7] Regardless, during the mayoral election, the UCL had supported Dore and campaigned for him.

In the elections of March 1932, 20,000 UCL votes were tallied for Dore. In the end, he racked up a total of 72,448 votes to Harlin's 41,212. The UCL had their man in office and rejoiced. Yes, they would still be faced with government interference, but Dore would fight for them, they believed. He understood that the unemployed weren't asking for a hand out, they simply wanted a leg up. He would provide jobs and give the Self-Help movement the boost they needed. Now the Dix Commission would be backed by the full weight of the mayor and with the County and UCL working together, the unemployed might yet be able to take back some control and help themselves.

Perhaps it would have been better had Dore won by fewer votes. But since Dore won by over 30,000 votes, and he believed he would have received many of the UCL votes anyway, he felt he owed them nothing. Therefore, with Dore's election, jobs didn't increase, evictions did. Water and lights were shut off in greater numbers.[8] Instead of maintaining wages, Dore began to cut wages. He stressed "efficiency" in government, rather than creating work for the unemployed. In the end, taxing the rich made good campaign rhetoric but poor policy, he decided.

To help in his "efficiency" campaign, Dore decided to create a commission to investigate ways of cutting expenditures. He proceeded to appoint businessmen and the well-to-do for the commission. Besides Dore, the UCL had helped elect two councilmen who remained true to the UCL vision. Those two joined others in the City Council to reject Dore's nominations. Dore aggressively labeled those who opposed him "public enemies." Demonizing his enemies, Dore went on to fire policemen, increasing the numbers of the unemployed. He threatened to lay-off 250 firemen if they refused to accept a pay cut. He cut work hours of other city workers. When he was running for mayor he had promised the UCL and labor groups that he would not reduce any workers' salaries if they were making less than $250 month. He lied about that as well.[9]

Just three months after his election, in June 1932, the Seattle Star, a previous supporter of Dore, printed a front page editorial entitled, "Why Did We Vote For Dore?" This was a question echoed by many Seattle liberals and unemployed.[10] His new nickname brought home his hypocrisy, "Revolving Dore." Having lost the support of those he had courted, Dore continued on his crusade to save money rather than tax the rich as he had promised. He fired 84 firemen and all 27 fire inspectors as well as shoving a 20 percent pay cut down the throats of the remaining firemen.[11]

Meanwhile, the number of unemployed in Seattle steadily climbed. From the beginning of March, when Dore came to office, to the beginning of May 1932, the number of families registering at the UCL for relief had increased over 27 percent. By April, 3,000 women had registered for Landes' sewing work. With spring coming, most assumed workers desperate for jobs would head out for seasonal work in the farms, and the numbers of unemployed families in the city would decline. Instead, they increased, even if at a modest 2.2 percent.[12] By June the commissaries were struggling to feed the 43,811 people who came through their doors. There were times when no fresh fruits or vegetables were available and the heavily starchy diet began to wear on the needy.

Despite disappointments and depression, both economic and emotional, the membership of the UCL tried to soldier on. A remarkable, if insular, resilience arose. The amount of volunteer hours contributed rose to the truly heroic. In the six months from January 1st to July 21st, men and women put in 2,306,415 hours of volunteer labor. On an average week, 5,078 members worked 79,532 hours to provide wood, keep commissaries running and to cultivate and ship food. Eleven thousand cords of wood were cut, 42,000 pairs of shoes repaired, 450 acres were cleared and farmed, and innumerable meals were served. They had even acquired houses on Capitol Hill and in th University District to help those who had been recently evicted.[13] If they couldn't do anything about the county intrusion or Dore's duplicity, at least they could muscle forward and attempt to provide for their own. There were still those in the UCL who believed that as long as they stayed united in their goals and grew as an organization, there was hope they still might rise, speak as a cohesive force and provide mutual support.

There was one final crippling contest, though, that the men needed to face. This was an internal struggle for the "theology" of the UCL. The organization had been founded on the shoulders of dedicated socialists like Carl Brannin and Hulet Wells. They were practical socialists who understood that live human beings were more important than party rhetoric. They realized that the ideal had to give way to the real and immediate. The Revolution could wait, the hungry couldn't. They and others like them created the UCL with the understanding that men would carry the load as best they could for as long as they could; that was the whole point of Self-Help. But when the people could no longer provide for themselves, the government would step in. The purpose of Self-Help was to give the government breathing room to organize work relief. This collaboration would allow the system to survive, altered and more humane, but intact.

Now a second front was moving in. These men, too, were socialists but they cared less about the present than the future. These men believed that the system, itself, was at fault and needed to be excised rather than altered. The government wasn't the solution, but the problem.

The new internal faction of the UCL called for less Self-Help, not more. The idea that the men could provide enough support for one another was simply snake oil, and those who peddled it were puppets of the system, they believed. This faction insisted that the men shouldn't beg the government. Instead, the UCL should demand a broader, more universal shift. Through mass movement and revolution, a Worker's Government would arise. The members of this faction were ardent Communists and International Workers of the World members. With the unemployed on the ropes from the dual assaults from Dore and the recent county requirements, this new faction decided it was time to inject their philosophy into the UCL.

Hardcore Communists in Seattle had a long history. They had attempted to disrupt the political and economic systems for years. They opposed private charity and did what they could to disrupt its distribution. Recently, they were known to join the IWW on Skid Road and attempt to drown out and chase away the Salvation Army by heckling and singing radical songs. They believed that charity simply helped the rotting system to continue and, therefore, they were justified in alienating those who offered food and shelter to the poor.

As the economic situation worsened, the numbers willing to listen to and join the Communist Party and its affiliates grew. Speeches by Communist leaders on downtown Seattle street corners could rally over a thousand men. It is almost certainly true that the majority of those who gathered were just curious. Still, the fact that a soapbox speaker could gather that many listeners speaks to the desperation of the times.

Many communist loyalists believed that all that was needed was a push to topple the entire system. As a result, they were willing to team up with like-minded radicals including the IWW. Because both the Communists and IWW wanted a fundamental change with the workers in control, the two organizations maintained an uneasy alliance.[14]

The weakened UCL was ripe for a take-over by this communist-dominated faction. By spring of 1932, the Communist paper, The Unemployed Worker, began to sow seeds of dissention in the UCL membership. They called Brannin and other leaders of the UCL "paid tools" of the bosses. They claimed that the Self-Help movement was a way of allowing the system to survive while forcing the workers to "help each other by sharing [their] poverty." This faction remained a minority, but they were an active minority.

As a result, by June, through publicity, propaganda, arm-twisting and innuendo, communists had taken over the leadership of two of the UCL locals, South Ballard and Columbia City. At first the original leadership reacted slowly, but with the take-over of the two locals, some began to understand the threat. In a two-pronged response to the Ballard take-over, the Central Federation tossed out the communist-backed leadership and regained control of that local. At the same time, Central Federation officials simply refused to recognize the delegates from Columbia City.[15] Unfortunately, this was only the first battle between those who cared more about the individual and those who cared more about institutions.

7

Shacktown: Mayor

Years after he was elected "Mayor" of Hooverville, Jesse Jackson wrote a brief autobiography of his time there. In it, he explained how the men came to inhabit these shacktowns:

"Most grown-ups remember the years back when great numbers of men roved around over the West, either walking the highways or riding freight trains, carrying big rolls of blankets over their shoulders. 'Bundle Stiffs,' they were called. They picked up jobs wherever they could find them, sometimes in railroad construction camps, or digging tunnels, or building dams. They never stayed very long in one place and then drifted on. They always wore rough clothing and cooked and ate their meals in the jungle camps and unrolled their blankets and slept either in box cars or out in the open, with the ground for a floor and the sky for a roof. The police always saw to it that they never stayed very long in one town...[The Bundle Stiff] was continually informed of there being plenty of work 'right over the hill' and that the best thing he could do would be to go and take on some of it.

"People often ask, 'What has become of the 'Old Time Bundle Stiff?'"Jackson continued, "They see great swarms of young men rambling around, but do not see the old timer of years ago. The answer is that the 'Old Time Bundle Stiff' has taken Mr. Gifford's advice and has built himself a shanty in some shanty town and has stopped drifting around. It is this type of men who predominate in Hooverville."[1]

Walter Gifford, the head of a Hoover-sponsored fact-finding committee on the unemployed, had advised those without jobs to stay put rather than engage in a futile cross-country search for work. Jackson claimed that Gifford's words kept many from wandering, but Gifford might not have been the best sage for Jackson or others down on their luck to follow. When called before the Senate to talk about his program, he was unable to tell them how many were unemployed, how relief was distributed or how money could be raised for the unemployed. Gifford was certain, however, that federal funds would simply cause private giving to decline.[2]

The fact was Hooverville was made up of a more complex mix of men than just Bundle Stiffs. A whole array of society ended up in the shacktowns. The only thing that linked their life-stories was the end, which usually went something like, "...and then I hit hard times and ended up here." For example, a man identified as Mr. B, around fifty years of age, had arrived at Hooverville after having been an Alaskan gold prospector. The previous two years were spent going from one temporary job to another. Just before claiming a shack on the waterfront, he had lived in a rooming house renting at $8 a month. After racking up a $70 debt with no way to pay it, he skipped out. He figured that living on his own was better than taking a hand out, even though it meant having to share toilets that simply left the waste in the bay and scrounging through the local market garbage after closing time to see what was edible. Regardless, Mr. B was proud of his refusal of charity. That pride was reflected in the neatness of his six foot by eight foot shack, partly dug in and lined with cardboard. A single small window let in light and two American flags advertised his loyalty.[3]

A second Hooverville resident, Mr. D had been a carpenter foreman in California. He, too, was about fifty. He had a family, wife and money until a car crash left him with a broken back and widowed. He had a solid nest-egg of $3,700 but his bank went under. He lost everything. His son had since moved to

South America and his daughter was in college living off a trust fund from his wife's people. Mr. D made some spare change by selling junk he collected but tried to send what little he could to help his daughter get through school. When he first moved north, he built a shack in West Seattle but was burned out. The next time he decided to use the base of a deserted steam-shovel to build his new home. The authorities had torn it down twice and he rebuilt it both times. But he decided he could build a larger place on the waterfront so moved to Hooverville where he had created a nice shack from three barn doors and two windows he had salvaged. He had even added a small front porch and a breakfast nook. Like Mr. B, Mr. D was not ready to accept charity and was satisfied with his arrangement for the time being.

Mr. K, a small man with a black moustache, was one of the few die-hard Communists residing in Hooverville. Inside his shack was a red Soviet flag complete with hammer and sickle. He was a veteran of World War I and resentful. He had tacked up a sign outside his door that read, "I FOUGHT IN THE WAR AND THIS IS WHAT I GOT!" After the war, he had worked as a boilermaker and a deck engineer on a freighter. He arrived in Seattle a year prior while working aboard a steamship. Upon arrival the crew found out that the company had gone bankrupt and they wouldn't be paid. Without money or a place to go, the ship's crew stayed put until the US Marshals arrived armed with two submachine guns to force them off. He now lived in a shack built on a cement floor which was left behind by the Skinner and Eddy plant and had a stock of canned goods given to him by a visitor.[4]

In the other shacktowns spread around Seattle the stories were also as individual as the shacks. At the Interbay shantyville lived Mr. L, a Chippewa Native, who had been a farmer in

Minnesota until bad weather and low prices pushed him out. He left his wife to find work and wound up on a series of boats as a fireman. From there it was downhill until finally he ended up living in a filthy shack, eating rotten food he had plucked from the local dump. He was trying to find work stoking a furnace for room and board, but even with his prior experience shoveling coal on ships, he realized that wasn't very likely.[5]

Mr. H originally from Slovenia lived at 6th and Massachusetts in an enclave of seventy other shacks, about ten blocks north of Hooverville. A miner, plumber and factory worker, he had found himself in Port Angeles, Washington earning $7 a day when the work just stopped. He had saved up some but spent $200 building and furnishing a shack on the Port Angeles waterfront. At some point, he completely ran out of money and was forced to sell his shack for $50. Afterwards, he bounced around from Portland to Chicago to St. Louis looking for and occasionally finding, work. But he returned to Washington State because of the temperate climate. He tried accepting charity but felt the conditions at the flophouses were too poor and the food on the soup line too lousy. Instead, he settled into the shack he made of packing boxes and scavenged wood. He'd had to raise the floor a foot off the ground to keep dry during the occasional flooding, but he believed he wouldn't have to stay long since he felt economic conditions were bound to improve soon.[6]

These stories, alongside those of the "Bundle Stiffs," could be multiplied by the thousands to make up the residents of Hooverville and the other Seattle shacktowns.

Jackson undoubtedly knew many of these stories in his role as unofficial mayor. For many of these men, he was the buffer between themselves and the authorities. He explained his duties this way, "At the time the settlement was founded, I was called a 'Contact Man,' a man to contact the city authorities and business houses, if the need arose. A few months later I was called the 'Mayor.'"

His role as mayor diversified as new needs cropped up. He was the man to talk to when any Hooverite felt the city was being unfair. He got "bawled out" by the city when the residents began causing problems. When someone in the village was sick and in need of medical attention, Jackson would make the call to hustle up help from Harborview Hospital up the hill. A couple of times a year, Jackson and his council would have to deal with a resident who died in their sleep. They would notify the authorities, check through their belongings and decide who got the shack. When a man became too intoxicated and threatened neighbors or the peace, Jackson contacted the police.

Drinking was a big problem for Jackson and others on the waterfront. Drinking, poverty and frustration made for a mean mix. While just about anything alcoholic that could be drunk was, the most common drink was "dehorn." This IWW nickname for denatured alcohol, used in homemade stoves and as a solvent, was nasty smelling, worse tasting and had a knock-out punch that was addicting. Unable to afford the also illegal but more expensive hooch, this was the medicine most men chose. And once chosen, its addictive quality and added kick sunk its hooks deeply in the men.

"Dehorn" was born out of a wrong-headed and malevolent streak in government policing. During Prohibition, the US government noticed that large quantities of alcohol meant for industrial uses were disappearing between manufacturer and the company that had ordered the stuff. It became clear that instead of being use for the purposed for which it was purchased, the alcohol was ending up in the stomachs of those who scoffed at the law. In order to prevent this, the government began adding poisons such as methyl alcohol and kerosene into this natural alcohol. The result was denatured alcohol, or "dehorn." And it was tragic for both the nation and Seattle's Hooverville.[7]

Most who drank dehorn weren't killed outright. Instead, this government developed cocktail usually took awhile to cripple and kill. Its immediate affect was normally a quick drunkenness and lots of laughs. But internally the deadly mixture was snaking its way into the brain, liver and kidneys. Depending on the amount used and the susceptibility of the individual, vision became blurred. Respiration was depressed and in many cases breathing slowed to two or three breaths a minute. The effect on the heart varied from rapidly speeding to a dangerously sluggish pulse. If dehorn was mixed with a high percentage of methanol, above fifteen percent say, rapid paralysis occurred. With less potent levels of toxins, however, it might take the mixture hours, days or even months to disable and destroy its victims.

South of Seattle in Portland, Oregon, Dr. Frank Menne reported on one batch of especially deadly dehorn. Twenty-two men died of this denatured alcohol within a two day period in that city during December, 1934. As the attending doctor, Menne felt compelled to issue a detailed analysis of those he had watched suffer. The men who hadn't died prior to admittance to Menne's hospital claimed not to have felt the result of the toxins until the morning after. It began with intense abdominal cramping. This was followed by a clammy sweat which soaked through their clothes. Vision varied from blurred to blind among the men. The slowing respiration caused a sense of suffocation which was quickly followed by cardiac arrest.[8]

At the Seattle Hooverville, dehorn was available for fifty cents a quart and was used to lubricate any occasion. One part-time resident recalled, "[I]ts nauseating orchard-spray aroma seem[ed] to be in good taste at all Hooverville social gatherings, formal and informal."[9] And by all accounts the effects were drunken brawls, unnecessary stabbings and pervasive illness that never left the men who drank it. Much of Jackson's time was spent on the mischief created by "Dehorners."

Jackson was also the unofficial contact for any who were interested in the men of or conditions in Hooverville. He received letters by the curious who asked questions of a sociological nature. Emotionally the hardest letters for Mayor Jackson to deal with were those in which the writers were attempting to track down runaway sons and husbands. He did his best to locate any that were, in fact, residing in the shantyville and let them know someone at home still cared. Many of the men, though, lived under assumed names due to trouble with the law or because they hadn't wanted to embarrass their kin. This made it difficult for Jackson to fulfill many of the requests of the families.

Jackson's shack also became the meeting ground for any who were looking to socialize or kill a couple hours. His was the only shack that had a non-crystal radio which had been donated by a local sporting store. Since his shack was the only one that also had electricity Jackson let the men sit on his porch or front yard while the radio played via loudspeaker. Music, news, and radio shows were broadcast to the homeless men who encircled the box. On the nights President Roosevelt spoke, men flocked to Jackson's shack. Particularly popular was the voice of Leo Lassen as he did the play-by-play for the Seattle Indians baseball team. His precise, rapid speech brought the men to Dugdale Field where the Indians took on the competitors from the

Pacific Coast League. When Dugdale burned down in 1932, Lassen set up camp in the Civic Field. For the length of the ballgame, the men shared the green grass of the outfield, heard the roar of the crowd as a home run ball flew over the left field wall and visualized a close play at the plate. They discussed the teams and players and rehashed the day's entertainment. Jackson's radio and his amiability helped many men pass summer days that verged on pleasant.

8

Shacktown: Aid

Before Franklin Roosevelt, the hope of the homeless and unemployed was local and state government, which was questionable at best, and private charity, which frequently came with strings or was sorely inadequate. The UCL tried to provide a third path by offering the option of Self-Help, but for many of the poor, joining the UCL was beyond their emotional capacity. These men were using every internal resource combating depression and fatigue brought on by an overwhelming collapse of self-confidence. Then, too, as the UCL contended with internal fighting, more members bailed out not wanting to get caught in a political squabble that had nothing to do with them and their problems. So while the UCL commissaries helped feed a certain section of the unemployed, for most others soup kitchens, breadlines and band-aid solutions were the only support they could count on. Organizations such as the Union Gospel Mission sprouted up to help the immediate needs of this group.

In April, 1932 Peter MacFarlane left the Saint Paul Mission in Saint Paul, Minnesota to travel to Seattle. The Mission in Minnesota had been around since 1902 and aided the poor and indigent. With the Depression gripping the nation, MacFarlane decided to lend his expertise and experience to other regions. Upon arrival, MacFarlane gathered clergy from around Seattle. The central question was what could be done to help those living in the shacktowns and wandering the streets? In the end, MacFarlane encouraged the representatives to form a single Christian community in order to pool their resources. The Apostolic Faith in Pioneer Square joined up. The Elim Swedish

Baptists of Wallingford and the Gatewood Baptists from the South End chipped in. Tabernacle Baptists of Capitol Hill and the First Presbyterian Church in downtown signed up. Since this would be a union of churches, they would call themselves the Union Gospel Mission. They open their doors on August 21, 1932 at 716 ½ First Avenue in downtown Seattle.

Reverend Francis O. Peterson, another Minnesotan, was placed in charge of the Union Gospel Mission. The location was perfect as it sat between two shacktowns and right next to the Society Candy Company. The Candy Company was civic-minded enough to contribute its large candy-mixing copper kettle, so the Mission could take whatever was donated and turn it into a soup for the men. With a first year's budget of $1,500 for rent, salary for Peterson and any other expenses, money was tight. Regardless, the Mission went right to work. As many as 500 a day lined up for potluck at the soup kitchen. The first year the Union Gospel Mission fed a total of 18,000 men with donations they received.[1]

There were many other soup kitchens and breadlines throughout the city, some existing years before the Crash. But it was with the onset of long lines and men in fashionable suits that the extent of the new need began to hit home. As early as February 1930, Volunteers of America was sounding warnings. They had run a breadline for years and had already seen the number of meals served in Seattle double from 1928 to 1929, climbing to 20,617 meals for the month of January 1929. A year later in January, 1930, that number had again jumped to 29,509. That same month, Volunteers of America watched as the 350 beds they had available for the homeless willing to endure an hour of prayer and hymns were filled, and they were forced to turn away an average of 40 men, nightly.[2] In November 1930, the Retail Meat Dealers' Association attempted to reassure the public that they could distribute enough meat through breadlines and soup kitchens to keep the poor from starvation.[3] But seeing the long lines of tattered men lined up outside the soup kitchen doors, sometimes hours before they opened, caused many to doubt their claims.

Walking the streets of Seattle any lunchtime or dinner showed how desperate the situation was becoming. The Catholic Church made it their unwritten policy to feed any of the hungry who showed up at their hospital. As a result, Providence Hospital had its own breadline.[4] The Millionair Club distributed bread to married men at 412 Main Street. Each loaf weighed a pound and the men could pick up one loaf for each member of the family.[5] The Blue Ox Lodge ran a soup kitchen on Western Avenue for single men.[6] The Seattle Star Newspaper boasted its own soup kitchen called the Sunshine Club. Here the food was cooked at James R. Boldt's Second Avenue restaurant and delivered hot to the city's Armory building. The Star reported serving around 2,000 meals a day. They proudly admitted that a quarter of those meals were for men who took seconds or thirds, one of the few establishments that allowed return visits.[7][8]

The Central Registry, the umbrella organization for many of the Seattle breadlines, helped to clearly define the extent of the need. In the single month of February, 1932, Central Registry's affiliate organizations supplied 45,689 nights of shelter for the homeless. Among other services, they began supplying day care for working mothers and home visits for the blind. Most importantly, though, they had been responsible for providing 151,156 free meals. All this private assistance was vitally needed since very little was contributed by government agencies to the shelters or breadlines.

Yet, many of the recipients of the aid were unwilling to call it charity and for good reason. The potluck meals were only given if the desperate men worked for it.[9] In other words, the food was not seen by many of the unemployed as charity but as forced labor for food. This was not a kindness given freely but a system that provided cheap labor to businesses in exchange for poor and inadequate food.

As to the quality of meals and the requirement to work for their dinner, however, there were contrasting opinions. The Seattle Times letter section presented two such views. Barney E. Johnsen wrote complaining:

"Have you, Mr. Reader, ever had the pleasure to be a member of a chain gang? If you haven't...then take a trip down to the Seattle central registry [sic] office, Second Avenue South...Honest workingmen in the clutch of unemployment some of the unfortunates with hardly a rag to cover their bodies are forced to work, rain or shine, sixteen hours per week without compensation except the magnificent generosity of two meals a day. And such meals! Breakfast: Mush, black coffee and a lump of bread – a la jail mode. Supper: By good luck, a plate of beans but mostly queer, Irish squeamish stew – Potato-mulligan, consequently Irish. There isn't a restaurant in Seattle which would be able to sell such meals at five or ten cents."[10]

Disagreeing was Charles Swanson who responded:

"I am on the so-called bread line (which can no longer be designated by that name, as it is far above that in Seattle) and can say that the writer of the letter did not know what he was talking about. [M]en who work sixteen hours a week receive excellent meals while they are working, in fact no restaurant could afford to serve those workers meals less than 25 [cents] and stay in business. Ninety-five per cent of the men who are registered and feed at the Volunteers of America are satisfied and thankful, as I am...And if more citizens would call at the Volunteers and see the kind of food we get, they would find out it is very far removed from the chain-gang element and after tasting some and seeing the clean beds supplied by the Salvation Army they would realize that men like Barney Johnson [sic] are only making it harder for the unfortunate and leaving the impression that Seattle is not doing her bit which she is. 100 per cent."[11]

A more balanced opinion was presented by Harold P. Levy, a reporter for the Seattle Times. He wrote:

"Mulligan stew...beans...bread. Multiply it by seven and you have a rough idea of the main – and only course on a Washington Streeter's weekly dinner menu. Only when you have stew you don't have beans and when it is bean night you get no stew. You always can count on the bread. But you take it without butter, or you don't take it at all...The line forms at 4 o'clock outside the Volunteers of America Building at Washington Street and Railroad Avenue: Old men, young, white, brown, black and yellow. As you step inside the door you show your work card, issued by the Central Registry...Then you march upstairs to the second floor. You show your card again to a man who punches it. You file past the food vats. A server sploshes [sic] a plate full of stew into granite dish and hands it to you. Another server gives you a tin spoon about two sizes larger than your grandmother's biggest serving spoon. You sit down at one of the numerous long tables, where little piles of four and five slices of bread are placed for each man. And you eat your stew and bread. An attendant comes filling tin cups with coffee, pale mud colored...They all agree it is clean...It is filling enough, but the men complain it is not strength producing...They tire quickly because their strength ebbs fast.

And, they say, their breakfast of mush, bread and black coffee don't help, either."

Levy wrote that there were reports roast beef was going to be served soon and sugar and cream might be available for the coffee, but if these things happened there was never any mention of it. Regardless of the quality, there was never enough and the lines seemed to always stretch down the street.[12]

While most understood the moral need for the breadline and soup kitchen, some were willing to recognize the practical reasons as well. Self -preservation dictated that the growing numbers of homeless and hungry should not be left to their own devices. If ignored, the desperate men and women might take matters into their own hands. Jim Marshall, writing for the Seattle Star's Sunshine Club, made it clear that he believed if the food were not available and the sympathetic declined to help, the jobless might become a threat to those better off. He wrote:

"As you stand there, and the Battered Battalion streams past you, ragged and hungry, you begin to get mad. You see the fine women- none of them rich – who come down to our club feeds every day and work...And you see the fishermen and fruit growers and truck gardeners and butchers and bakers – none of them rich – who pile in food for the foodless...And you see far away, others – lolling in limousines, strolling thru art galleries, chuckling over profit-and-loss accounts...and then you wonder! What would happen if these fine women and these fishermen and butchers and bakers and fruit growers and these cooks and dishwashers, didn't stand between greedy exploiters and that tragic battalion?...Suppose, you say as you turn away, that shadowy line falters? As the door swings shut, you can hear, faintly, the rumble of the guns..."[13]

Some men shunned the breadlines and instead took to prowling the back alleys and garbage cans for edible refuse. Store owners would sometimes set aside day old bread or overripe fruit or damaged cans for the homeless, placing it on top of or near garbage cans. But one of the reasons that so many shacktowns were located by city dumps was because of the access to yesterday's meals. A reporter, only identified by the initials U. M. went out to one of the dumps to see firsthand those who picked through the debris. As he approached he was startled by the number of seagulls that he saw from a distance swarming the piles of trash. As he got closer, he realized that the squawking of the birds was in response to the men who were fighting the animals for scraps.

Hooverites picking through garbage. May 6, 1937. *Post-Intelligencer Collection, Museum of History & Industry.*

"Men with long dragging sacks tied to a harness-like rope across their shoulders, a forked stick in their hands eagerly scratched around through the filth...Artificial flowers, blood stained rags, a dead hen, entrails from some large animal, decayed vegetables and fruit, helped to make the sight more unbearable," U. M. reported.

It was worse when it rained and the men waded into the muck and mud. This, though, is where these men found most of their food. Carrot peelings, lightly-molded bread, watermelon stuck to the rind, and over-cooked rice could be salvaged, although meat was discarded for safety's sake. When asked why they didn't eat at the soupline, the men answered that they had no desire to be investigated and picked at to receive a voucher. Their biggest complaint was that competition at the garbage dump was growing and that made life harder still.[14]

No one was proposing soup kitchens or breadlines as permanent solutions, however. What the men needed was more than a hand-out, they needed a job. Everyone recognized that. Unfortunately, the city and county had tried to find work for the unemployed and failed. The state was weak and in many ways disinterested. Local solutions had been found wanting across the nation. A national solution needed to be found.

9

The City: An Idea under Assault

In Ballard, the communists in the UCL local hadn't fully relinquished control. They had been denied representation in the Central Federation and lost some leadership positions, but they maintained their grip on the commissary. Since the commissary was responsible for distributing food, communists inside the Ballard UCL maintained power in fact if not in name. They used this power to give their supporters preferential treatment in the way of extra rations and goods.

This inequality didn't go unnoticed. Some sided with the communists for ideological reasons, others simply to get additional food for them and theirs. Others, still, thoroughly resented the blatant manipulation and resisted communist control. Eventually, the failure to equitably distribute food led to a small riot. But because the Central Federation never granted itself power over the locals, there was little they could do to control the infighting in Ballard short of booting them from the organization entirely. To do so, though, would have meant abandoning non-communist supporters who were still in the Ballard UCL. Besides forcing the Ballard UCL out of the Central Federation could create a backlash in other locals where communists continued to gain strength.

Other problems began to challenge the Central Federation. In Fremont, the commissary manager was charged with selling donated food to a restaurant for his own personal profit.[1] This joined other rumors of corruption, graft, fraud and racketeering within the UCL. As talk spread, there were those who began to ask whether they were working for themselves or helping support organized crime. Throughout the summer of 1932, the ideologues and criminals caused some to question their faith in the UCL.

Despite the doubts, though, the Unemployed Citizens League movement continued to grow. The UCL had spread across the western portion of Washington State. On the east side, farmers had also been meeting and forming their own organizations. It seemed the next logical step was to gather together the various leagues and determine what common ground they shared. Perhaps, they could form a united force that would demand the attention of politicians across the state.

As a result, on May 29-30, 1932, a convention of 400 attendees was held in Tacoma to unite 112 locals representing unemployed workers and impoverished farmers. Hulet Wells was called to be chairman of the new United Producers of Washington and Charles Gilbreath, the man who had formed the second UCL in West Seattle, joined him on the executive committee. Carl Brannin was called to head the publicity duties for the new organization. His experience in writing and publishing The Vanguard equipped him to be a superb evangelist. Through his efforts, many heard of the UCL and its Self-Help philosophy. Business Week, Survey, New Republic, Nation, Fortune, Atlantic, Reader's Digest, and Colliers were just some of the nationwide magazines that printed articles on Seattle's ambitious unemployed in part due to Brannin.[2]

Meanwhile, Seattle Central Federation President Cronin continued as if the communist take-over of local UCLs was an unimportant sideshow. Instead of solidifying control over the endangered locals, he talked of expanding the Self-Help movement. Cronin discussed plans of creating a UCL-operated bakery which he believed could lower the price of baked bread to three and a half cents a loaf. He also looked into the possibility of creating a UCL bottling plant to supply milk for their members.

Unfortunately, Cronin failed to acknowledge that other attempts at expansion had not been successful. A quilt manufacturing enterprise had gone under and an attempt to sew and sell overalls had also folded. He also never addressed the need to somehow consolidate power in the Central Federation. Had he been more politically astute, Cronin might have been able to block the communists from grabbing control. Instead, Cronin opted to build political connections outside the association, and by extending his reach through new initiatives and alliances rather than strengthening his gains, Cronin opened the door for the more single-minded attack from his rivals. In the end, this meant that mainline socialists like Cronin and Wells and Brannin would soon watch as their influence as leaders of the unemployed quickly ebbed. The first major warning signs of trouble for the old leadership occurred on Independence Day, 1932.

Washington State Governor Roland Hartley had been urged by five mayors, including Seattle's, to organize a meeting on relief and the unemployed but he had refused. With rare support from Mayor Dore, Cronin decided to organize a UCL sponsored march on Olympia scheduled for July 4, 1932. The demands of the march were stated in a front page article in the Seattle Times. First, the State should enact legislation to provide adequate relief to the cities and counties. Second, money should be freed up to create jobs for the unemployed. Third, there should be a state-wide program for public improvements. Additional proposals called for a 30 hour work week to spread the available work around, a state income tax to make the state tax collection more progressive and unemployment insurance for the workers.

Cronin called for 50,000 to turn out for the march.[3] When Governor Hartley heard about the march, he let it be known that he would be unable to meet with the leaders of the protest. Claiming he had a previous engagement, Hartley recommended that the United Producers send a written request to the Governor's office instead of marching on Olympia. Carl Brannin, joining Cronin, made it clear that they would not back down. He said, "We will camp on the Capitol grounds until we are given an audience. There will be no use for the governor to leave Olympia to avoid us."[4]

On the day of the march, rather than 50,000, a mere 600 protesters showed up. Cronin had vastly over-estimated the power of the UCL and United Producers to bring out their people, and even those few who showed up were split into two rival camps. A communist faction appeared, aligned in purpose it seemed but refusing to be led by Cronin or Brannin. Instead, they attempted to elbow the United Producer leadership out and take over the protest themselves. But when that failed they divided from the other protesters and marched separately to the Capital Building.[5] Once both groups arrived at the statehouse, Brannin addressed the crowd. A small cadre of communists began booing, heckling and making alternative demands. The communist faction wanted a flat $15 a week for each unemployed person with $3 for each dependent. The United Producers' leadership realized this was a pipe dream and continued to stand by their original demands. Arguments broke out followed by a scuffle. A few punches were thrown and an arm was broken. Cronin's failure to rally 50,000 marchers as promised, and the fact that he couldn't even keep the few that showed up in line, called into question his leadership.

Later, Brannin reiterated that the whole problem was that the organizers refused to "permit the Communists [to] assume control of the demonstration." In the end, the protest broke up after only a couple of hours, and the leadership never met with the governor. It was reported later that the reason Governor Hartley was too busy to meet with the unemployed of Washington State was because he was "picknicking [sic] with members of his family in Everett."[6]

Upon his return, the governor did agree to a meeting with a select few of the United Producers leadership, including Wells, Gilbreath and Cronin. A few days later under less pressured circumstances, the two sides got together.[7] It ended up being an aggravating and useless meeting. Hartley refused to consider any of the United Producers' requests. Instead he took the opportunity to lecture the leadership on the problem with the poor. He claimed that the central reason there were so many unemployed and poverty-stricken was a lack of foresight. According to Hartley, they were destitute "because of their extravagance during the period of good times." He added that he was certain he, personally, "could go out without a dollar and make his way in the country."[8] This stunning condescension and refusal to understand the legitimate plight of the unemployed, highlighted the gap between the man in power and the men on the unemployment line. Also, the failure of Cronin and the inability of the United Producers to make any headway in the political realm opened up the gate even wider for the communist faction.

Problems piled on top of problems for the UCL. Complaints about the quality of food available at the commissaries became more insistent. The competent Dix began to experience health problems and had to resign from the Community Fund. All these difficulties were celebrated by the communists.

At the same time, the communist faction used the July 4 march to regroup and plan. There was much soul-searching in the meetings afterwards. Why were they not able to convince the mainstream members of the UCL of the superiority of their cause? Didn't the unemployed understand the numbers were in their favor and a revolution was at hand? Perhaps, it was decided, the presentation of issues they were advocating was too remote and esoteric. They might need a watered down version of revolution before common workers were ready for stronger stuff. Maybe a second march could be organized. This time, though, they would be less confrontative and echo more intimate demands. If the second march focused on the need for food, shelter and basic necessities and if the revolutionary movement took a temporary backseat, the people might be more open to the ultimate goals of communism down the road. This was seen as the best way for the communists to turn the UCL and gain control. As one of the communists leaders said, "[I]t was obviously necessary to organize another march [in] which we would aim to lead and control."[9] Only afterwards, would they educate the people on true communism, and eventually they would escalate until a full revolution bloomed.

In reality, of course, the communist movement in America never understood the unemployed. It is true that people were desperate and frustrated, but they were also law-abiding and afraid. As one of the unemployed said, "The dominant thing was this helpless despair and submission. There was anger and rebellion among a few, [but] by and large, [there was] that quiet desperation and submission."[10] Very few in Seattle, or anywhere else in the US for that matter, wanted to tear down the system. They were less angry than frightened. They were afraid that boom times might never return. They were searching for jobs not a new government, so if communism only offered more turmoil and destruction, why go that route? The people wanted security not upheaval.

That isn't to say that communism wasn't garnering attention. Across the nation, the unemployed and needy were protesting, marching and, in a few cases, rioting. Communist meetings took place in big cities like Seattle, Los Angeles and Pittsburgh, but they also occurred in smaller, out of the way places like Grand Forks, North Dakota. This was not a signaling of the need for revolution in the US, this was simply the manifestation of the people's discontent and dissatisfaction. Congress finally recognized the national frustration and attempted to respond. On July 9, Congress passed a relief bill for $2.3 billion.

President Hoover, however still rejected the idea that the government had a role in individual assistance, and many who were still living in comfort applauded the President's veto. Unfortunately for Seattle's unemployed, Mayor Dore was one of those. Dore not only didn't raise money for the out-of-work but looked for any way he could to cut city expenditures. By the end of July, Dore had sliced deeply into the city budget hacking out $2.5 million. Business owners and the wealthy sighed in relief; public employees, the unemployed and the poor groaned in exasperation.

At the August 24, 1932 meeting of the Central Federation, another battle was looming. When the leadership of the UCL was put up for a vote, the stalwarts – Cronin, Wells, Brannin and Gilbreath - were challenged. Communists pushed their new agenda and nominated W. H. Murray for Chairman. Murray had made a name for himself by helping to organize and lead the Bonus Expeditionary Force. This group of World War I veterans had marched to Washington, D. C. just a couple of months previously to demand an early payment of a bonus promised them. In the end, Hoover had sent in the army to remove these men, burn out their shacktowns and roust the ex-soldiers.

Murray also had a history with the International Workers of the World and had been involved in directing one of the local UCLs in Capitol Hill. When the election was held IWW and communist members bound together. Murray was in and Cronin out. An IWW member also from Capitol Hill, C. J. Boardway, took over the vice-chair. P. M. Larson, a Crown Hill Communist was voted in as executive secretary.[11] The coup was complete.

Immediately after the communist take-over, the Self-Help movement waned. In the last week of August, 1932, members compiled over 103,000 hours of volunteer work dedicated to the movement. Once the communist and IWW members gained control of the UCL, this number rapidly decreased until four months later, in December, less than half as many hours were recorded on voluntary programs.[12] Instead, the emphasis under the new leadership was mass movements and direct action. The UCL would gather large groups to protest and disrupt. Time currently used to further Self-Help would be spent on organizing marches and working to further the Cause. They would confront not compromise.

With the communists in charge of the UCL and a change in tactics, the constitution was rewritten. This new constitution stated that the only hope for the workers was if private ownership was "replaced by complete public ownership." It also made clear their intention to rid the commissaries of any influence by government officials. Commissaries, under communist control, would be run for and by the UCL only.[13] This was a direct challenge to the order issued by Ernst in January.

When Ernst had been appointed to oversee relief for King County, he had made it clear that professionals would take over UCL commissaries. The men and women of the UCL who started the commissaries and who worked there on a voluntary basis

97

took this as an affront. They had attempted to stop the transfer to professionals from happening, but finally Ernst decided it was time and sent in his hired managers. The new UCL leadership decided to make a stand at the Georgetown local.

Hearing that salaried county workers were coming to take over their commissary, Georgetown volunteers went on strike. On September 8, 1932, between 900 and 2,000 unemployed men and women milled around the building. Mayor Dore, who had been supported by the UCL in the election also decided to make a stand. In order to show the UCL who was in control, he sent fifty police officers to break up the crowd. Dore supported Ernst and the King County paid managers of the facility and refused to have relief blocked by what he considered a mob.

Dore came down to the strike personally. Once there he decided to address the crowd himself, even as Murray, the new UCL Chairman, was already speaking to the assembly. As Dore slid past Murray to speak, he said, "I'm going to show you today who's running this town."

As Dore began to talk, some in the crowd heckled. Finally, taking a defiant stand, Dore bellowed, "Get this and get it straight, we're going to bring groceries out here and we're going to distribute them...Anyone looking for trouble is going to get it – plenty of it – today, even if some of you are dead before it's over."

County Commissioner Don H. Evans, supporting the militant move by Dore, declared, "We will have a showdown. It's got to come sometime and it might as well be now."

Evans blamed the volunteers for the trouble. He insisted that the reason for the change to paid managers was because of the faulty organization and corruption under UCL volunteers.

Evans wasn't entirely wrong. Clearly, there had been sloppy administration and some outright graft. A special deputy, T. R.

Millard, had been assigned to trace rumors of theft of county acquired food and supplies. Just the day before the Georgetown confrontation, Millard had raided some houses of UCL members and confiscated roughly $500 worth of pilfered supplies. Millard insisted that there was widespread theft, listing six locals in which his investigations had found stolen goods bought by county funds. The morning of the strike, Millard had even found a note slid under his door saying, "Better lay off raiding our houses and leave our commissaries alone or you will wake up on a marble slab. 'The Committee of Action of Capitol Hill.'"[14]

While Evans might have had some evidence of the UCL's sloppiness, it's hard to find any systematic or large value losses. Even the day after the Georgetown strike, when Millard did track down two more examples of thievery, both were of little consequence. John McGinnis was found with two hundred bars of soap and John Carroll had taken $12 worth of groceries, all coming from commissary stock.[15] Once again, though, the volunteers had to wonder if the managers' salary would take more out of the budget than would be lost in theft.

Despite the threat of violence and despite bluster from Dore and Evans, the conflict at Georgetown was resolved peacefully by the promise that the paid manager would be withdrawn. While this calmed the crowd and allowed both sides to withdraw without violence, the promise was never fulfilled. Paid managers were the new fact of life.[16]

Continuing the philosophy of confrontation, the UCL attempted a second strike that September. This was in reaction to the lack of meat and the overly starchy diet served at the commissaries. This strike failed to get much traction, however. Next the UCL threatened to strike for milk. This never even got to the action stage. Protesting the scarcity of shoes for children, the UCL encouraged their membership to keep their children home from school on September 19. This was met by less than tepid response by parents who saw this as an attempt to use their kids as pawns. The mass action that communists saw as their ticket to revolution was proving to be more difficult in execution than they had assumed.

Unbeknownst to the communist movement, however, an even greater threat was forming that would slow their momentum and rob them of their membership. On September 20, a train pulled into the King Street Station and was welcomed by a boisterous twelve thousand people. Supported on one side by his son James and on the other by Seattle Police Chief L. L. Norton, candidate for President Franklin D. Roosevelt hobbled out. A Seattle Police Band preceded the car carrying Roosevelt, and an estimated one hundred thousand lined the parade route. Six blocks from Hooverville, at second and Washington, an especially loud cheer warmed his arrival even though other parades had been "received with apathy" at the same location.[17] It was clear that here was a man that carried the hope of something better or at least something different, and the people of Seattle were ready for change. In fact, he would give them the one thing Hoover hadn't and communists couldn't - jobs. That, however, was in the future.

Meanwhile, investigations into UCL fraud and corruption continued. Three members were arrested for grand larceny. They were accused of taking King County wood to Yakima, trading it for produce and selling the crops to fruit stands on the way back. They protested their innocence saying that the produce was brought back to be distributed among the unemployed in King County. One of the three even claimed to have affidavits to support his version of the story.[18] With threats of strikes and continued arrests, the two sides, UCL and local government, were becoming more adversarial.

Then, on September 26, the County escalated the conflict. A memorandum was sent to the paid commissary managers warning them that they were now fully responsible for making certain that those receiving relief provided work in exchange. In addition, the managers were commanded to take control of the gardens started under Self-Help and track the food coming from there. They would also be responsible for distribution of chopped wood and requests for all clothes, shoes and housing.[19] This was plainly an attempt by Ernst and the County to strip the UCL of all control and power. The men who had birthed and nurtured the idea of Self-Help and self-reliance were being pushed to the curb, and all the infrastructure they had built from the ground up was being ripped from them. Unfortunately, the new UCL, rather than looking for any negotiated or political settlement, fed on confrontation and talk of revolution and so welcomed the fight.

The following month, the County upped the ante with another attack against the UCL. During the berry picking season, the UCL had gathered more berries than they could eat at the time. The UCL had all the supplies required to can the left-over berries but needed a place to store the canned fruit. At that point, the Port of Seattle came to the rescue and provided a warehouse for storage. Now, several months later, County Commissioner Evans had gotten a temporary restraining order to prevent the UCL from retrieving 175,000 pounds of fruit stored at the docks. With winter coming and a lack of fresh fruit or vegetables, this was a serious blow to the UCL.[20]

About the only good news the unemployed in Seattle heard was, surprisingly, from the federal government. After Hoover had vetoed the relief bill passed by Congress, the legislative branch went back to work. They trimmed and massaged until they produced a bill the president would accept. This was a

$300 million package of loans, rather than the $2.3 billion originally recommended, that would be available for states which were "absolutely unable to finance the relief of distress."[21] It excluded any outright gift which could be used for direct relief for the poor but provided some source of federal loans for states that were willing to admit to desperation. At that, though, Hoover required that states show that they absolutely needed the money. In order to do that, each county had to prove complete poverty, which, of course, required each individual to show they had nowhere else to turn. Governor Hartley refused to make any such concession. His state was doing just fine, and it certainly needed no interference by the Federal government. Therefore, there was no call for the state to pay for any survey.

A sympathetic federal agent who was responsible for monitoring loans to Washington State, Pierce Williams, knew this to be a lie. He had seen the homeless, the breadlines and the ragged army of unemployed. Williams knew that Hartley was opposed to relief, believing it would only go to those too lazy to find work. Further, Williams believed that Hartley was a hard man who was "admitted by all who know him to make negotiation an exceedingly difficult thing."[22] Unable to convince Hartley of the wisdom of accepting the money, Williams began to contact the individual counties. In an open act of defiance, Williams began to instruct the individual counties on how to apply for aid directly, bypassing the governor.

Beginning with King County, Williams began to make headway. Despite King County Commissioner Evans aggressive stance against the UCL and past resistance, other Commissioners understood the severity of the problem. They listened to Williams and approved a move to conduct the appropriate surveys. When the results were tallied, it was clear that Governor Hartley and Commissioner Evans were in denial. The problem was deep and wide. King County was awarded the first federal loans in the state starting in October, 1932.

Considering how badly the Self-Help movement was floundering, the loans had become a necessity. The communist-controlled UCL had come out firmly against Self-Help as a way forward. Organizational time and resources were siphoned out and redistributed to other areas, such as mass movement and political plotting. On top of that fewer people were participating, and even those who remained active in Self-Help started to see cracks develop. Claims of selfishness and laziness replaced the pride of unity and purpose. The amount of hours donated declined. There were arguments about who was and who wasn't pulling their weight. K. O. Lynch of the Green Lake local wrote a poem expressing his and others' frustration. In this poem called Who Cuts the Wood? Lynch began with the lines:

Does your conscience ever hurt you,
When you're sitting safe inside,
With the fire warm and cheerful,
And your hunger satisfied?

And ends with the stanza:

Sitting 'round and always beefing,
Doesn't do you any good.
If you'd keep the home fires burning,
You must go and cut the wood.[23]

Mayor Dore added to the pressure on the UCL. He began a nightly radio show under the City-County Home Defense League to lambaste his enemies. In mid-October while on air, Dore launched an aggressive assault against the UCL-supported candidate for County Commissioner, John Stevenson. In part, he said, "I want to say, if this man should be elected...I would declare that a public emergency existed, and that I would arm householders to protect the lives of themselves and family...[I]f this man were elected county commissioner, I believe the streets of this city would run with blood inside four months...He believes that the crosses should be torn from our churches, and that it should be a crime to mention the name of God in this country...Commissaries will be turned back to agitators, to anarchists and Russian agents."

A year after they had so loudly endorsed Dore's candidacy for mayor, the UCL membership understood how wrong they were. Brannin's and Wells' UCL newspaper, The Vanguard, printed a large front page headline which read, "Mayor Dore Public Enemy." And even though they strongly disagreed with the current communist leadership of the UCL, the co-editors did agree with their evaluation of Dore. The article included a resolution passed by the recently communist elected leadership of the UCL Central Federation which stated Dore was "incurably addicted to making malicious and unfounded remarks concerning matters of public importance." He had "double-crossed the unemployed with unfulfilled promises and violent persecution" and had "assumed the position of dictator..."[24]

It seemed as though the current UCL management was failing miserably. They were unable to get the membership to actively engage in strikes. The constant barrage of attacks by Dore, Evans, Ernst and others had destroyed UCL control of the commissaries and weakened their political influence. The Self-Help movement was staggering. But despite all these setbacks, more people were joining the UCL. November set a record for total membership with twelve-thousand. Perhaps, the unemployed realized that they would have to unite to keep from being reduced to paupers and charity-cases; perhaps, they felt they had nowhere else to turn.

Unemployed Citizens League members. *Courtesy of Paul Dorpat.*

Or perhaps, the membership believed the fight for control of the UCL wasn't completely over. In a November 2, 1932 election of officers, a confused message was sent by the association. Hulet Wells was returned to the Executive Committee. This was a repudiation of the communist drive for control. But then William K. Dobbins, a deeply entrenched communist, was also voted into the Committee. Meanwhile, new Chairman, Phil Pearl advocated an increase in political activism, a move vehemently opposed by the communist faction.

Regardless of what message was being sent by the UCL elections, Pearl went forward with his plans. Under Pearl, the UCL supported the elections of two new candidates for county commissioner, John Stevenson and Louis Nash. Both ran on the pledge that they would return control of the commissaries to the League. One of the UCL's own, Marion Zioncheck, ran for the United States House of Representatives and Pearl gave his and his organization's full support. Zioncheck, UCL attorney from The Junction's chapter, spoke passionately for the poor and unemployed and was an unrepentant liberal.

In December the two UCL-backed candidates for county commissioners won. Stevenson and Nash were both helped by Pearl's support. The two would be called upon to pay back this support several times during their terms. In the short term, their election would be a mixed blessing, however, as the lame-duck commissioners let their dissatisfaction at being defeated be known. They pushed for and received cancelation of all remaining funds which were headed to Self-Help projects. This was a significant hit. With all their other problems, Self-Help was already struggling and this was another nail in the coffin. Without financial support and with the recent withdrawal of donated gasoline by Standard Oil, Self-Help took another nosedive.

Zioncheck also won his race for House of Representatives. In fact, his margin of victory was a clear indicator that his message had been popular with the voters of Washington's First Congressional District. Zioncheck received over 57% of the vote compared to second place Bert Ross who managed only 32%. Franklin Roosevelt also received 57% of the vote of President in a progressive wave that swept the country that year. It was clear that a desperate nation was demanding a new political track. Pearl had anticipated this and attempted to tie UCL's fate to these fresh ideas.

Unfortunately for Pearl, the communist faction of the UCL saw any alliance with politicians as treachery. Pearl further angered communists by using his connections to increase funds for the organization and convince supporters of the UCL to provide jobs for members. This, too, was anathema to the

Communist Dream. In essence, communists were looking to control the organization so as to swell their numbers. At the same time, they hoped that desperation could be increased until society collapsed and the UCL could then be folded into the larger communist movement.

In January 1933, a second hunger march on Olympia was organized with UCL leadership. This time government officials seemed more ready to meet with the protesters. A thousand marchers stood on the grounds in front of the Capitol Building. Some carried signs reading, "We Demand Food and Winter Clothing" and, more interestingly considering the internal fight for the UCL, "The Communist Party Leads the Struggle of the Workers" and "Down With the Commissaries." The Washington State Senate and House created a combined committee to meet with representatives of the unemployed. This time no punches were thrown. Communist, socialists and those who simply couldn't find a job all marched together.

Officials for the government acted as mediators between the newly-elected Governor Clarence Martin and the committee for the marchers. Among the demands of the protesters was $10 a week for each unemployed man and $3 a week for each dependent. Additionally, the marchers wanted an increased taxation on corporations and the rich.[25] While the reception and the meeting were cordial – women and children were even allowed to sleep in vacant stores – little was accomplished.[26] All were politely listened to, respectfully addressed and subsequently ignored. When there was no follow-through after the meeting, word spread. Kind statements without action were useless and perhaps worse than outright opposition. It was deceptive and disarming, leaving the protesters feeling powerless and manipulated. Dissatisfaction gripped the unemployed.

Just a few days later, perhaps as a feeble protest against the ineffectiveness of the march, a thousand men descended on the Volunteers of America relief station near Hooverville. They rallied around three men who encouraged them to reject the requirement that they work to get their food. But when the police showed up and the three were arrested, the crowd dispersed without incident.[27] Anger and frustration were strong, but fear and hunger were stronger.

On January 18, 1933, at a raucous meeting of the Seattle UCL, the failure of the second march on Olympia was blamed on Pearl's leadership. Pearl was accused of acting in bad faith by the communist contingent who questioned both his competency and integrity. Additionally, an internal audit exposed some misuse of funds. This was clearly the responsibility of the president, communists insisted. Whether this was Pearl's doing or not remains unclear but regardless, Pearl was suspended from his duties the following day.

Hulet Wells fought the attacks on Pearl. A week after Pearl's suspension, Wells lead another loud and prolonged discussion that narrowly reinstated Pearl by a vote of 49 to 47. It didn't matter. The communist faction was used to protracted battles and continued to harass and pressure the old-line leaders. Finally, on February 1, 1933, Pearl had had enough. With his resignation, the final roadblock was removed. Those who fought for ideology over relief had won.

This was the end of the battle for UCL's soul. Communists had gained control this time and would never again relinquish it. They had organized an internal revolt, created support from the men who were too busy staying alive to question motives and elected their own. "Fighting" Bill Dobbins, a 35 year-old jobless father of three became UCL Chairman.[28] Later they would admit that this was the moment they forever "abandon[ed] the old habit of the UCL leaders of making friendly deals with politicians..." Instead, they would push for a "militant struggle..." Conflict, not compromise was victorious.[29]

Washington State Governor Clarence D. Martin.
Photo by William Manto . *Governors' Portrait Collection*. Washington State Archives

And if conflict was what the UCL wanted, the new governor was happy to oblige. At first, Governor Martin appeared friendlier to the unemployed than Governor Hartley. Instead of rejecting federal loans under the Reconstruction Finance Corporation, Martin submitted requests for the money.[30] Martin also pushed through the McDonald Act in the name of helping the unemployed. This created the Washington Emergency Relief Administration (WERA), an agency to dovetail with the Federal Emergency Relief Administration (FERA). This facilitated the flow of money and assistance between federal and state governments. Unfortunately, the McDonald Act was a wolf in sheep's clothing as it instituted a voucher system. This meant that men working on relief projects would no longer get cash, but chits that could be used for food. This was strongly opposed by the unemployed as it restricted where they could shop. Further, vouchers might also be discounted by stores. Finally, the McDonald Act weakened county control over planning and hiring for relief projects. Allowing Martin to determine where the relief money would go was clearly a power grab by the governor. It meant that Martin could direct the relief money to friendly counties and officials as he saw fit.

On January 25, 1933, Martin made clear his feelings about the unemployed. He appointed Charles F. Ernst director of WERA. The unemployed and those who supported them were stunned by the choice. Ernst had shown his disregard for the opinions of the unemployed in his work for the Dix Commission in Seattle. He had ignored the wishes of the unemployed, implemented paid managers at the commissaries and revealed a striking lack of sympathy for the poor. Ultimately, he was fired by UCL supporter County Commissioner Stevenson when it was clear that Ernst's goal had been the destruction of the Unemployed Citizens League.[31] No matter, Governor Martin made his choice and staked his ground.

Under WERA two types of relief were provided. First, "home relief" helped the unemployed by giving direct assistance. The point was to provide "shelter, food, clothing, water, light, necessary household supplies, medicine, medical supplies" and other needs which were vital to maintaining a residency. Second, was "work relief" which was a temporary job given by a "municipal corporation" in order to help the unemployed earn enough for the "necessities of life...during the emergency period."[32] With Ernst in charge, the decision as to which type of relief to emphasize was left, in many respects, up to him. Reverting back to his belief that those who relied on home relief needed to be kept in tight rein, Ernst developed a statewide plan to track and investigate all those who received this form of direct assistance.

The new method of distribution of home relief under Ernst would eliminate the commissary system entirely. Instead, the unemployed needed to come to an office to register. Afterwards, an investigator would show up at the door of those requesting relief and interview them at their home. The investigator would examine the food and resources at the home of the applicant and determine what was needed. Then, the investigator filled out a voucher that could be redeemed at a local market. The voucher would list the types of food and how much the merchant would be reimbursed for them. Based on the reimbursement, the merchant then filled the order deciding on the brand and amount given. Then the voucher was submitted to relief offices for payment. Every two weeks or so the investigator would return to reevaluate the family's needs and the cycle started again. This convoluted and demeaning system was lauded by Ernst and WERA officials as less humiliating and more efficient than standing in line at the commissary.[33] In fact, it infantilized the recipient by taking away all decisions and handing them to the investigator and store owner. Further, this method applied to all who received home relief even if they were simply too old to work, wounded veterans from the recent World War, blind, bedridden, or paralyzed – all were stripped of their adulthood.

Those who received work relief were treated better, but by no means as equal to "real" – that is private industry - workers. They labored for a pittance and still were made to feel like they were accepting charity, although the underlying message from WERA was that at least they weren't simply sponging off the government like those on direct relief.

To aid WERA in providing help for the poor, three organizational units were developed. The first section was the Federal Surplus Relief Corporation. Its job was to buy surplus food from farmers and distribute it to the destitute in the cities. Since this was federally run and food was a perishable commodity, few in the state seemed to object strenuously to this program. The second section was the Self-Help Cooperative Program which provided services for groups like the UCL so that they could continue to barter and exchange for necessary goods and services. Ernst would later make it clear that he had no intention of utilizing this part of the organization. He thought the Self-Help Cooperative Program simply gave resources to political activists to manipulate for their own causes. The final unit was the Transient Services for Washington (TSW) which was established for those passing through or stuck in transit due to lack of funds like many of the shacktown residents.[34]

TSW was authorized by WERA, and Colonel Hudson T. Patten was appointed director in Seattle. The TSW took over the Central Registry from the Community Fund. TSW also teamed with Seattle and the Salvation Army to coordinate services at three shelters for homeless men: one at 213 ½ Second Avenue

South, another at 117 ½ Main Street and the third at 84 Union Street. The organization also consolidated food distribution to the unemployed at a single location, 87 Lenora Street. Allowing TSW to run these services helped free the Volunteers of America and Salvation Army to concentrate on their traditional missions.

Patten's TSW also took on responsibility for transient boys. Young boys who became hobos often ended up being taken advantage of by more experienced men. Realizing they had nowhere to turn, Patten teamed with the Boy Scouts. He received permission to use the Boys Scouts' Camp Parsons and there housed fifty boys under age 21. While at Camp Parsons, the boys received education as well as entertainment and supervision. A second program focused on the older and tougher young men. In collaboration with the Elks Club, an additional fifty boys were helped to find part-time jobs. At the same time, they were encouraged to attend school. [35]

Some of the WERA programs such as TSW did good work and helped those it was intended to, but others, such as the home relief became bureaucratically entangled. This was not always unintentional. Ernst and Martin were in sympathy with one another. They saw the state as responsible for work relief but believed home relief should be administered by locals. As a result, their main job, as they saw it, was to make sure that no one received more than the absolute minimum needed for survival. Besides, in their minds home relief was simply another name for the dole which they felt was almost universally unnecessary.

10

Shacktown: Roy

At first, Donald Francis Roy walked the mud and dirt paths of Hooverville without notice. Soon, though, the suspicious nature of desperate men couldn't help noting his odd behavior. The new boy, a 24 year-old in the midst of middle-aged men, seemed to be walking with a strangely measured pace. And yet his path was ambling and led neither to the privy nor to any particular shack. He talked to everyone. While he had no permanent pals or guys with which he regularly shot the breeze, he liked to talk - or rather to listen. He was persistent in his questioning, too. Rather than a conversation, some felt they were being interrogated. Though always polite and never snooty, this Donald Roy was high-toned and had something about him that just aroused suspicion. He bought a shack for $15 and moved in with a partner, but within a day or two the other guy was gone. Something else was strange, too. He had enough money to eat at a restaurant nearly daily.

Mayor Jackson pulled Roy aside at one point. He noticed that while Roy walked, he was drawing something. Oh that, Roy said, I got a job at the Civil Works Administration to sketch out a map of the place. Not one to criticize a money-making scheme, Jackson left him alone, but others talked. Maybe he was a welfare worker looking to get the skinny on the men here. In fact at a drinking session with some of the guys, Roy was flat out accused of being a "stool pigeon" for the government. Just before it got rough, one of the other men helped Roy out. "Oh, Red is all right," he said, "I've known him for a long time. We worked together at camp ----!" In truth, Roy had never been to that camp or any other for that matter.

Bored men with little to do theorized about the young man during that Seattle winter of 1934. He could just be a magazine writer looking for the inside scoop on slum life, some thought. Another bit of gossip that was making the rounds was that Roy was fishing for homosexual favors. He was young enough and everyone knew that there were enough lonely men that he could survive pretty well on their generosity. At one morning meeting, with Roy present, a member of the vigilance committee made the accusation literal. The man stared at Roy and threatened "to run all the punks out of here!" Roy was able to avoid any violence that might accompany those words, but it was clear that any open solicitation would be dealt with aggressively. Roy was not homosexual, though. Three men knew that for a fact. One suggested a trade of oranges for a dalliance with Roy, another made the offer of a happy home and the third offered cold, hard cash. Several others were less direct but clearly not less inclined. Roy turned them all down, though he never seemed to take offense.

One day, Roy showed up with a stack of 6X8 cards with the word "Census" printed on the top. Keeping close to the truth, he claimed he was gotten relief work through WERA. He admitted to the men that from all his pacing, he had constructed a map of Hooverville and said the Civil Works Administration which was tied to WERA was so impressed they hired him to gather more information. Now he openly sidelined the men and asked them questions, recording their responses on these cards. Most of the questions were standard – name, age, race – but a few went beyond that. In particular, Roy was asking how they were "getting by" and did they get any relief money. Frankly, most resented his intrusions. They had received enough of this type of prying by those at the relief offices or employment agencies.

Some suspected their information might get back to the police; a few were afraid because they had ties with radical political movements. Still others thought that these questions might wind up in their deportation. Stories went around that he was on the pay for one of the government agencies that were bent on rounding up the men and shipping them off to camps. When confronted with this, though, Roy laughed it off. He even had a ready explanation as to why that was impossible. He said that the government didn't need to collect a census if they wanted to cage them, all they had to do was surround the place and pack them off.

The truth was much more mundane but more significant for history. Roy was writing a paper. He was a University of Washington graduate student working on his masters in sociology. With the support of WERA, Roy had dressed in worn clothes and set himself up in a fifteen dollar shack in the middle of Hooverville. He became the only person to do an organized study of the men in the shacktowns anywhere in America during the Great Depression. His was the authoritative study of life among the hundreds of thousands of lost men of a generation. Fortunately, Roy was observant, skilled and persistent.

While the men resented his constant nagging for information, Roy returned two, three and four times to get what he needed. It was through him that we get the most reliable descriptions of the houses the men lived in and that we know that there were five hundred shanties built in the former shipyards. His map was precise and the most detailed of any shacktown anywhere in the US. He also left behind a system that separated Hooverville into sections. Each section was assigned a letter from A through J (skipping I since it could be mistaken for a 1). From there, he laboriously numbered each shack, thus providing the postal service with the ability to deliver letters. And the data he produced gives us a picture, not just of the location, but of the men as well.[1]

Aerial view of Hooverville. 1936.
HistoricAerials.com

During February and March of 1934, Roy counted 639 men and seven women. There were no children running around the dirt pathways. "Hooverville is no place for kids," Jackson had said. Although a few daring kids wandered through the shantyville on a lark, none lived there. Jackson went on to say that there was a woman who came with her 15 year old daughter, but the police were called and better housing was found by a relief agency. Only 4 residents were under 20 and an additional 76 were under thirty. Hooverville dwellers tended toward those too old to hop a train or to be lured by fantasies of jobs and hopes elsewhere. In fact, well over a third were in their fifties or older. Without homes or families, they congregated with men much like themselves.

Many of the men had no support because they had no family in America. Only 164 of the men living in Hooverville had been born in the US. Almost equaling the number of native-born were those from the Philippines which was the place of origin for 120 men. Fifty-nine percent of the men on the waterfront – a total of 172 individuals - had come from Nordic countries. In fact, out of all European nations, Sweden contributed the most men to Hooverville with 77. Eastern Europe was represented by 44 men from Austria-Hungary and Russia. If ever one needed proof that the depression was worldwide, all one had to do was take a walk along the waterfront.

Even of those who were American citizens, it was almost as though the people of the nation were shaken up and dumped out at this one shacktown. More men came from Michigan – 18 – than from Washington State – 16. Ten Pennsylvanians, thirteen Wisconsinites and twelve Minnesotans also gravitated here. These statistics made an interesting contrast with a poll taken at the Central Registry. Of those receiving assistance at the Registry three-fourths were Seattleites. The matter of where those from other nations and from out of state were going for food - or if the survey was legitimately taken - can only be left to conjecture.[2]

While most Hooverites were white, Roy found 29 blacks, 25 Mexicans and two Japanese alongside the Filipinos mentioned previously.

There had been much speculation as to the educational level of the men who ended up in the shacktowns across America. Some said the slums were crowded with languishing college graduates. At least in Seattle, that was not true. Only five had a college degree and almost 90 percent hadn't gotten past eighth grade.

The job history of the men placed Jackson among friends. Logging was commonly listed as the primary profession of the squatters along with mining, fishing, farming and construction work. As Roy said, "Hooverites look like 'shovel stiffs,' behave like 'shovel stiffs,' and possess the educational qualifications for pick and shovel work." Even what was listed as white collar work was really blue collar redefined. Janitors and night watchmen were among the 80 occupations listed as white collar in Roy's paper.

The marital status of the Hooverville residents was overwhelmingly single. Less than two percent were currently married and, of course, the majority of that two percent was separated. Just under fifteen percent had been married at one time in their past. Twenty-one men, including Jackson, were widowed. There were only six couples living together. The women who temporarily visited the shacks were not counted by Roy, but he did say they could be had for as little as 10 cents. Some kept the men company for a drink.

Hooverville's was a fluctuating population. Just under half had lived there for 13 months or more, and many came and went depending on the season. Summer meant an exodus to farms to pick fruit and factories to can fish. During their time away, many simply snapped locks on their hovels and returned when the work dried up.

A variety of odd jobs allowed most men to pocket a bit of change even if they couldn't find seasonal work. One hundred and five men collected paper for their cigarette money. A hundred pounds of newspaper gave them 40 cents; 100 pounds of cardboard, 20 cents. They also collect other scrap but metal, bottles and rags were tougher to collect so brought in less overall. Copper netted five and a half cents a pound and lead two cents a pound. Five men collected driftwood and sold it for $3 a cord. One worked at a junk shop; another cleaned a bakery. A black man shined shoes on Saturday and Sunday. A couple worked at the fish market or washed dishes. Thirty-six had some semi-steady work around the city.[3]

This was the picture Roy painted. Near the end of his thesis, Roy summed it up this way: "Ruthlessly, albeit impersonally, rejected by the industrial chameleon that once wooed their services, these men have no way of obtaining money to pay their way in modern society. Not only has the tap been shut off, but the faucet has been disconnected and the pipes taken out. The Hooverites are 'up against it'...Customary city haunts, the cheap hotels and lodging houses, don't offer free shelter, nor do restaurants big-heartedly provide the nourishment necessary for metabolic upkeep." Instead, he continued, the men constructed their own houses and scrounged their own food. This became their society. "And there remains Hooverville scrap-heap of cast-off men, junk-yard for human junk..."[4]

11

The City: An Idea Suffocates

In February 1933, Seattle and King County were preparing to put the new state relief plan into action. Not all parts of the system were complete, though. In particular, the investigators who would do the home visits were not quite ready. In preparation for full implementation, W. D. Shannon, the relief officer in charge of King County, decided the first step would be to close the commissaries where the needy had been receiving their food and supplies. Instead, the unemployed would go to one of thirteen distribution centers. At these centers, anyone who had been eligible for commissary privileges would be welcomed and handed vouchers that could be exchanged at a thousand grocery stores in the area. Once all the details were worked out, the state investigators would begin to weed out the ineligible and trim the list of recipients.

Shannon was convinced that this was a superior system. It would help the grocers derive some benefit from the relief and provide a more independent source of food for the needy. A second benefit, according to Shannon, was the eventual ability to more thoroughly regulate who received the resources.

Shannon also sent a veiled warning, "For the present, we will issue vouchers to everyone on the county commissaries' rosters. These commissary lists, however, are in our hands and our trained supervisors and investigators will immediately scan them to determine the actual needs and financial status of individual families."[1] This warning was clearly aimed at the UCL. In effect, Shannon was saying that Seattle Mayor Dore had won, and the UCL no longer had any say in who would receive help or how it would be distributed. UCL President Dobbins was more than ready to meet this direct challenge. In fact, it aligned perfectly with the long-term plan of the Communist Party. Conflict was always preferable to compromise.

Dobbins leaped at the opportunity to stir up his people. Calling for a halt to any plan that eliminated the commissary system and demanding that every family receive $13.50 a week, Dobbins sent out word to rally supporters. He organized a protest march on the County-City Building and created a new buzz among the unemployed. It was clear that their organization had been cut from any discussions and their voice was now muted. Dobbins gathered the UCL and other unemployed to participate in the march, scheduled for Valentine's Day 1933.

"Trailing behind a shabby little middle-aged drummer man, 2,000 organized men and women – some carrying placards and banners, some little children – marched down Seattle's Third Avenue and massed outside the King County Courthouse just before noon on February 14," observed reporter Harold P. Levy.[2] Once inside the courthouse, "their calm, able young leader" Dobbins insisted that a meeting between public officials and twenty representatives of the unemployed take place to talk about the rules for relief.

Two county commissioners met with Dobbins but admitted that they couldn't commit for the entire council. So Dobbins turned to his followers and asked, "You're running this. Do we stay here until Shannon and his board comes?" The mob roared in the affirmative. They would stay until the council agreed to sit down with their leadership. Dobbins then told the protesters to station themselves throughout the building. Warming to the conflict, Dobbins sent out a call to others across the state to join him in Seattle. Phone calls were made and the cry went up, "Two thousand now and 20,000 by nightfall."

Volunteers then organized food for the masses, bringing down sandwich makings, donuts, oranges and coffee from the seventh floor soup kitchen. The county jail chipped in by sending over additional sandwiches and coffee later that night. County Commissioner Louis Nash, a UCL supporter, tried to convince Mayor Dore and director of relief Shannon to meet with the marchers' representatives. Nash explained to Dore and Shannon that this meeting was the only demand the UCL had made. Once the meeting took place, the protesters had agreed to evacuate the building. Surely, nothing would be lost by just sitting down with them, he said. But everyone knew the first meeting would need to be followed by others, since the protesters clearly expected further negotiation on other issues. It really didn't matter, though, if there was one meeting or a hundred, neither Dore nor Shannon had any intention of getting together with this self-appointed rabble. Instead, Dore used the occupation of the building to create additional stress for his political enemies, Commissioners Louis Nash and John Stevenson.

Stevenson, another county commissioner helped by UCL support, watched as Dore withdrew Seattle police from the building. This put the responsibility for any failure to keep the peace squarely on Nash, Stevenson and the rest of the County Council. Further, Dore would not intervene unless a specific written request was issued by the County. In other words, Stevenson and Nash would have to provide written proof that they were turning against their old supporters before they could expect any help from Seattle. Fortunately for the two men, the marchers filled in the gap left by the vacancy created by Dore by appointing their own police force. Trusted men were given white cloth to tie around their arm as a symbol of their new rank. These men were authorized to keep rooms from becoming overcrowded and to prevent those who were intent on causing problems from entering any area. Dobbins and the marchers' leadership were being careful not to fall into the trap of being declared a mob. Dore, they knew, was just waiting for the opportunity.

While some protesters left, approximately 900 stayed the night. They made speeches, listed grievances, sang and tried to convince the press to give them more publicity. About midnight, they found room on the wood benches or marble floor and did their best to rest. By five in the morning, though, they were roused by the call from their own organizers to help clean the hallways. They swept and picked up trash on the second floor where they had settled in.

By eleven o' clock that morning 3,000 protesters had shown up on the steps and in the building.[3] The next day, Tuesday February 15, the process was repeated. Once again, food was gathered, the marchers' leadership tried to meet with officials and bored men stationed themselves on benches and talked. Some went home, but many stayed. That night the marchers policed their own and cleaned up after themselves. They ate what was donated, sang and made more speeches.

On February 16, two days into the take-over of the County-City building, a meeting between Dobbins and County Chairman Stevenson took place. Unfortunately, no headway was made. During the day, the business of the courthouse proceeded as best it could, and after hours the men settled down for a third night on the cold floors and hard chairs.

Stevenson decided by Thursday the 17th that he had done all he could do. With the intransigence of Dore and Shannon, it was time to accept the inevitable. He sent out an order to those occupying the courthouse to leave by 5 PM. Dore provided smirking support for Stevenson decision. The County Welfare

Board Chairman, J. C. Black also backed Stevenson's move insisting that those inside the building in no way represented the real unemployed anyway. According to Black, the real unemployed were "home minding their business and waiting for the start of the new system..."

Having lost his primary supporter in Stevenson, Dobbins began grasping for straws. He made an unrelated, almost bizarre, demand at that point. Dobbins agreed to evacuate the building if IWW members convicted of killing American Legion members in Centralia in 1919 were released from jail. Dobbins told the crowd that they would "go home – quick, too" if the prisoners were released. The gathering applauded his demand, but some must have been confused as to what that had to do with the new relief distribution. Dobbins also tried to reassure the public that only "one-fourth of 1 percent of the demonstrators [were] communistic." This was a strange statement as well coming from someone who was, in fact, communist and who knew what he said was false.

Meanwhile, Stevenson announced that the next day he would release the names of the 1,294 stores that would be accepting the vouchers. He also let it be known that he had already sent the list of purchasable foods to the sellers.[4] Stevenson then packed up and left the building having finally come to the realization that the political battle for control of relief distribution was over.

It was rapidly becoming apparent to most everyone that all the cards had been played and UCL had lost. A last minute stand was attempted by Robert Gordon, a young, black secretary of the UCL, who grabbed the podium and called out, "Do we go or stay?"

"Stay," was the response. But enthusiasm was waning quickly.

With several hundred spectators lining the hill above the building, 120 policemen backed by 30 sheriff deputies moved into the courthouse and escorted the men out. It was a surprisingly peaceful exit. Deputies who had been on standby were not needed; the machine guns which had been prepared for use at the local armory remained idle. Four minor arrests were recorded and only one injury was detailed. A IWW leader had been hit with a blackjack and had to be hauled out on a stretcher. Several men came out of the building singing, "Solidarity Forever." But the police joked with the men and coaxed, rather than pushed the last stragglers.

As the police began moving the men out, Eugene V. Dennett, a Communist Party member who had stayed with the protesters inside the County-City Building hurried across the street. There, watching from the roof top of another building, was the Chairman of the local Communist Party, Axel Noral. Dennett asked for direction on how to proceed. Noral looked dazed. He told Dennett that what he was witnessing was the "glorious demonstration of the rising militancy of the working class and that's what a revolutionary uprising looks like."Stunned by the futility of the Communist leadership, Dennett walked away. Dennett understood as did most participants that the march and the sit-in had been failures. All they had shown was that the unemployed were at the mercy of the political leaders. Noral believed this to be the beginning of the Revolution and would later claim credit for the protest. He bragged about the role the Communist Party played in sparking the demonstration.

Dennett put the record straight in a book he wrote in 1990 called "Agitprop" in which he said, "Little did our critics know or understand that the Communist party did not cause that demonstration. Neither did we lead it." Despite the fact that this was a UCL organized protest and that UCL president Dobbins was a dedicated communist, Dennett made it clear that this was less a communist dominated protest, then a "'spontaneous' demonstration." [5]

The police continued to act patiently and respectfully. Once the building was fully vacated, though, a few protesters tried to reenter. At that point, the fire department was called in and hoses were turned on those remaining. Mayor Dore showed up and used the opportunity to let it be known that there would be no more parades or demonstrations. He also cast out a challenge, "We'll have no more foolishness. The police also will stop any attempt of marchers from outside Seattle to enter the city."

Those who had already come to Seattle for the County-City Building protest were provided with gasoline to get them back on their way. For those who had no transportation, it was provided for free of charge. With that, Dore stationed a police guard around the building and left.

The next morning there was a much smaller second demonstration at the Volunteers of America relief station. About a thousand men showed up. There was little enthusiasm and the whole group was dispersed by six policemen. Later that day, those who showed at the commissaries were fed as usual, but they also received a card which told them where to go to get their vouchers the following week. [6] The battle to maintain the commissaries was over. Dore, Shannon, Martin, and Ernst were the clear winners.

Meanwhile, some of the less radical element of the UCL tried to use the failure to push out Dobbins. They hoped to reinstate ex-president Pearl who had attempted to build alliances with politicians and community leaders. Pearl's supporters called for the resignation of Dobbins. The communists, however, were firmly in control and had no intention of allowing any internal voices to question their power. Opposition was squelched and Dobbins remained Chairman. [7]

A new politician was on the horizon, though. One who in November, 1932 would win election, not as mayor or governor, but as President. The president-elect would soon become the hope of a generation of the downcast. He would lead an administration that would find work, food and support regardless of the machinations of lesser politicians. He would not blame the unemployed for their predicament, as had Governor Martin, or plead that helping the poor wasn't the job of the government, as had his predecessor, President Hoover. Instead, he took the bit in his mouth and moved the nation forward. It would take awhile, though. In 1933, the new President was not inaugurated in January, but in March. And on February 15, 1933, in the midst of the courthouse take-over, the new President almost became John Nance Gardner.

12

The City: A Ghost of an Idea

Even as the majority of unemployed began to accept that their power was limited and they would have to acknowledge the reality of the new demeaning voucher system, the communist-led UCL continued to fight, hoping to resurrect the issue. A meeting was called of four hundred representatives from 87 different UCL locals and other unemployed groups from around the state. The purpose was to plan a third march on Olympia in order to force a return to the commissary system. They envisioned an army of 5,000 protesters parading through the capital city. With that large of a gathering, the leadership also decided to include previous demands for relief of $10 a week for single men and $3 for each dependent.[1]

A week before the march, an organization called the American Vigilantes met in Seattle and agreed to travel to Olympia to intercept the protesters. The Vigilantes were a quasi-military, secret association. They believed themselves to be protectors of society and thought the protesters were a sinister force bent on destroying America. The extent to which they would go to prevent the march was illustrated by a secret Vigilante memorandum which included the following advice: "Temper your severity to suit the occasion and if forced to fight don't forget that nothing so swiftly sickens a mob as brutal, stomach-wrenching, soul-sickening force swiftly, fearlessly and judiciously applied."[2] All members were encouraged to be fully armed including "automatic weapons [which] should be carried with a full magazine…" Approximately one thousand Vigilantes traveled south to meet the marchers. Upon arriving in Olympia, instead of being sent away, this untrained, self-appointed mob was incorporated into the two-hundred-man police force already employed. The sheriff even went so far as to deputize the Vigilantes, giving them the authority of law.

On March 1, 1933, an approximately 1,500 protesters from the UCL and other organizations began the trek to Olympia in an attempt to spike the State Relief Act. They set out in the morning with the goal of meeting with the governor and the State Relief Commission, but unlike the previous march in January, the reception was far from cordial. As they approached the city, someone signaled an Olympia mill that the horde was coming. A siren from the mill sounded an alarm. Stores shuttered in anticipation of trouble, and the Vigilantes drove out to meet the incoming protesters. Just outside the city border, the road was blocked and the two sides met. The Vigilantes and deputies, well-armed and prepared to fight, halted the marchers and made it clear that they were not going to be allowed to enter the city. There was a brief council between the leadership of both parties where it became quickly apparent that there would be no negotiation. Instead, the marchers were given five minutes to make a choice. They could either go to a nearby park or turn around and go home. The other options of continuing the march or standing their ground weren't given. Discussing it among themselves, the organizers decided to spare bloodshed. The unemployed agreed to turn off into Priest Point Park. At the same time, they were allowed to send an attorney with a handful of their leadership ahead to attempt to get legal permission to march on to the state capital.

The rest of the protesters were then herded into Priest Point. Vigilante sentries encircled the encampment, refusing to allow any to leave the park. Marchers created their own internal line to match the Vigilante's. The unemployed chose guards to stand watch over their watchers to ensure that the Vigilantes stayed on their side of the line. The volunteer guards also searched all incoming vehicles to make sure that guns and alcohol were not brought into the already volatile situation.

That night, as they waited for a response from Olympia, a cold rain fell on the assembled. Most had no shelter and were forced to endure the rain, although a few were able to get out of the weather and sleep in the available cars. Huge bonfires and hot coffee did little to stem the cold. The Seattle Post-Intelligencer was given permission to send a photographer in to record the conditions. The thick mud and increasingly deteriorating state of affairs were noted, but no story was ever written.

Under the dark, rainy sky with little to do but talk, rumors began to spread. The Vigilantes had two cars loaded with machine guns. The Vigilantes were attempting to sneak in liquor to get the unemployed drunk so as to spark an incident.[34] On the Vigilante side, a different line of gossip stirred the mob. Radicals were attempting to spark a "Soviet Dictatorship controlled by Moscow..." [5] The marchers were led by foreign agitators. None of the rumors proved true, but the tensions they inspired kept both sides on edge.

Late that night a real problem did emerge, though. Protesters thinking they would have shelter in Olympia were unprepared for the cold and rain. As the conditions worsened, several became ill. Some passed out; one went into convulsions. The marchers approached the Vigilantes to discuss the situation. Both sides realized that a middle ground had to be reached. It was decided to let those who were sick through the lines so that they might go to the local hospital and get help. After further discussion, the Vigilantes suggested that all of the 300 women and children be sent home to prevent further illness. A quick conference was held on the marchers' side and a decision was made: Due to the conditions, the leaders of the unemployed decided to accept the proposal, leaving the march with approximately half of its beginning strength.

At the same time, those leaders who had gone on to negotiate with the officials at Olympia returned with further bad news. Once again the governor refused to meet with the leadership, and Superior Court Judge Wright had denied the request to march in Olympia. In essence, the unemployed were told to turn around and go home. Eugene Dennett, one of those in charge of the camp, talked with a counterpart on the Vigilante side and they both agreed that something needed to happen quickly before more people began to get seriously ill. They created a plan to allow the marchers to return quickly and peacefully to Seattle which "was carried out smoothly and agreeably even though with great reluctance on our part to admit a second failure," said Dennett.[6]

On March 2, 1933, in a short article on buried on page 11, the conservative Seattle Times simply reported that the protesters had decided to call off their parade. There was no mention of the Vigilantes. There was no mention of the town shutting down in anticipation of violence. Instead, the Times suggested the marchers left solely because they hadn't been allowed to protest on the steps of the capitol.[7]

Far from being disappointed, though, the Communist UCL leadership was fully satisfied. This fit neatly in with their plan. The marchers had been shown the futility of conventional protests. They had earned personal stripes standing in the rain, and the membership's anger and bitterness had been allowed to fester in the process. This was the road that would lead the followers to radicalism, many communists felt.

The failure was also used by the leadership as an opportunity to attack their internal UCL enemies. In the March

132

25 edition of A New Weekly, the Communist Executive Board of the State Committee of Action stated, "It is necessary to point out by name and warn the workers about Phil Pearl and J. Rohan of Seattle, who were in the state capitol the night of March 1, trying to obstruct the attempts of our committees to get housing."[8] Thus slinging accusations while providing no evidence, they hoped to create suspicion of Pearl and so torpedo any plan he and his mainstream supporters had to reestablish control over the UCL.

Meanwhile, trouble was brewing at the newly established voucher locations. At Seattle's South End Voucher Station, those seeking relief were told they would not be given any assistance unless they did assigned work. They needed to contribute one day's labor for a $2 voucher. At the order of W. D. Shannon, King County director of welfare, a notice appeared on the door of a South End relief station which read, "...those who do not report and work will be denied relief from this agency...At this depot for every $2.00 worth of food vouchers one days [sic] work is required of the recipients."[9] This was rejected by the UCL as "forced labor." Some unions were also concerned that work was being taken from them and performed at half the cost by the unemployed. With the county unwilling to rescind the demand, Dobbins called for a strike. He also worked to recruit the local grocery stores to the cause. Dobbins warned the store owners that those who didn't support the strike would never see another voucher. The South End continued to insist that no work meant no food. Pressure built. The UCL, organized labor and the businessmen hurt by the lack of trade, leaned on the South End Voucher Station. After the UCL strike passed the one month mark, the Welfare Board decided to raise the payment from $2 a day to 45 cents an hour in vouchers, thus raising the wage to $3.60 for a day's labor. The county felt this was fair since it was the going wage for all county work, but the UCL and Dobbins remained unsatisfied. Forced work was slave labor.

As time dragged on, some of the unemployed began to weaken. With no money coming in, many found it difficult to hold out. People needed to eat. Unemployed men not affiliated with the UCL began to cross the line. Occasional acts of violence erupted as jobless fought jobless, principle against necessity.[10] Since it was the state that supplied the money for the vouchers, eventually WERA was called to weigh in. In one of the few decisions that supported the rights of the unemployed, WERA declared that the intent of federal loans to the county was relief and carried no requirement to work. Therefore, forced labor could not be demanded to receive the vouchers. Also, they made it clear that projects that were done with work relief funds should only be those that wouldn't have been done without the additional funding.[11] In other words, unions shouldn't have to fight the unemployed for public works. This was a rare victory for the unemployed and the UCL.

"Mass action" became the catchphrase under communist controlled UCL. That is what the marches and the voucher strike were about. They believed that activating the people would cause greater change. Instead, what the communist leadership should have paid attention to was the declining numbers. By March, 1933 membership in the UCL had plummeted to 1,000. This was down from 12,000 members only four months prior. Those who had joined to alleviate the effects of the Depression were tired of the internal squabbles, disappointed in the direction of Self-Help and unimpressed by communist rhetoric. The leadership ignored these complaints, however, and believed a new round of mass action would inspire the troops. Evictions of the unemployed were growing, and they were certain they knew just how to invigorate the mass action movement.

In early April 1933, the Blonder family was threatened with eviction from their South Ballard home. The father, Frank, couldn't do anything about it as he sat in jail. His crime was turning on the lights in his own home. It seems that Frank had been unable to pay his electricity bill and his wife was ill. When his electricity was cut off, Frank's neighbors decided to intervene. They managed to illegally hook up his house to receive electricity so that he could heat his home for his sick wife. When it was noticed that his lights were on, the police were called and he was arrested. At that point, with Frank sitting in a jail cell, his landlord served papers to evict his family for non-payment. In fact, Frank had been buying the house and had paid $3,000 of the $4,200 price when he lost his job and had to shift to renting. In effect, the Blonder family had lost $3,000 worth of equity and their home due to bad luck. While Frank was incarcerated, deputies were sent to remove the rest of the family. The police arrived to evict the Blonders but were met by 250 members of the local UCL. After a brief stand-off in which the crowd refused to allow the police inside, the officers finally relented and left.[12]

The next day, 200 people met at the Blonder house to ensure that the deputies didn't follow through with the earlier threat. One of the 200 who defended the Blonders demonstrated the pervasiveness of the eviction problem. Mr. Wickland had spent the morning at the Blonders but decided to return to his own home to have lunch. As he approached his house, he found his wife, two children and all of his furniture on the street. Inside the house were the landlady and two deputies. Wickland and his family had been evicted for non-payment. Wickland walked back to the Blonder house, gathered a hundred men and returned home. These men pushed past those inside and returned the furniture to the house. The landlady called an attorney. More deputies arrived and, Sheriff Bannick was called. Bannick decided that the extent of the police responsibility was the removal of the furniture, which they had already done. A rather civilized debate, considering the circumstances, ensued. It was decided that a committee consisting of two UCL members, the landlady's attorney and a deputy would meet with the county housing committee the next day. There the group was able find alternate housing.[13]

Meanwhile, Frank Blonder, with the eviction still hanging over his head, was freed from jail. Soon, however, he was arrested again for turning on his lights and this time sentenced to fifteen days.[14] Finally, on April 11, with only twenty-five workers on guard, fifty deputies entered the Blonder home and removed the family and furniture. Sheriff Bannick had had enough. A call for more UCL members was issued, and they began to put the furniture back. At that point, Bannick made it clear that he would arrest those who continued to violate the order of eviction. His officers returned the furniture to the street and ended up arresting two men who tried to interfere.[15]

While Frank Blonder was fighting for his home, Ernst was busy at the state level working to lighten the relief rolls. With Ernst in charge and his demand that the needy demonstrate complete destitution, it was easy to find cases to remove. From April 1 to 14, 1933, state-wide Ernst's WERA expelled 20,000 from relief. In the same two week period in King County, 227 families lost food allowance due to the stricter rules under King County Welfare Board Director Shannon.

Meanwhile, those who were physically unable to work were in dire straits. The maximum a person on direct county relief in King County could receive was a single dollar a week. As historian Richard C. Berner aptly puts it, this dollar "possibly might be stretched to cover critical non-food items as well, if one believed in the efficacy of prayer."[16] Pierce Williams, the Federal Emergency Relief Administration agent, was concerned about the lack of empathy displayed by the executive branch of Washington State. It was his job to monitor the state to determine if they were in compliance with the federal directives. He was becoming more doubtful as time went on.

While relief was being slashed across the state and the unemployed were struggling to subsist on their dollar a week, the eviction crisis continued. The next major conflict in Seattle was over the eviction of the Frandsen Family. In 1926, Frank Frandsen bought a house in Rainier Valley for $3,700. With a down payment of $600 and consistent monthly payments he had whittled the principal to $800. Unfortunately, Frank lost his job in 1931. On top of which, the $1,000 nest egg he had in the bank was lost when the bank went under. The woman who held the deed, Wilhelmina Peterson refused to negotiate or give Frank any additional time to find the money. She wanted the house and the windfall that went with it.

On April 24, 1933, Frank and his family were scheduled to be put out on the sidewalk. Under Dobbins, the UCL gathered 200 men to prevent eviction. For three days they stationed themselves around the perimeter of the house. Peterson called the Sheriff and insisted the Frandsen family be kicked out. Sheriff Bannick brought 20 deputies to carry-out the order, but by the time police arrived, the crowd had grown to 300. Frank's sixteen-year-old son, Leonard Frandsen, took it upon himself to prevent the police from ousting the family and scuffled with Deputy William Sears. Another officer testified that Leonard knocked the deputy down and was "sitting on [Sears] and hitting him on the neck with a short length of broomstick."[17]

When Sears finally began to get the better of the teen, a rock was pitched at the deputy. This was quickly followed by a shower of stones thrown by members of the crowd. According to one observer, an unnamed deputy then threatened to "shoot anybody who [threw] another rock." That threat kept any more debris from being hurled and things began to calm down.[18] According to Grant Nevels a black representative of the Home Owners' League, the group was warned by himself to remain orderly and calm and not interfere with the deputies in their duty. The police, then, approached the house, broke a window to gain access and pushed both Orland Frandsen and his father Frank. Nevels realizing that things were getting out of hand again, decided to flee, but as he left he saw Sherriff Bannick hit a man and brandish a gun toward the crowd. The end result was nine deputies injured, though none seriously, and sixteen members of the crowd arrested for inciting a riot and injuring officers in the line of duty.[19]

A petition signed by 10,000 asking for release of the arrested men was sent to the judge in the case.20 Ultimately, seven of the rioters were convicted and sentenced to between twelve and eighteen months.21 This was the last major mass action campaign by the communist controlled UCL.

13

The City: A New Idea

If things had gone differently on February 15, 1933 in Miami, Florida, the Great Depression might well have claimed significantly more lives than it did. If Giuseppe Zangara had been taller than five foot; if he had something more stable to stand on than a wobbly metal chair; if little Leona Merrill hadn't yelled out so quickly; if Lillian Cross weren't quite so fast to react, there might never have been a New Deal. Had there not been a New Deal, more people would surely have starved and many more would have lost the little they had. More homes would have been repossessed. More families would have splintered under the weight of debt and hunger. Shacktowns might have spread and grown, progressively gobbling up more and more of Seattle and other cities. The men in Hooverville might well have become more rebellious and increasingly radical as their numbers grew and their desperation became more acute. The whiff of revolution that began to waft from the UCL could well have spread in the more combustible mix of rough men in the shanties. And the spark and tinder might have formed flames that could have ignited this nation.

Fortunately, because Zangara was short he needed to stand on that rickety chair in order to see Franklin Roosevelt. Because of that he didn't quite have the balance need to take careful aim with his. As a result of having to take extra time to aim, nine year old Leona Merrill was able to yell out, "That man has a gun!" Once Zangara missed with his first shot and once Merrill's warning registered, Cross was quick enough to grab his arm and force the other shots awry. Roosevelt survived the assassination attempt and his New Deal reached down into the shacks, shanties and skid roads of cities like Seattle to feed and give respect to the destitute.

A month after the assassination attempt and one week after Roosevelt's March 4th inauguration, Harry Hopkins began actively working to alter the mission and role of the Federal Government with regard to the unemployed and needy. Hopkins had been in charge of work relief in New York when Roosevelt was governor. Hopkins' new role in President Roosevelt's administration was to take the Federal Emergency Relief Administration (FERA), which under Hoover simply oversaw loans to the states, and turn it into an organization to directly help the unemployed. The objective was simple: Provide grant money to create temporary work for those who couldn't find a job but were employable.

Harry Hopkins (Left, front) director of President Roosevelt's relief efforts meets Seattle John Dore. *Acme.*

Hopkins understood the need for immediate action. Unwilling to waste even the short time it would take to rearrange office space at the Reconstruction Finance Building, the new FERA Director simply plunked himself down at a desk in the hallway and got to work. He believed that the government's primary responsibility was to help its citizens, and at the moment, that meant getting them back to work. Hopkins labored tirelessly. On May 12, 1933, just two months after taking charge of FERA, Hopkins, with FDR's backing, was able to coax Congress to put up $500 million to implement FERA's new mission.

Hopkins and Roosevelt agreed with those who said work should be paired with relief. FERA was not simply a hand-out. Men and women were assigned jobs for which they would receive pay. FERA also was designed for the truly needy, requiring those who requested jobs to show evidence of their need. These aspects of the new FERA program were similar to what had been done on the local level under the old system in Washington State. What was different was how it was done. Pay was in cash not vouchers. Men went down to the offices to apply; no one showed up at their house. There were still embarrassing questions, and there were still some sanctimonious officials in charge. It was by no means a perfect system, but most of the unemployed were encouraged by the new direction.

Also, Hopkins made certain that FERA money flooded into areas that needed it, rather than arrived in dribs and drabs. For the unemployed, it was a welcome rain after the drought. They had room to breathe again. Businesses throughout the area came alive with the influx of cash. There were new shoes for the kids, food on the table and bills paid on time. There were still loads of problems. Not everyone could get a FERA job. Many had been unemployed for so long their debts were still a crushing burden. For the first time, though, someone in government was reaching down to them. For the first time, men of power and influence seemed to understand that they weren't lazy and irresponsible, just folks who needed a break.

In order to make sure the money and effort wasn't wasted, Hopkins funneled the federal funds through local agencies which understood the needs of the community. These agencies wrote up plans for local projects, but identifying and designing these projects took awhile. In the meantime, FERA continued to pay for work started under Hoover's loan program. Under the new rules, FERA would provide direct grants for approved projects as opposed to loans. This allowed the local government officials to concentrate on needs rather than worry about how to repay mounting debt. For the next two years FERA continued to build bridges, provide shelter, produce food, sew clothes and do hundreds of other jobs that needed to be done to encourage a nation on its knees. In that time, FERA would supply $3 billion in relief across the United States. Some criticized FERA, saying that pumping this much money this quickly was a poor strategy in the long run. Harry Hopkins response was, "People don't eat in the long run, they eat every day."

At the state level, FERA expected Washington to chip in $3 for every $1 of federal funding. This was a dream that would never be realized, not in Washington and not in most states across the nation. The federal government also required that each state list the resources, public and private, that were available to team with the Federal aid. Also, recipient agencies were to have a plan on how expenses and relief would be monitored. Finally, the state was to be the funnel through which all local requests would be submitted.

This new source of jobs became a godsend to the unemployed in Seattle. They had attempted to fend for themselves by creating the Unemployed Citizens League only to watch their organization collapse under doctrinaire leadership. They had been accused of laziness by the local and state agencies. They had watched as government requirements and benefits had shifted and turned without their input. The new federal regulations promised stability and real assistance. Not all of the unemployed were willing to completely trust Roosevelt, Hopkins and the New Deal, but most were willing to give them the benefit of the doubt for now.

Not everyone in state government was so enamored with all aspects of the new federal program, however. In particular, Washington State Director of Relief Charles Ernst resented one aspect of FERA. Like WERA before it, FERA authorized money to assist self-help organizations. Once again Director Ernst made certain to block this piece of assistance. Still bitter over UCL opposition, Ernst would never allow the money to encourage Self-Help. As much as he admired the intent, he said, he believed that organizations that developed self-help movements had demonstrated that they couldn't stay politically neutral.[22] Instead of facilitating assistance and aid, Ernst continued to trim the relief rolls. Even as FERA put the unemployed to work, Ernst cut more state jobs. Between May 1 and July 14, 1933, WERA found an additional 8,008 people to cut from state rolls.

14

Shacktown: Crime

On the waterfront, Mayor Jesse Jackson and Police Chief Reuben Washington patrolled Hooverville looking for stolen goods and signs of trouble. During these walks, they inspected abandoned cabins and looked for purloined goods. On one of these trips, Jackson searched a vacant shack and found 400 pounds of sugar, a case of canned peaches, another of apricots and three cases of canned coffee. As was his custom when he became suspicious, Jackson contacted the police who were able to trace the cache to a nearby boxcar which had been looted earlier. [1] Among broke and hungry men, theft was common. Drivers and deliverymen who were near shacktowns were advised to keep their car doors locked and their keys with them. A donut delivery truck driver learned the hard way. The driver parked his truck at the King Street Railroad Station and went in to drop off his goods. After making his delivery, he came out to find his truck gone. He contacted the police who searched the area. The stolen truck hadn't been taken far, but when located by the police the two rear tires had been removed along with hundreds of donuts. The policemen assigned to the case were able to follow a "trail of doughnut crumbs [which] led to a nearby 'shacktown'. From the recesses of the huts came the steady 'munch-munch' of hungry men devouring doughnuts." [2] Hooverite Clyde Massey, 45, put it plainly. When he was caught inside a nearby apartment with stolen packs of cigarettes still in his hands, he said, "Lots of other Hooverville men prowl around nights just like I was doing." [3]

Shacktown dwellers were told to keep quiet about any treasures they might have hidden to prevent just such a theft. A. S. Vincent provided an example for those too obvious with their wealth. He returned one night to his shack to find he had been robbed of a camera, drafting set, gold necklace and two gold watches. [4] Theft among the down-and-out in Hooverville was a fact of life, and most likely few of the break-ins were ever reported. Smart men kept padlocks on their shacks to deter the less determined thieves.

Jackson watched out for theft and tried to anticipate trouble. Once, Jackson brought in the police when a resident, Nich Osinivitich, 48, decided to make some spending cash by raising dogs and selling them to those headed to Alaska. His kennel had grown to fourteen dogs, and the constant howling was keeping the other residents up at night.[5] Jackson was forced to call the police and have the operation shut down. Jackson was well aware of the danger of allowing this sort of thing to continue. A year prior another man, Paul Como, also had kept dogs in Hooverville. Their barking had gone on for several nights when Como's neighbor J. D. Rainier visited him and told Como to control his animals. An argument ensued and Rainier punched Como. Not willing to let it go at that, Como grabbed a couple of bricks and followed Rainier back to his shack. Once there Rainier pulled out a gun and shot Como, killing him. [6]

Murder was not exactly unknown to Jackson and the other shacktown dwellers. They had seen enough careless killing over trivial issues to harden them. Louis Cruz crawled into the wrong shack at one in the morning and ended up stabbed to death by the three men inside.[7] Drunken brawls left the dead in their wake, like the one in Hooverville in which Antonio Flores was stabbed in the neck while three men and a woman looked on. [8]

145

At another, five were arrested when a fight broke out and a man only identified as "Jimmy" was found dead. [9] At other times, friends or relatives wore on each other's nerves, like when Steve Paulos killed his cousin, Pete Aarapis. [10]

On occasion, the true value of life was measured in the shantytowns and found to be startlingly cheap. Cicero Hawthorne caught Arthur Hopen as he attempted to steal from him. A fight ensued and Hopen was killed. Hawthorne was charged with second degree murder. The argument was over fifty cents, and for that half-dollar Hopen lost his life and Hawthrone lost twenty years in prison. [11] [12] But even that was not the lowest price paid for a life in Seattle's slums. Milo Booker, 48, borrowed $1.25 from Henry Chapman, 38. Booker later paid back a dollar. When confronted about the missing twenty-five cents, Booker refused to pay. Two men watched as Chapman drew a gun and fired, killing Booker for a quarter. [13]

The most notorious Seattle shacktown murder occurred not in Hooverville but in the shantytown across the way at the Duwamish mudflats. Mary Kelly was born in Russia. She lived as a housekeeper in the shack of Otto Johanson, and like many among the dispossessed Mary and Otto drank to pass the time. On January 16, 1935, according to Mary, she, Johanson, and a friend, Dick Brown, were sharing a gallon of moonshine whiskey. The party began at Johanson's shack at 2:30 in the afternoon. Sometime later it moved to Brown's shack and then returned to Johanson's place throughout the course of the afternoon and evening. The party was still going strong at eight that night when the drunk Johanson tumbled to the floor. Mary bent over the prostrate man to check his condition. When she realized he was fine, she kissed him. In a fit of jealousy, Brown pulled a knife from his pocket and attacked Johanson. From somewhere, a geologist's pickax was produced and Brown stuck his victim a fatal blow. As he lay dying, Mary cradled his head while Johanson spoke his final words, "I don't blame you, dear. He did it."

Mary Kelly rushed out in time to see Brown throw the pickax into the river. She, then, headed to the nearby Bates Valve Corporation, the closest place with a working telephone, to call the police. When they arrived Mary directed them to Brown's shack. Brown was handcuffed and arrested for the murder of his friend, Otto Johanson.[14]

Had that been the end of the story, it would have simply been just another sordid love triangle. But further investigation began to reveal a more interesting Miss Kelly. In fact, Mary Kelly had been born with the last name Yermani. It was discovered that during the First World War, she had fought for the Russian army as a member of an elite all-women fighting force called the Battalion of Death. They were so-named because each person was issued a vial of poison and pledged to die rather than surrender. After the war, while the Russian Revolution was in progress, Mary decided to leave her homeland. While in Vladivostok, she met Mr. Kelly, an American soldier. They were married and she used her new citizenship to come to the States. What happened to her husband is unclear, but she found herself alone. Needing to pay her own way, she disguised herself as a man and got work on a fishing boat. At some point, her true gender was discovered and she lost that job. Afterwards, she drifted down to the Duwamish squatter's town. For a time, she worked as the accused, Dick Brown's, housekeeper. One day, Otto Johanson approached her with an offer of more money. She took Johanson up on his offer and moved out of Brown's shack and into Johanson's.

Detectives immediately began questioning Mary Kelly's story. Then, an investigator wading through the swamp behind

Mary's room, found the pickax just under her window. An autopsy showed Johanson had been hit with a prospector's hammer six times. After which, his throat was cut with a knife. Also, it was discovered that a hundred dollars had been taken from his pocket.

Further investigation revealed an interesting gap in Mary's story. While Mary claimed to have called the police as soon as she could get to a phone, witnesses were located who had seen Mary at a downtown bar that night. In fact, a limousine driver said he had picked her up from the bar and driven her back down to the Duwamish. Where the money for the limousine had come from became a point of contention.

At the trial, Mary's attorney asked for sympathy for his client. She was a poor woman in a foreign city with no means of support. He claimed that she was a victim of the "vicious system of poverty, who has fought against adversity, hunger and abuse."[15] The truth, though, was in the prosecutor's corner. He summed it up by calling her a "vicious, cold-blooded" murderer. It was only after Mary Kelly was convicted and sentenced to up to 20 years that her true nature came out. At that point, she admitted she was simply tired of Johanson. He was, in her words, nothing more than a "piece of human tideflat driftwood."[16]

While murder was frequent if not exactly common in the shacktowns, assaults most probably were common. Mayor Jesse Jackson felt firsthand the pent-up anger that caused others to attack. One night, a Hooverville drunk threatened his neighbors with an axe. Jackson was called out and tried to defuse the situation, but nothing could calm the irate Hooverite. Finally, a group of men came out to help. They surrounded the threatening man. At that point, the assailant threw a coffee cup at Jackson leaving a large gash on his head. After a brief scuffle,

Jackson and the others were able to subdue the drunk. The police were called, and he was carted off to jail. To prevent his return, the cabin in which the arrested man lived was dismantled, and the best wood and material was hauled off by the other men.[17]

This wasn't the only attempt to assault someone with an axe in the shantytowns of Seattle, but the other shacktown resident was less fortunate. He was actually hit by the axe-wielder twice, front and back. When he went to report the incident, the police arrested the assailant and, to add insult to injury, also took the victim into custody.

More common were the stabbings. Many instances were reported in the Seattle newspapers. Walter Blackburn was stabbed twice while at the shantytown at 6th and Lander, but unwilling to tell the police what had happened or who was involved, the attacker went free. Ed Anderson, 45, "was wounded slightly" when stabbed in the neck at Hooverville.[18] Two black men were stabbed at a party by "a black man with a gold tooth... [at] King George's Palace" in Hooverville. Remarkably, the victims were held without charges, but there is no further report about the assailant.[19] Two men, Clarence La Pierre and James Burns were stabbed on the same day and probably by the same two assailants. La Pierre lost $62 in the attack.[20] And the list of stabbings goes on.

For some the violence, depressing surroundings and the lack of hope gave rise to darker thoughts. Others found mental illness which predated slum-life exacerbated by the bleak conditions. Suicides sprouted from this toxic soil. They were frequent, though probably also underreported in Seattle shacktowns. Frank Innana, 45, stepped in front of an oil truck. Neighbors said he was delusional and thought somebody was out to get him. Even though he lived in the slums, he was found with $140 on his person.[21] Enough other shacktown residents were hit and killed by passing cars to raise questions as to whether they were accidents or suicides. Meanwhile, the body of Ole Hagen, 50, was dredged out of Eliot Bay as he either fell or jumped off of Pier 12.[22] Louis Johnson of Hooverville was also found under Pier 3 on the waterfront. Missing a month, he was only recognized from the keys in his pocket.[23] Some of the drowned were never identified. A 55-year-old man, with a broken nose and missing tooth was discovered near the Diamond Cement Company Pier in the Duwamish Waterway. The unknown victim wore a gray overcoat, two pairs of pants, a pajama shirt, a blue denim shirt, a serge vest and black oxfords.[24] Another questionable death was that of Henry Frost, 68, from the South End waterfront shacktown. Frost was believed to either have jumped or fell from the bridge over Dearborn Street around 11:30 in the morning on December 1, 1939.[25]

Suicide was not limited to the Seattle shacktowns, but county-wide the increase in suicide was blamed on economic hardships. Reports of suicide throughout Seattle's King County show a considerable jump during the Depression. In 1929, there were 129 reported suicides in the county but by 1932, the nadir or the Depression, that number had climbed to 190. More significantly, in 1929 according to investigations only 8 people killed themselves because of economic trouble. By 1932, 72 people did so because of "pauperism, unemployment, 'business trouble.'"[26] All these factors were clearly evident in Hooverville.

Even death by natural causes takes on a more depressing hue when looked at through the lives of the shack-dwellers. Kenneth Horton, around 40 when he died, had been a salesman but "lost interest in his work and 'drifted' in recent months." He had lived in his shack for only a few weeks, and when he died a "soiled and crumpled Christmas card" was in his pocket.[27] Hannah Costello, 67, from Hooverville died at the end of August, 1934. The report of a woman's death is rare enough to make it notable.[28] Another Hooverville resident with the unlikely name Otheim Olger died at age 59 on Christmas Day 1934.[29] For most, the newspaper simply acknowledged that the deceased was from a shacktown, or Hooverville if they were being specific, but for Emil Dahl, 62, who died on the 4th of July 1935 the actually shack location was included, 41 M, Hooverville.[30] Whether by suicide or natural causes, once again, it was Jesse Jackson's job to visit the dead men's shacks, attempt to find a next of kin and divide the goods when no family was found.

While Jackson continued to deal with the myriad of problems that alcohol brought, it wasn't until after Prohibition and nearly the end of the Great Depression that law enforcement began to take serious notice of the illegal hooch. At that point a concerted effort was made to prevent the potent beverage which was being brewed in the shacktowns from invading nearby neighborhoods. In August 1940, a raid found 212 quarts of homemade beer in Hooverville. The distiller, Harry Tripp, 57, pled guilty and was remanded to King County Jail.[31] By September, five raids on shacktown brewing operations had been executed; the latest brought in 32 quarts of beer and 37 gallons of mash.[32] The next month, four more men in a shacktown at the foot of Atlantic Street were charged with making and selling liquor when 241 quarts were discovered in their hovels.[33] The confiscated booze was found to contain twice the legal limit of alcohol. The reason for the increase in arrests was the low price and the additional calls the police department had received. At a twenty-five cent price for two bottles, both shantytown residents and decent citizens were sneaking down Atlantic Street to cop a drink. The alcohol had become so pervasive that Investigator A. D. Sales said he had received numerous complaints from women who claimed their husbands had spent the entire family budget on the booze.[34]

Beyond the murders and assaults, the thefts and suicides, the drinking and despair, there was one shacktown resident whose secret life remained undetected for years. Perhaps more infamous than any other for the destruction he caused and the massive potential for loss of life, though no death was ever directly traced to him, was Robert Bruce Driscoll.

Driscoll was a Washington State native, raised in Spokane. The oldest of seven children, he ran away at age 16. From Spokane, he headed to Texas and later resided for a time in California and Oregon. For a while, he boxed professionally and was a fair hand at the violin. In Oregon, Driscoll held a job as a stenographer, but his odd behavior concerned his employer who said that Driscoll "was on the borderline between genius and insanity." After turning to logging for awhile, Driscoll ended up in Seattle and settled on a shacktown along the tideflats. Balding and with a moustache, Driscoll stood five foot five inches tall. His photograph shows a man with a cold, detached stare. In all his travel, he had had the normal run in with the law resulting in a series of vagrancy arrests. In Portland, Oregon, Driscoll fell ill but couldn't afford to pay for a doctor's visit. Instead, he threw a rock through a window and waited to be arrested so that he could get free medical attention in jail. He had one lone serious crime on his record. The details are unclear, but he apparently entered a house where he was caught assaulting the woman inside.

It wasn't until May 3, 1935, that Driscoll's real secret came out. Marie Melikoff, owner of Seattle's Moscow Restaurant, was cleaning her place of business. Looking out her window, she spied Driscoll at the Russian Church nearby but thought little of it. A few minutes later, however, her manager V. P. Tellason, also observed Driscoll near the church and saw flames jump from the spot where he was crouched. Tellason signaled Melikoff and the two headed across the street toward Driscoll. When Driscoll saw the witnesses coming toward him, he took off running. Fortunately, Tellason was faster and after a short pursuit, Tellason tackled Driscoll. With additional help from Melikoff, the two were able to subdue Driscoll until the police came. The fire was easily doused.

Driscoll insisted that he hadn't set the fire.[35] Under intense police questioning, however, he began to unravel. Yes, he admitted, he had set that fire. In fact, he said, he had set others as well. At that point, he began listing a series of fires that had been, up to now, unsolved.

Once he started confessing, it seemed Driscoll couldn't stop. By the end of the night he confessed to lighting fires all across Seattle. He was asked why he would do such a thing. His only answer was he was "sore at the world."[36]

Unfortunately, Driscoll had set so many fires that he became confused and was unable to remember the location of all of them. Most everyone involved in the investigation was convinced of his desire to help, so, after some discussion, firemen decided there was only one way to refresh his memory. They packed Driscoll into a car and took him on a tour of all the locations of fires in Seattle over the last two years. Driscoll looked at the area and then, according to the Seattle Times, "Sometimes answering, 'no, not that one,' but more often shaking his head affirmatively, Driscoll cleared away doubt about all but a few of the blazes." He admitted to setting a $65,000 fire at the Globe Feed Mills and an $80,000 fire at the Ehrlich-Harrison Hardwood Lumber Company. Total damage in the hundred fires to which he admitted was estimated at $300,000.[37]

By May 9, Driscoll added another 23 fires to his list, including the Pacific Coast League Dugdale Park. Using baseball programs and kindling, Driscoll torched the stadium on July 5, 1932 causing the Seattle Indians to have to relocate to Civic Stadium. He also admitted to the Albers Milling Company fire of June 9, 1931. On that same night, Driscoll set fire to eight industrial plants and six railroad cars. That one night cost its victims $500,000, bringing Driscoll's total up to around a million dollars in damage. Surprisingly, even with all the mayhem and destruction, Driscoll faced only second degree arson charges.[38]

While no deeper motive was ever established for Driscoll's obsessive need to light fires, an anger at the world and a self-loathing expressed itself in notes he left at the scenes of many of his crimes. At one he had written, "Look Out! So long as I am blackballed for not being in last war I will continue my many big fires in industrial plants."

At another he wrote, "I was offended (rather tried to be offended) by capitalist tools or stools or those who try to bother me because I was man enough to stay out of last war and tell Catholic Church to go to hell. That happened day before your fire. I burn some place every time so offended. Get wise or get fire or worse. White citizen slacker to Wall St. Fire Bug."

At still another, his note left a clue as to his situation. It read: "If that ticket puncher at breadline has a job 24 hours from now I burn you out. A Fire Bug."

He may have purposefully misspelled or feigned a lack of education as in, "Dismiss that Negro janitor at Central library within 30 days or we start wrecking trains. He abuses whites without reason to do so. No excusess [sic]!!! We will raise hel [sic]!!"

A final note also hinted at his shacktown residence. It said, "Long as Bruce B. at window 8 at 84 Union St. has a public job I will cause fires!!! I burnt them corn flakes on 1st So. He insults white citizens like me who ask for cloths [sic] I need fire him of all jobs or I fire."[39]

After pleading guilty, Driscoll's attorney claimed that the fires were a result of a distorted sense of injustice, but that he never meant to cause physical harm to anyone. When the judge asked Driscoll if he wished to add anything, Driscoll, indicating his lawyer, said, "I guess he told the truth." He was then sentenced to a maximum ten years in prison.[40] One of the chief investigators, Ed Smith, later admitted, "I grew to like this fellow. He was always careful never to set fires in buildings occupied by people. He was disturbed terribly about one fire in which a watchman was nearly trapped by flames. He had been sure the building was empty."[41]

It would later come to light that despite what his letters said, Driscoll was a World War veteran, and when all his fires in Seattle were added up, the total reached 147. That wasn't the end of his story, though. Throughout his incarceration, police continued to question Driscoll about fires in Texas, Oregon and California. With further probing, he admitted to an additional 150 fires around the country.[42] If true, this would put the Seattle Shacktown Firebug in the list of the most notorious arsonists in American history.

Along with the more serious issues, petty crimes, small fires, quick fights and a variety of disturbances added to the rough-and-tumble life that came with residing in this male-dominated, desperation-driven village. Eventually, the violence and danger added with the frightfully unsanitary conditions to become a toxic stew that made many question why shantytowns were allowed to continue to exist. Working citizens and home-owners began to organize a call for their elimination.

15

The City: An Idea Haunts Still

Most unemployed had abandoned the hope of the UCL and resolved themselves to being a dependent of the federal government. They were able to feed their families, fill their gas tanks and sleep in homes paid for at public expense. But a few remained committed to the independence granted by maintaining their own organization. These few remaining mainstream members of the UCL tried one last futile attempt to reclaim the organization from the grip of communist control. In late August, 1933, a group, labeled the "Splitters" by the Communist newspaper Voice of Action, rose up. Their local was Phinney Greenwood, and at the next meeting there, the Splitters voted to separate from the Central Federation. By doing this, they hoped to rebuild Self-Help and reignite the organization they had originally joined.

Dobbins and the Communist leadership, hearing of the attempted split, attended the following meeting at Phinney. Local membership was not intimidated by the presence of the Central Federation leadership. They held another vote and rejected the Communist-infused constitution. They also agreed to do away with all political offices instituted by the communists and only retain the positions of chairman and secretary. Dobbins demanded to address the meeting to argue against the split. The majority of the members was in no mood to listen and voted to deny him the podium. Regardless, Dobbins began to speak. Ignoring him, the Splitter held a vote to adjourn which passed. As people collected their belongings and began to exit, Dobbins disregarded the vote of adjournment and continued to address the remaining attendees. He said that if they split, they could not use the UCL name or material. Further, he urged those who stayed behind to continue to battle for the UCL and organize their own loyalist faction. In essence, he sought to split the Splitters.[1]

Meanwhile, the communists attempted to strengthen the Central Federation in order to make the organization "harder to split up" and quicker to mobilize. While communist dominance was constantly denied by the leadership throughout this period, the machinations of the Communist Party are easy to identify. The Central Federation advocated that 20 or 30 "best minds," which of course meant communist ideologues, meet weekly to plan further action in each district. They also advocated uniting with "any working class organization..." which strongly inferred they should attach themselves to the Communist Party. While they still insisted that the point was to help the unemployed, the rhetoric became increasingly and alarmingly communist.[2] In fact, the UCL leadership began to question the very motives of the founders of the organization. The Voice of Action claimed that the Self-Help movement was not created to help the unemployed at all but to "enable local authorities to escape responsibility of the problems of feeding and caring for the jobless..." They continued to attack any that disagreed with their new goals. The Voice claimed that when Pearl was elected to lead the Central Federation, his real mission was to destroy the UCL. The founders were also guilty, according to the Voice, of being controlled by the politicians they supported. Instead of latching onto politicians, the current leadership wished to attach the UCL to a nationwide Unemployed Council which was begun in 1930 by the Communist Party.[3]

The Splitters tried to expand their own following and wrest back control of the UCL. The Splitters called another meeting. This time they offered a motion supporting FDR's programs and advocating for political action. In other words, they attempted to reestablish the original purpose of the organization, Self-Help and jobs. This move was attacked in the next issue of The Voice. The communist leadership claimed it was "insanity to imagine we could take everything from the capitalist class 'peacefully.'"[4] In the end, the older presidents and leaders - Pearl, Cronin, Murray and others - couldn't muster the numbers or enthusiasm. Ultimately, the Splitters lost control of the treasury. Communists then used UCL finances, much as they had used the commissaries earlier, to cement support by shifting money to their followers.[5]

The once strong organization that swayed the city to create a work relief program, inspired a national Self-Help movement and took over the county courthouse was now flaccid and weak. A few isolated protests, perhaps connected to the UCL, perhaps not, were staged. In November 1933, eighteen men at a Seattle lumberyard being operated by the Central Registry went on strike for cash payment instead of vouchers, but this was quickly quelled and only one of the strikers, Henry Staff, was arrested.[6] Less than a week later, police were called back out to the lumberyard when some of the men were refused vouchers because they hadn't worked that week. The dispute led to a gathering of a hundred men who were once again easily dispersed.[7] The internal fighting in the UCL had destroyed the unity and eliminated the one source of power the men had. They became rudderless against the will of the State.

Without an organization, the unemployed had to accept whatever burdens the government decided to lay on them in order to get relief. Fortunately, the federal requirements were becoming the standard for work relief just at the time the UCL was weakening, and while federal requirements were usually annoying, they were not as thoroughly humiliating as the state standards. Those unable to work, however, were forced to follow the state demands which continued to demean the poor.

In 1931, the Washington State Supreme Court had ruled that in order for a person to receive state relief they must be completely destitute. This meant that all money, valuables, and resources must be emptied before the state would provide any help. Further, the Supreme Court had ruled that before turning to the state for assistance, the family - including any parents, siblings, or grandparents - must help the indigent first. When the UCL was strong, diverse and unified, the organization had enough political pull to mitigate this ruling somewhat. As communists gained control, the UCL weakened and began losing members and influence, which left the unemployed and desperate nowhere to turn for help. With no help, they were forced to acquiesce to whatever the State demanded.

From the beginning The Vanguard had spoke for the UCL. But it began to falter when Brannin was called back to Texas to take care of family business. Wells remained as the sole editor, but Wells needed Brannin's money and inspiration. Eventually, Wells found himself in financial straits. He realized that he could either be the editor of The Vanguard or feed his family; he couldn't do both. Reluctantly, he handed the reins over to another. Wells continued to write for the paper but was no longer in charge.

The new Vanguard editor, too, struggled to keep the paper going. As The Vanguard suffered, the communist Voice of Action prospered. The Voice told its readers that if they were approached by the editors of the Vanguard, they should respond by saying, "The capitalists have the Times, the P.I. and the Star – do they need the Vanguard, too?" The Voice went on to say that the Vanguard was in fact more dangerous than the other newspapers. At least the others didn't claim to back labor and the workers. In particular, the Voice angrily resented the support The Vanguard had shown for Roosevelt's measures. Roosevelt, after all, only sought to feed the poor and prolong the whole rotten system.[8] In December, 1933, The Vanguard, unable to attract new readers or pay their bills, closed the doors. The Voice now claimed sole representation of the UCL.

The Voice of Action carried the torch of the hollowed-out UCL. A column in the paper gave a weekly update on the UCL activities, but it became a death-watch. At first, the articles clung to the advances being made under communist leadership. They were few and unimpressive – thirty men skulked around the house of Mrs. Page, a welfare worker who turned down a request for firewood;[9] an investigation was held into whether or not a PI newspaper fund was being used for children's shoes as they had promised.[10] Mostly, the UCL spent its time raising money simply to keep the Voice of Action newspaper going.

Later, several articles began to emphasize the coup aspect of the takeover by the Splitters. Eventually, the Voice even feasted on their own leadership. UCL chairman Dobbins who had been put in place with enthusiastic support of the communist faction was deposed, and the headline in the Voice of Action lauded the move saying, "Dobbins' Resignation Is Step Forward Says CP [Communist Party]."[11] Finally, the Voice itself struggled to find anything in the UCL to promote or applaud. The newspaper dropped the weekly column. Instead, individual articles, struggling for any reason to publicize the UCL, printed absurdly trivial accomplishment such as the UCL providing free tuition for a child to go to Pioneer Camp, a communist camp for children, and another article in which a UCL member won $2 for a story he had written.[12]

By 1935, the UCL was grasping at anything to stay alive. An obviously dwindling membership forced the organization to propose a new method of expansion. Up to this point they had advertised themselves as an organization of unemployed people, but the new proposal encouraged the locals to immediately "unite with whatever groups exist in their territory. Commonwealth Builder units, Technocrat clubs, trade union locals, civic, fraternal and church organizations."[13] This was clearly a desperate attempt at survival.

By 1936, in spite of these efforts, the UCL had lost all credibility. They were reduced to begging for a seat at the labor directed Washington State Commonwealth Federation meeting in Everett. They request was rejected by the Federation for having elected William Murray, "an avowed Communist," as president of the Seattle UCL.14

By this point the UCL had cast aside their original purpose. In May of 1936, they were no longer fighting for the unemployed but became entangled in an argument with the Seattle School Board over allowing a meeting of the Second Northwest Congress against War and Fascism at Broadway High School. The proposed meeting was a front for a communist rally and strongly supported by the ragged remnants of the UCL. In fact, one of the main defenders of the assembly was Wesley Randall, dean of the "Communist College."[15] An internecine battle between Murray and King County Communist Party Secretary Al Bristol caused the final collapse of the UCL. A juvenile argument between the two men centered on whether or not Murray had been "expelled" from or "quit" the Communist Party.[16] In the end, communists had stolen, crippled, trivialized and destroyed the Unemployed Citizens' League.

16

Shacktown: Events

Little would change in Hooverville over the next several years. Tired men would move into worn shacks or scrounge material to build new ones. Crime and despair would be the daily diet. Suicides, hunger and the stench would provide the grist for gossip. Each day was pretty much like the last. Every once in awhile, a new event or a significant change would occur, but rarely.

In 1934, Stephen A. Eringis and John J. Feroe came together to create a unique plan for Hooverville. What if they could form an institute of higher learning right down in the middle of the shacktown, they wondered. They could help educate those who needed new skills and at the same time employ the underemployed professors and literati who couldn't find appropriate work. The two men put the pieces together. They convinced the Port of Seattle to donate a section of the shantytown. They solicited wood to build the classrooms and found willing donors. They were even able to persuade the Seattle City Council to pay for water and lights.

Eringis, who had a passing resemblance to the ex-heavyweight champion Jack Dempsey, had come to America as a child, having been born in Lithuania. Eringis lived in Baltimore before moving to Seattle in 1927. He was a geology professor at the University of Washington until an unexplained controversy sparked his firing. He was convinced that the only reason he was forced to leave was due to political rivalries. As a result, he insisted that politics would play no part in his shacktown college.

163

For a time after leaving the University of Washington, he was forced to rely on relief. This provided a mere $2.50 a week for both himself and his wife. After searching for work for some time, Erngis was finally able to use his Master's Degree to finagle a position at the Warren Avenue School making $7.50 a week. Unfortunately, this was a short-term job, and he was never able to count on the money. He said it was at that point he arrived at the idea of a Hooverville College. This college would allow an alternative to the unemployed and down-and-out. Further, it would combat the rise of radicalism in the shacktown. "The purpose of the college is to combat isms," he declared. He didn't want the desperate to be lured toward Communism, Socialism, Fascism or any other ideology except Americanism.

Eringis was optimistic as the numbers of enrollees grew. He said, "Already 2,000 have registered at Hooverville. Of those we've found 276 Hooverville people are high school graduates, 83 had more than two years of college and one is a medical doctor." He also had lined up eight teachers who agreed to donate their time, as well as some University of Washington professors who were willing to offer occasional free lectures. Eringis had even convinced the United States Army band to play as part of the festivities for the opening day of Hooverville College.[1]

Eringis' Vice President John F. Feroe claimed that Hooverville College would "replace agitation with education." Feroe, a broke but enthusiastic partner with law degrees from two universities, was tall, gray-haired and sturdy. Three years earlier, he had moved to Seattle from Iowa where he had taught as an assistant professor. In order to provide an appropriate education for everyone involved, Feroe said, Hooverville College planned on presenting education at all levels, elementary through college. Things seemed to be on track when tragedy struck.[2]

On August 17, 1934 almost exactly a month after an article in the Seattle Times introduced the soon-to-be opened college, a second article appeared entitled "Teacher Killed When Struck By Rebounding Car." Eighteen-year-old Gordon Wilson, son of Renton Mayor Ernest Wilson, was driving down a residential street in Central Seattle. Somehow he lost control. After careening off of a second vehicle, Gordon's automobile spun, jumped the curb and struck John Feroe, killing him.[3]

From that point on, there is no more mention of any Hooverville College in the pages of the Seattle Times except for a brief article explaining that Sarah Feroe was filing suit against the drivers for killing her husband. Speculation is that the college failed to materialize because the city refused to help with the funding, but it is just as likely that the development of such a large undertaking was simply too much for one man.[4] Either way, the dream of providing an education for the downtrodden died with Feroe.

A more common occurrence at Hooverville was visits by various luminaries. As Mayor Jesse Jackson was fond of telling, a series of local political celebrities felt compelled to visit Hooverville. Marion Zioncheck, UCL lawyer and later a Congressman as well as a ferocious fighter for the unemployed, came to Jackson's cabin. Washington Senator Lewis Schwellenbach, strong supporter of Roosevelt's New Deal and later Secretary of Labor under Harry Truman, sat in a chair at Jackson's place. Jackson claimed that Secretary of Commerce under Roosevelt, Daniel C. Roper, also came to his Hooverville hovel to "see a town named after a former Secretary of Commerce..." While no documentary evidence showed he actually stopped at Jackson's cabin, Roper at least passed near there when leaving to Alaska via a ship docked at the foot of Charles Street. Upon spying the shacktown, he is reported to have said, "Every city has a place like this." But sitting next to Roper was Alfred Lundin, president of the Seattle Chamber of Commerce, who replied with more than a little pride, "Yes, but all are not as clean and sanitary as this one."[5] This was a nod to Jackson, the Hooverville committee and the continued acceptance of the agreement between the city and the shantytown.

One famous visitor who Jackson appeared to be less than appreciative of was the famous writer Ernie Pyle. In October, 1936, Pyle visited Jackson and was clearly unimpressed by Jackson's name-dropping. Worse, from Jackson's perspective, Pyle entitled the article, "Dictator Rule In Shack-City." This, said Jackson, was wrong. He wasn't a dictator but a contact man for the residents. In fact, Jackson resented the implication so much that he never included Pyle's name in the list of visitors even after Pyle became the most famous columnist of World War II.[6]

By 1939, Jackson had to have been tired. For eight years, he had been unofficially in charge of a rabble that by nature resented authority. He had done his best to be a mediator, coaxer, and friend to those who lived on the ragged edge of a society that only wanted them to go away. Whether his efforts were appreciated is hard to say, but sometime in late October, Jackson threw in the towel and resigned.

On Sunday, October 23, 1939 a second election was held among the residents of Hooverville. A new council of five was voted in. George Parish became the new mayor. Sixty-two year old Parish had been unemployed for some time but listed his profession as restaurant worker. According to the way these things were judged, he was a long-time resident of Hooverville having living in shack 7 L for four years. The new council's spokesman was Lawrence Oertli, who declared that council meetings from then on would be held every Monday evening. Oertli also made it clear that the council would resist any attempt to rid the city of the shacks. The first official act of the new council was to obtain an arrest warrant for a noisy Hooverite who had threatened another resident with a shotgun. Oertli said their goal was to "make Hooverville a decent place in which to live."[7]

17

The City: The New Idea Strives

The end of the UCL meant the last inclusive organization of the unemployed was gone. The Communist Party continued to recruit and attempt to lead whenever possible, but most of the men rejected their leadership. For many the shift from private to local to state relief had been the key factors that determined their lives, sometimes for the better, often for the worse. One moment they had a job or relief, and the next they were unemployed and homeless. They were given cash, food through a commissary, or vouchers, depending on the whims of politicians. They signed up at a depot, were investigated at home or were simply informed they no longer qualified. They were the troublesome pawns of an ever-changing system over which they had no control. It wasn't until Roosevelt and Hopkins and the drive by the Federal Government to recognize the exceptionality of the times that the needy and destitute were accepted as more than a burden. The agencies continued to change under federal control, and rules were not always consistent or uplifting, but at least the unemployed could expect warning before modifications occurred, and they understood that the men at the top wouldn't abandon them. Now, instead of watching for the shifting of winds across the various governments and politicians, they could concentrate their attention on federal actions. A sense of calm began to take hold.

A justification for that calm presented itself that winter. With cold weather coming, Roosevelt was convinced of the need for an additional work relief program. As a result, he created the Civil Works Administration (CWA). The CWA was placed under FERA and Harry Hopkins. Hopkins' new task was to help see that the unemployed had jobs to last through what would be a difficult winter of 1933-1934. The CWA was purposefully a short-term bridge to get the unemployed over the rough winter months, but it was not done on the cheap. With a budget of $200 million a month, Hopkins was able to assist approximately four million people across America in the four months the CWA existed.

Hopkins understood that the jobless would need a reasonable wage to heat their homes and keep fed over the cold months. Therefore, he set salaries to accommodate those needs. Unskilled labor received between 40 and 50 cents an hour, skilled workers between a dollar and a dollar and a quarter an hour and white collar workers between $12 and $18 a week. In order to spread the work around, CWA employees were limited to thirty hours a week.[1] But Hopkins also decided that the intrusive and resented inspections to prove poverty would not be used in determining eligibility for CWA. Those applying for work were assumed to need the job.[2]

The program began in King County on November 8, 1933 and immediately led to the employment of 3,500 men. By the end of the month 12,700 were employed. Winter months were always the most difficult, so the jobs offered were a godsend for many of the men and families, especially after the constant battles by Ernst and others to cut jobs and relief money.

The tasks that the CWA took on were spread across Seattle. The CWA helped repair roads just outside Hooverville on Railroad Avenue. They painted bridges at Montlake and 8th Avenue. They filled in a swamp area at the Green Lake Park, as well as cleared a new trail in Lincoln Park in West Seattle. Ballard High, Broadway High, and University Heights Schools, as well as the Seattle Public Library all received sprucing up.

Tuberculin testing and improvements at the Firland Sanatorium north of Seattle were provided by CWA. The landing strip at Sand Point Naval Station was improved, and work and training was provided in furniture, piano, typewriter, and sewing machine repair.[3]

Civil Works Administration road crew working just outside Hooverville at Railroad Avenue South near Washington Street. February 1, 1934. *University of Washington Libraries, Special Collections, UW13059.*

The money from the CWA had several lives as well. It went from the workers' hand to the grocery down the block to the clothing store. It helped the ailing restaurants and shoe stores. It gave a lift to gas stations and movie theaters. The combined effect caused a ripple that, while not solving the long-term problem, elevated the spirits and primed the economy.

The CWA reinvigorated many. One Civil Works employee in Butte, Montana took some loose change from his pocket and showing it to a friend said, "Do you know, Frank, this is the first money I've had in my pockets in a year and a half. Up to now I've had nothing but tickets that you exchange for groceries."[4]

Those in Seattle felt much the same way. Vouchers would not be given for federal work.

While the federal government sought ways to build respect and help those in need, Washington State remained in the regressive grip of Governor Martin. Earlier, the state legislature had passed a $10 million bond to provide relief for those who were unable to work or simply couldn't find a job. The Washington State Supreme Court finally ruled that the $10 million in bond money could be used for direct relief for those unfortunates. With the federal government supplying the resources for those who were fit enough to work, the ruling meant the state could now help those who couldn't work. However, Governor Martin and Director Ernst still refused to spend any of the funds on these needs.

By January, 1934, the federal government was firmly staking out ground as the strongest defender of the unemployed. The Civil Works Administration had grown and was now supplying 17,173 jobs in King County. Meanwhile, the national government waited in vain for Washington State to send its financial share to the relief effort.

The CWA was established with the idea that the state would provide the bulk of the funding. For every dollar contributed by the nation, the state was supposed to chip in three more. Many states, including Washington, ignored this requirement. It wasn't that Governor Martin couldn't have made an effort to pay the state's portion. If he was reluctant to spend the $10 million bond money on direct relief, Martin could have made partial payment to the federal government for the state's share of work relief. Instead, Martin used the bond money to create some of his own work relief programs and pay for other state expenditures.

171

In fact, Martin called Hopkins to let him know that, not only could the federal government not expect payment, but Washington State would need an additional $600,000 for each of the next three months to maintain the present relief levels. Martin still had $1 million dollars left from the bond but that money, he made clear, was going to be spent on his own work relief. Harry Hopkins, angry but unwilling to let the unemployed go hungry despite the callousness of political maneuverings, gave in to the blackmail and provided the funds.

Meanwhile in Seattle, the mayoral elections were held in March of 1934. To no one's surprise, except perhaps for Mayor Dore, Dore was soundly defeated and Charles L. Smith became Seattle's new mayor. Dore's failure to keep promises to the unemployed and the leeriness of the businessmen, who remembered his earlier promises to tax the rich, cost him the election. Smith was the leader of the King County Republican Club and had firmly committed to support the businesses of the area. Once again, the unemployed realized their needs would not be upper-most in the mind of the Seattle executive.

Back in Olympia, another relief crisis was rearing its head. On March 30, 1934, Ernst made a panicked call to Harry Hopkins. It was less than three months after Governor Martin had extorted relief money from Hopkins, but Washington State needed more assistance. The situation was dire, Ernst told Hopkins. Washington State would run out of money for relief in two days. Once again, the state refused to allocate any funds, and once again Hopkins realized that the only ones hurt would be the ones without work. Hopkins reluctantly put up an additional $1,750,000 of federal funds to cover the next month. This established a pattern that would be repeated throughout the coming year. By the end of 1934, FERA under Hopkins had given Washington State a total of $8,398,988. During this same period, the state supplied an anemic one percent of all relief given to its own unemployed.[5]

18

The City: A Revolutionary Idea

As the winter of 1933-34 came to an end, the Civil Works Administration concluded as well. FERA once again became the primary agency responsible for federal relief. The shift from CWA to FERA meant that the cash to begin new projects dried up. Projects that were still in process were given additional time, and some essential personnel were transferred to FERA. Only about 6,000 workers statewide were retained while the rest were told that they would have to wait to see if money for additional jobs might be forthcoming. They were encouraged to continue to apply for relief as that would keep them eligible for upcoming work.[1] Unlike CWA, FERA required that workers prove their need which meant a return to the despised interviews and investigations.[2] This was seen by the unemployed as a step backwards.

At the same time, the state-run WERA program finally took over complete control of the county system in 1934. Ernst was given overall command. He divided the state into six districts, pulled the decision making power out of the county, and made the district administrators answerable to him. Ernst did get rid of the hated voucher system and began cash payments. At the same time, he was adamant that direct relief was not to be paid equal to work relief. This meant that those on state work relief earned $45 a month for a family of four while those on direct relief would receive $34.

In the private sector, workers were paid nearly double what work relief paid. A 1935 survey showed the average factory worker brought home $86.28 a month, a white collar employee pulled in $89.96 and a supervisor received $177.33. Most everyone agreed that relief was never meant to be a substitute for private industry jobs, and even those on relief agreed they should receive less for government work. Still, the father on work relief pulling in his meager $540 a year and watching his children have to do without, knew that luck had as much to do with finding a good paying job as ability. They would have gladly traded their government check for one signed by private industry; just as they would have gladly worked the extra fifteen hours a week for a livable wage. Most believed the relief job was only temporary, to get them through the rough patch. For the worker, it didn't matter whether it was FERA, WERA, CWA or any other agency that provided the job so long as it translated to food in their stomach and a roof over their head. At the same time, most recognized that the federal government was less likely than the state to quibble over investigations, vouchers or cash, and exactly how poor was poor.

After limping along with FERA for nearly a year, it was clear to Roosevelt and Hopkins that a more aggressive program was needed. As a result, on April 5, 1935, the Works Progress Administration (WPA) was created. This was meant to be more like the CWA. New projects were identified by the local governments with the federal government footing the bill. WPA legislation set aside $4 billion for work relief and an additional $800 million for direct relief.

From 1935 to 1940, WPA would be responsible for the employment of eight million people across the nation. These people eventually received eight billion dollars for their labor. WPA directly touched more lives than any other New Deal program. Ultimately, the WPA provided income for nearly one-quarter of the US households at one time or another during that five year period.[3] For many, the WPA was the New Deal. As writer Cabell Phillips said, "...People came onto and went off the rolls as fortunes varied...But no one was a stranger to the program. Some families were shielded from it by luck or pride, but many were not. It was a part of daily experience, and it was a major preoccupation of mayors and governors and congressmen and the President."[4]

WPA, like many federal programs, paid attention to the earlier complaints of the unemployed. Pay continued to be in cash, not vouchers. The wage was to be at the prevailing hourly rate, depending on the job performed and location. The federal government was very explicit in requiring that wage data be taken not just from government agencies but from "labor groups, trade unions, employers and their organizations...and other available sources." This made it more difficult for the local politicians to peg wages to the lowest "average" they could find. Hours, too, were progressively regulated. "The maximum hours of work for project workers...shall be 8 hours per day, 40 hours per week and 140 hours per month." The only exception to the wage and hourly rulings was for supervisors and administrative personnel.

Age requirements limited WPA work to those 18 and older, but those under 18 were eligible for National Youth Administration or Civilian Conservation Corps jobs. Likewise, physically handicapped individuals were excluded but only if the handicap interfered with the safe performance of their duties. Non-citizens, too, were restricted from receiving WPA help. Since the WPA was a relief organization, ninety percent of all workers were expected to be from the relief rolls. In other words, it was only open to those who were not currently employed. Also, in order to spread the work around, each "family group" could only have one member working for WPA at a time. Finally, WPA workers were expected to be registered at approved employment offices, and if a WPA worker could find a job in the private sector, he or she was expected to take it.[5]

Once the rules were written and the policies established, the federal government rolled out the WPA to the states. In Washington State, there was a six month window allowed for the unemployed to apply for WPA jobs beginning on May 1, 1935 and ending in November. Applications flooded in, and the number of people employed by WPA in the state climbed rapidly. The very day applications were closed, November 1, the WPA notified 2,457 people in the state that they were no longer part of the unemployed.[6] Employment increased rapidly, and within a month, 28,789 were engaged in WPA projects.

Seattle was in Region 4 of Washington State. By the end of December 1935 Region 4 already had 120 projects going and 7,373 people employed.[7] For the first time, women were actively included in relief efforts. A statewide women's director, Nancy Beaver, was appointed. Beaver, later replaced by Julia Donovan, hired four hundred fifty women to provide hot meals for needy children. An additional 107 women were brought in to create "wearing apparel, bedding, rugs and curtains to be distributed to unemployable and needy persons by welfare agencies."[8]

WPA State Administrator George Gannon was proud of the inclusion of women in work relief. In his March 17, 1936, press release Gannon trumpeted the fact that the WPA state projects employed 4,000 women alongside 40,000 men.[9] Unfortunately, Gannon was a political appointee who used his position to favor his supporters and became a thorn in the side of Harry Hopkins. So in May, 1936, Gannon, was pushed out by Hopkins and replaced by Don G. Abel.[10]

Abel carried on admirably, and by May 15, the number of WPA workers employed in Seattle region 4 alone had grown to

9,897 of which 2,105 were women. These nearly ten thousand workers logged 522,620 hours in the first two weeks of May alone.[11] A month later, though, on June 15, 1936, the number of workers employed had fallen to 6,976 in Region 4.[12] Fluctuations were fairly common since WPA projects began and ended, necessitating more or less workers. Throughout the life of the project, though, the work performed for Washington State was surprisingly safe without a single fatality in 24,638,556 hours of labor.[13]

Despite Washington State's abysmal record at providing state funded aid, 1936 became a banner year for relief in the state due to federal assistance. Once again, Washington collected more than its fair share of federal aid. The state ranked eighth of all forty-eight states in employment from work projects, nearly all of which were funded by the federal government. Perhaps part of the reason the state benefitted so disproportionately from federal assistance was due to the ruthless policies of Ernst. In January, Ernst ordered all those who were employable off the state rolls. This meant they had to either find a job on their own or starve. Certainly, many of those forced off state relief were simply accepted by WPA to assure the workers' survival.

In March 1936, the redoubtable John Dore made an unlikely come-back. This time in his run for Seattle Mayor, Dore didn't try courting the unemployed or business. Instead, he aligned himself with labor. Dore, in turn, was strongly supported by organized labor and its boss, Dave Beck. Also, Dore played up Mayor Smith's unwillingness to tame Seattle streets. In his two years as mayor, Smith had done little to quash police corruption and the free-wheeling vice that permeated the city. This, too, became a central issue of Dore's campaign. Smith's inability and Dore's strengths combined to give Dore a second chance. He had learned his lesson, though. He would no longer dabble in the troubles of the unemployed.

By the middle of March, 1936, the WPA still played a huge role in the economy of Washington. The agency employed a record setting 49,523 people across the state. Typical among the work done in Seattle during this time was a street improvement plan which cost $375,000. The bulk of the financing was paid by the federal government with the city responsible for a mere $7,500.[14] Don G. Abel summarized WPA victories for 1936 in an open letter to the people of Washington State. Not only did the program employ "tens of thousands" to improve the state but their wages helped "rung millions of WPA wage dollars into [merchants'] tills...WPA wage dollars go into circulation immediately, turn over frequently."[15]

Unlike Dore, Clarence Martin's re-election as governor would continue to have negative consequences for the poor. Martin considered Dore a political enemy and sought ways to hurt his administration. Martin would later admit that his refusal to help Seattle fund relief was based at least partly on spite. Martin also kept Ernst in charge of much of the state-funded relief even though WERA was eliminated and Ernst was nearly universally opposed by all of those who defended the unemployed. This translated into an increase in suffering for the indigent and unemployed of the state throughout the subsequent two years.

Martin's reelection coincided with a particularly vicious recession. By August 1936, unemployment surged and the streets and shacktowns began to fill up once again. The rate of unemployment hit levels not seen since 1932-33, the pit of the Great Depression. Adding to the misery, federal relief was cut based on promising employment figures from the previous years. As a result, living in Seattle at that time meant an uninterested mayor, an antagonistic governor and a federal government caught off-guard.

Unfortunately just as in the UCL, communists saw the WPA as another opportunity to gain converts and to bolster their ranks. The communist controlled Workers' Alliance, for example, managed two sit-down strikes in Seattle within two weeks in 1936. The first strike was at the Welfare Office at the Burke Building. The second strike was at the Blue Ox, a shelter and welfare office. At the Blue Ox, one hundred and twenty-five members of the Alliance walked in and refused to leave. The police were called in because those who had come there to apply for relief couldn't even fight their way to the window to get an interview. The Alliance demanded that those who received direct relief and work relief be allowed to form unions, presumably under their banner. Since the protesters were calm and well-organized and never resorted to outright violence, the police took no action. This only encouraged the Alliance to continue to disrupt relief work.[16]

Seeing this as an effective strategy, the Workers' Alliance continued to implement and escalate this tactic the following year. The first major attempt to strike against the WPA in Seattle began on January 25, 1937. WPA wages had been increased during the preceding years until the minimum WPA wage in Seattle had climbed to $65 a month. While Seattle received a relatively generous salary based on prevailing local wages, other areas across the nation which received lower wages felt shortchanged. To placate these objections, the federal government reduced the highest minimum WPA wage to $55 a month. This was a shock to many in Seattle who depended and budgeted based on the $65 a month.

The Alliance saw its opportunity and shut down ten WPA projects in Seattle in protest. The Alliance, then, demanded not only a return to the $65 minimum but union scale for relief work. Further, they demanded additional concessions to settle the strike including shelters for outdoor workers and laborers' voice in how WPA was to be run. There was enough dissatisfaction that the Alliance hit a chord. More men joined the strike and more projects were forced to stop work. At its peak, the Alliance led strike shut down 25 job sites in King County. Eventually, between 1,700 and 4,500 WPA workers in the county were unable to work because of the strike. The Alliance saw this as a victory, but many workers became frustrated. WPA officials warned the men that staying away from their jobs for over five days meant they would have to re-register for their positions. The fear of a return to the breadline forced many to rethink their commitment to the strike. Beginning on February 8, a stream of men came down to the County-City Building to re-apply for their jobs. The Alliance formed picket lines at many of the job sites. Seven hundred men broke the line held by roughly 200 men and returned to work that day. There were arguments between strikers and those wishing to return, yelling and cursing, but police kept things peaceful. County commissioners threatened to reopen all the projects with those who re-registered or new men, thus excluding the hardcore supporters of the strike. Battle lines were being drawn, but the Alliance appeared to be blind to the declining support. Not understanding the shift that was taking place, and assuming they had the WPA officials against the wall, the Alliance requested the County provide 7,000 cans of food, five tons of dried fruit and use of the Civic Auditorium for a mass meeting.[17][18] Their requests were denied.

Tension finally spilled over into violence when WPA laborers returning to work at the West Seattle Golf Course were confronted by about 75 picketers. Returning workers accused picketers of jumping two men as they headed to their stations. Several fistfights broke out and the police were finally called. The workers were allowed to file in to work, and the protesters were sent to jail.

Works Progress Administration protest, Seattle, 1938. *University of Washington Libraries, Special Collections, UW10014.*

The Alliance made it clear that their main concern was not a single defeat at a golf course. Momentum was the issue. Individual battles could be lost so long as the front remained strong and enthusiasm for reform remained high.[19] But the politicians and many of the WPA workers, who simply wanted a paycheck, were getting tired of the interference. By February 11, police began wholesale arrests of strikers. Forty-nine were arrested in strike-threatened areas in Seattle and nearby Bothell in order to stem possible trouble.[20] In the largest of the round-ups, forty-two accused were brought before Judge William Bell.

In a jammed courtroom with scores of men at the window overlooking the proceedings, Bell questioned the reasons for the arrest. Sergeant E. C. Griffin claimed the police were given a hostile welcome when they arrived at the strike site. The fact that Griffin interpreted a "Bronx cheer" as a sign of trouble was made light of in the court. But the sergeant, feeling he had a duty to protect the men who wanted to work, divided the two angry groups into those who were headed to work and those who were there to protest. If they weren't here to work, he told them, they needed to go home. Many of the picketers questioned his authority to demand they leave and refused to go. Feeling they would start trouble as soon as the police left, Griffin arrested them.

The defense asked if the men were ever physically threatening. Griffin responded by admitting that all the men were peaceful. If the men were peaceful and doing nothing to disrupt the workers, why were they arrested, the defense attorney continued. Griffin could only fall back on his assumption that this was an illegal gathering. With no solid legal rationale for the arrest, Judge Bell released twenty-one of the men on their own recognizance.[21] Soon thereafter, Bell released the remaining defendants saying that with no evidence of threats or intimidation by the strikers, they broke no law so had to be freed.[22]

In order to prevent an escalation of trouble, a conference was held between the two sides. Charles Ernst represented the work relief administrators and Harold Brockway, a leader of the Workers' Alliance, stood in for the strikers. At this conference an agreement was reached. The compromise "peace proposal" gave the Alliance the right to bargain for the men but didn't meet the demand of a $10 bump in pay.[23] The Alliance originally agreed to let the workers vote on the proposal, but after discussion by their executive committee the Alliance rejected the compromise outright and refused to allow the promised vote. WPA director Don Abel warned that snubbing the peace proposal could cause the WPA to close projects in King County.

Abel sympathized with the workers. He had tried to reinstate the $10 wage cut, explaining to those in authority that the decrease had made it impossible for some families to maintain a "decent living." When Abel was informed by the federal regulators that the raise was not possible, he refused to give up. He asked the state legislature to petition Congress to improve the wages and work conditions for those on WPA. This, too, failed. Having done what he could, Abel felt he had no choice. He warned the WPA workers that he would have to drop 2,000 of them from the rolls for failure to show if they didn't return to their jobs quickly.[24]

The warning worked. The next day, a second organization calling itself the American Project Employes'[sic] Association was formed. Two days after Abel's warning, on February 20, the Association had recruited 3,000 members, held a meeting and voted to return to work. The Association met at the Eagles Auditorium and carefully screened those who came in. All Workers Alliance members were turned away, providing for an obviously skewed vote.[25] Therefore, the Alliance decided to hold its own vote on the matter. Much to their surprise, the results mirrored the Association's vote. WPA workers wanted to return to work even if it meant they would not get the pay raise. In the end, the Alliance and the strikers had to settle for a promise of no reprisals for the strike and a reduced work week consisting of six hours, five days a week rather than a pay raise.[26] Over eighty percent of the strikers voted to end the strike and by Thursday, February 25, workers began to return to their jobs.[27]

With the recession continuing into 1938, Ernst searched for more ways to tighten the state's belt. In March 1938, the recession hit a low point. Two-thirds of the economic gains made since 1933 had vanished. Stock market values were sliced nearly in half. Businesses were watching profits plummet.[28] As relief rolls began to once again grow, Ernst made his decision. On March 10, 1938, Ernst announced that no more relief for unemployed would be available through the state starting April 1. In King County, this meant that 13,000 people were set to lose their income. The federal administer of WPA, Don Abel said that the removal of these workers was unnecessary. He laid out the conditions needed to retain assistance. The state would have to release matching funds, and Ernst needed to pass county requests for projects to the federal level. Even this was too much for Ernst. He did agree to provide aid to some of the unemployables through Social Security, but otherwise, those without jobs were on their own as far as the state was concerned.

The failure of the state to provide aid didn't cause the government's fiscal problems to disappear. It merely shifted the weight to the counties and cities. The state could hide from the down-and-out, but local officials passed by them on a daily basis. Governor Martin reassured local politicians that there would be another relief program soon but no details were forthcoming and no timeline was given.

When no new plans were presented by Ernst's deadline of April 1, 1938, King County Commissioner Jack Taylor made it clear he believed that the state might renege on promised funds. This meant, Taylor said, the county was completely liable. Also, Taylor warned that the county, despite a lack of funding, would need to finance more relief since those kicked off state relief had nowhere else to go. In the meantime, King County relief had already been reduced to providing a few vouchers for food and distributing federal surplus food and clothes. The chaotic and confused nature of relief caused the communist Workers' Alliance to organize another protest. About 400 people met outside of the County-City Building.[29]

With the additional burdens brought on by the elimination of state funding, King County needed to trim its relief budget. So the county sent out an order to close the Blue Ox. The Blue Ox had provided food and shelter for the needy for years. This had been the home of the desperate even prior to the Great Depression, and now it was being taken away. About 300 residents of the shelter decided this was a step too far. They entered the County-City Building and hiked up to the seventh floor. There the men sat on the benches and stood in the hallways. Where else did they have to go, they asked.

County officials put their heads together. After hurried discussions, they arrived at a possible solution. There was an old Civilian Conservation Corps camp up near Fall City. Perhaps those who were kicked out of the Blue Ox could use that facility. The men on the seventh floor gathered around to discuss the proposal. Fall City was twenty-five miles from Seattle and was surrounded by farms, woods and not much else. Some likened it to a "concentration camp." One of the leaders gave a more valid reason for rejecting the proposal: if the unemployed leave "the city, [they] lose all chance of getting employment." It was certain there wasn't any work up there. The consensus seemed clear but a vote was taken anyway. No, they decided, they wouldn't be moving to Fall City.

While the search for other solutions continued, the county attempted to make the protesters comfortable. Sympathetic county workers pitched in to buy donuts and coffee for the indigents. County officials gave permission to the protesters to stay the night with the understanding that the men police themselves and not spread to other floors. The officials reassure the men that they could still get food even with the Blue Ox closed, either through vouchers or by surplus supplies. Also, county representatives let the protesters know that the WPA would soon be providing more jobs if they could just hold on a little longer.[30]

Unfortunately, there was nothing that could be done to ease the worry of those on the seventh floor. When it finally became clear that no compromise could be reached, King County Commissioners huddled once again and decided to reopen the Blue Ox shelter on their own authority. So the commissioners, trailed by the protesters, walked the few blocks to the Blue Ox. Upon arriving, they found the shelter was already in the process of being dismantled. The deconstruction was halted, and the men were allowed back in. Emergency food was brought and served, but everyone understood this to be a temporary solution. Still, for the time being, the reopening at least allowed both sides some breathing room.[31]

Unfortunately, the Blue Ox was quickly overrun. By Sunday, April 3, many of the men who had been kicked off of relief on the previous Friday under Ernst's decree realized that there were few options. Almost 2,000 men showed up for meals that day. This created an additional problem since the cafeteria only had 284 dishes. This meant that meals had to be served in shifts. The morning meal took three hours to serve, and no one expected the lines to shorten anytime soon.[32]

This was apparently too much for the county, so on April 5, they announced that the Blue Ox would be closed within three days. This decision to shut the facility so soon after reopening was justified based on the claim that many of the men receiving food were not local. People were coming from other regions and states because King County was seen as a soft touch, officials said. A new policy was established to prevent outsiders from benefitting from the county's generosity. After proving they were King County residents, local men would be given chits for rooms at neighboring hotels and for meals at nearby restaurants. The county also began pushing the WPA to speed up the application process.

In the midst of this battle, a man who had figured prominently in the rise and fall of the Unemployed Citizens League and had shaped Seattle politics for most of the Great Depression died. Ex-Mayor John Dore, 56, passed away from what was described as "a general physical breakdown" on April 18, 1938. The Seattle Times obituary was stunning in its non-appraisal of Mayor John Dore, saying, "To catalogue things promised, tried, done and left undone would be an inexcusable departure from the simple requirements of the occasion." The article went on to say that Seattle's "opinions are submerged in sincere sympathy for the bereaved." In his place Arthur Langlie officially became the new Seattle mayor.[33] Just as Dore before him, Langlie, too, would defer the shantyville battle to his council.

Meanwhile, the Workers' Alliance teamed up with two other organizations to once again call for a march on Olympia to protest the cuts in relief and to encourage an increase in WPA funding.[34] This march fizzled as only about a hundred attended and they were denied a meeting with the governor. They did, however get the opportunity to meet with Ernst who informed them that he had seen too many able-bodied slackers on relief. "Many people have been on relief so long they don't want to do anything else," he said. "The problem now is to force them off relief and to work."[35]

Just as Ernst and Governor Martin continued to look for ways to cut aid provided by Washington State, the national government was recognizing the need for increased relief. With the recession stretching into 1938, those in charge of WPA realized that relief rolls would have to be expanded. A record 3,300,000 people nationwide were employed by the federal government in WPA projects by November 1938.[36] For many, WPA was their only life-line, a fact that Roosevelt and most of Congress recognized as well.

By 1939, though, the political battles were taking their toll. New distractions, like a looming war, were drawing attention away from the needs of the desperate. While it wasn't feasible at this point for the conservative faction in Congress to totally curtail WPA, they searched for other ways to weaken it. In March 1939, anti-New Deal lawmakers were able to pass a resolution forcing all WPA employees to forego any political campaign activity. In essence, that meant that those involved in WPA had to quit work or quit civic involvement.

A month later, in April of that year, one of the last significant protests was held at the County-City Building. Once again, cuts in the county welfare program meant that another shelter was scheduled to shut down. The county director, L. L. Hegland said that the step had to be taken because of severe cuts in funding. "We just haven't the money to continue paying [the $190 a month] rent on the premises," he said. Therefore, the 440 men staying at the shelter at 213 ½ Second Avenue South were told to vacate by 8 o'clock in the morning of April 1. Instead, they instituted a "sleep-in strike" refusing to move from their beds and rooms. Meanwhile, three of the protesters went to a local judge to request he intervene. Judge Chester Batchelor told Director Hegland, he would have to appear and explain why the shelter must be closed.[37] Until then the men would be allowed to occupy the premises.

Hegland tried to get alternate quarters for the men several days later but found it difficult. In the meantime, a group of the protesters under the guidance of the Workers' Alliance set up a "starvation camp" on the lawn of the County-City Building. About 600 men unfurled tents and squatted. Seattle Mayor Arthur B. Langlie ordered the protesters to leave. When they ignored his order, Langlie demanded the police remove them on April 7. Eighteen officers were called in and ousted the men, then gathered up the tents and shipped them to Alliance headquarters. The crowd remained non-resistant and silent during the action, but refused to vacate the grounds.

On the same day the tents were coming down, the relief rolls were once again cut. As a result, there was a flood of unemployed at the county relief offices asking for food and vouchers. By this time single men were reduced to 20 cents a day, while married men received $2.80 per month per person along with some supplemental food. This was about half what had been given just a month previous. Further, Hegland begged the unemployed not to rush down to the offices to demand payment as the budget cuts forced staff reductions along with relief.[38]

The indigent who had instituted the sleep-in were eventually given a replacement shelter at 118 ½ Third Avenue South. This didn't stop the protests, however. The relief cuts, the lack of housing and continued agitation by the Workers' Alliance led to protests in front of the courthouse[39] and a second, smaller "starvation camp" on April 10. Meanwhile, thirty men refused to leave their beds at the original shelter, and those who did ended up at the Third Avenue South location where they found the only place to sleep was on the floor.

Others complained saying that the new shelter had poor lighting and little heat.[40]

Eight years of hearing of protests, seeing ramshackle shacktowns and living with the results of poverty had worn thin the patience of many Seattleites. The problems of the unemployed became stale and seemed to have no permanent solution. And while there had never been substantial empathy for the single unemployed man, even some who were married with children began to sense resentment.

The final significant protest of the unemployed even exasperated the architect of the New Deal, Franklin Roosevelt. This protest was not simply a Seattle phenomenon but a national one. Conservative law-makers were finally able to effect direct changes to WPA. New regulations for WPA workers came out in July 1939. Workers were required to put in 130 hours a month regardless of their classification in order to earn their salary. New wages were reduced nationwide to $52 a month. This meant that the prevailing local wage for a job no longer applied. There was also a requirement that workers could only be on WPA for eighteen consecutive months. After a year and a half, the worker would be laid off for at least thirty days and would have to reapply afterwards.[41]

One hundred thousand WPA workers across the nation went on strike against these new requirements including many in Seattle. Nationwide tens of thousands of strikers were fired. In Seattle, workers who walked out were also threatened with firing if they didn't return to the job. Seattle WPA workers held a rushed meeting at City Hall Park on July 12, and about a thousand voted to return to work a day before the deadline.[42] Finally, on July 14, President Roosevelt made it clear that WPA workers "cannot strike against the government."[43] While there were minor protests afterwards, none had the determination of earlier times.

By 1940, serious changes altered the WPA. All art and theater programs were cut from WPA and were forced to rely on local governments for support. Workers were told they were going to need to put in longer hours for the same or lower pay. This, of course, meant that WPA workers were significantly cheaper to employ than union workers. WPA employees sometimes had to labor triple the hours in order to make the same salary as their union counterparts.[44] Soon thereafter, a loyalty oath was required of all workers to prevent any with communist ties from receiving a job.[45]

What finally caused the WPA to become less vital was the growing European war. First, business was called on to shore up America's military and to supply materiel for England. Then, in September 1940, the Selective Service and Training Act was signed into law. In Seattle, young men lined up at the Field Artillery Armory to register in October 1940. By the end of that month, 45,341 men aged 21 to 35 had registered in Seattle and King County and anxiously awaited the lottery. Due in large part to the escalating military situation between July 1940 and March 1941, 855,000 individuals nationwide were able to get off public work relief and find jobs in private industry[46].

By July 1941, only a million people were left with WPA jobs and nearly half of the projects across the nation were being curtailed or cancelled. Of those still on WPA, a third were now dedicated to working on military preparedness. Then, on December 8, 1941, the day after Pearl Harbor was attacked, state and local WPA administrators were sent this message: "You are instructed to close off rapidly as possible all construction of projects of nondefense nature using critical materials or labor where they can be effectively used in defense activity."[47]

The unemployed of Seattle now streamed into the employment offices at Boeing near where the UCL had planted one of its gardens and Todd Shipyards where the Duwamish shacktown used to be. Many young men found employment in the military. The next employment problem would be too few workers rather than too many.

19

Shacktown: Clubs

The final fight to maintain the shacktowns was a long one. Even before the Depression, when shanties had sprung up in various locations around Seattle, people had objected. The city had tried to burn out the hovels but they always sprang back. With the advent of the Depression an uncomfortable stasis had developed. The city recognized that there were simply too many homeless men to ignore their need for shelter, and the homeless realized that the acceptance of their shacktowns would only come at the cost of recognition of the city's authority and acceptance of basic rules for conduct.

By 1936, though, some thought the balance had shifted from acceptance to actual assistance in maintaining the shacktowns. At the city-owned Sears Tract near Beacon Hill for example, water was being supplied to squatters by a nearby spring that flowed openly through the city. Everyone recognized this as a danger, so the city promised to provide water to the six families residing there. The Water Department Superintendent even went so far as to agree to lay pipe out to the shacks, although the residents were required to do the manual labor and reimburse the department for most of the materials.[1] Soon after, nearby home owners objected to the use of open flame for cooking in the Sears Tract saying a fire was inevitable. The solution arrived at by the vagrants was to apply to City Light for electrical hook-ups for their shacks. This drew the attention of Seattle City Council to the growing shantyville. Some of the Council agreed that the indigents posed a fire threat, and their application for electric service nearly caused them to be expelled from their rent-free land.[2] The threat of expulsion

194

didn't cause the residents to maintain a low profile, however. Two months later they complained that the one-inch pipe that the city was planning on laying to give them access to fresh water would be too narrow, and they needed at least a two-incher to supply the needs of all the residents.[3] This demonstration of seeming ingratitude by the Sears Tract squatters became the epitome for all shacktowns in the minds of many citizens.

For many Seattleites, this request tested their patience. Those left in the shantyvilles were there by choice and were of the lowest element, or so thought a growing number of "good citizens." The shacktowns were seen as unnecessary, unsanitary and too-long tolerated.

By 1937, there began a fresh assault on Hooverville and its companion shacktowns. Despite its persistence and expansion, it was a surprisingly peaceful attack and never reached the level of vigilante action such as had happened with the UCL. It began with a complaint by Lawrence E. Barrett, president of the North End Federated Clubs in March of 1937. The North End didn't object to Hooverville, but they had noticed that the shacktown near them at Interbay was growing. Barrett made it clear that "[m]embers don't want to see a second Hooverville at Interbay" but "[a]n increasing number of shacks are springing up at the dump and conditions are rapidly becoming more unsanitary and troublesome." As a result, the Club met to draft an official request to the city to clean up the Interbay shacktown.[4]

From that point on, the various community clubs spearheaded the attacks on shantytowns in Seattle. Smoke drifting up from the Interbay garbage dump next to the shacktown drew the next complaint filed by residents of the area.[5] To placate the objections and to create more healthy conditions, Building Superintendent H. C. Ritzman suggested that any unoccupied shacks be taken down. This was in response to a petition by the Gilman Park Community Club which claimed that only thirty-one of the seventy-seven cabins in the Interbay area were occupied. Destroying the vacant shacks, Ritzman believed, would discourage new boarders.[6] The North End Federation which included the Gilman Park Community Club and five other community clubs, agreed with Ritzman. North End Federation President Barrett supported the idea of razing the empty shacks, saying, "In this manner, no one will be forced into the streets, which appears to be the principal objection to a much-needed clean-up not only in the Interbay district but in other parts of the city." The city, however, refused to act.[7] The cost for the destruction of abandoned shacks was estimated at $1,000 which would have to come out of the budget of the Board of Public Works. The officials whose authority was required refused to release the funds.

Centrally-located Beacon Hill Community Club, which had two shacktowns, echoed the North End's objections. These slums were unsightly and a nuisance, they said. Once again, Building Superintendent Ritzman joined protesters urging the city to destroy the vacated houses.[8] Two days later, the Beacon Hill Club prepared to team with the North End Federation to create a united front against the continuation of shacktowns. This alliance was precipitated by the recognition that if the North End clubs were successful, shacktown residents would simply move further south invading the Beacon Hill area. In fact, just the threat of eviction had already caused some of the homeless to move to Beacon Hill in anticipation of the destruction of shantyvilles up north. The combined groups hoped to end the "trading, selling or transferring 'titles' to shacks" anywhere in Seattle by city ordinance. Barrett reiterated that this gradual method of eliminating squatters was preferable to the "mass eviction."[9]

On April 20, 1938, the Consolidated South District Commercial Club joined the shacktown fray. With the north and central parts of the city pushing along the vagrants, they saw what was coming. They complained that the Sears Tract shantytown on city owned property was growing in South Seattle. They also noted that Hooverville had been tolerated on city land many years. The South District urged Seattle Council to send them all packing.[10]

Despite the united force of Community Clubs across the length of Seattle, little was done by the city. One of the originators of the war against shacktowns, the president of North End Federated Clubs Barrett, pledged to "redouble efforts to obtain the removal of the shanty settlement at Interbay." A clearly annoyed Barrett continued on to say, "The federation's protest against the shanty town was placed on file with the Council after being referred to the safety committee. We were assured it would be brought up at a hearing and we appointed a group to appear in our behalf, only to find the issue had been sidetracked."[11]

With the city still unresponsive, the fight moved to the county. The Consolidated South District Commercial Clubs approached the Board of County Commissioners and asked for an investigation of growing shacktowns on county property. The Board appointed John P. Angel to look into it.[12]

Six months later, with no overt action from Seattle or King County, someone decided to take matters into their own hands. Forty shacks at the Duwamish slum were destroyed. While it appears that the shacks were taken down by some governmental agency, it was never clear which one or under whose authority. Certainly, no hearings were held, since the

Chairman of the Public Safety Committee, Councilman William L. Norton, hadn't been notified of any meetings on the subject. Men from Duwamish visited Norton and said that the destruction was scheduled to continue. On October 12, 1938, Councilman Norton heard complaints by the Duwamish shantyville residents about the tearing down of the shacks. Norton decided he would investigate.[13] Within days, Hooverville residents also found signs posted demanding that they vacate their houses. The explanation they were given was the WPA needed the area for a project. Soon there were signs tacked up throughout shacktowns across the city even though it was clear that the WPA had no intention of using all the acreage from all the shacktowns in Seattle. Questions began to arise in the various shantytowns: Was this a ploy by the community clubs? Could the city be testing to see if the vagrants could be tricked into leaving without complaint?

The Workers' Alliance sent James Riley to the city to defend the squatters. Riley said the signs "have been posted in shacktowns all over the city waterfront notifying residents to vacate in thirty or sixty days, and if the shacks are torn down the city will have to find houses for 20,000 persons." No one seemed to know who had placed the signs and no one ever took responsibility. After investigation, Norton found that only the original signs in Hooverville were legitimately placed by the WPA which had a project planned. The people of Hooverville were willing to accept the dismantling of those shacks if it led to jobs, and there was no further protest regarding the legally posted WPA signs. Norton's inquiry gained him the reputation as an honest defender of the rights of the homeless.[14]

Norton had been elected to Seattle City Council in 1937 with the rather dull promise that he would give "Seattle the same type of efficient service that I have given the City of

Seattle for the past several years in my public service activities..." He was an ex-Seattle policeman, but despite this he never joined others on the police force who looked on the homeless as just a public nuisance. Instead, the 37-year-old ordained Episcopal minister, was a straight-shooter who had a heart for the men in the shacktowns.[15] Time and again Norton intervened to prevent any capricious attack on the shacktown residents.

Meanwhile, the Consolidated Clubs accused the City Council of not just allowing building in Hooverville but issuing permits to build there. It decided to send representatives to the next city council meeting to register these complaints.[16]

By now, Hooverville residents were beginning to understand the stakes. The illegal signs and ire of the various clubs inspired the men to do what they had always resisted - they organized. A large group travelled to the city council meeting to protest. If their houses were destroyed, where else could they go, they asked. The Consolidated South District Commercial Clubs essentially ignored the question, and instead renewed their request that those evicted should not be allowed to build or rent other shacks. This was especially important, they felt, with the forced evictions caused by the WPA project. Many of the Club members were afraid those who were pushed off the waterfront would end up in the Sears Tract or other shantytowns in their district.[17] Councilman Norton issued the official response of the City Council, saying that the destruction of shacks would be stopped given the objections of the shantytown residents and the controversy that followed the WPA evictions. This declaration sat poorly with the Club, but Norton remained unmoved.[18]

Perhaps with urging from the Seattle community clubs, the Seattle Police waded into the debate in November 1938, saying they favored the razing of the shacks on the waterfront. Sergeant E. C. Griffin, the same officer who had arrested Alliance workers for failure to disperse during the WPA strikes, said that police had "constantly made arrests in the shacktown for offenses ranging from murder down to the smallest kind of crime." Griffin didn't advocate for any immediate destruction of the entire town but was supportive of the gradual process in which vacated cabins would be taken down. Norton refused to be swayed by his fellow officer or to hurry any decision. Instead, he continued to look for a solution that would help the unemployed men in the shantytowns find alternate housing before starting any concerted eviction.[19]

On November 22, the two sides - community clubs and shacktown residents - were brought together in a city council meeting. Both sides were adamant but polite. The Consolidated South District Clubs, represented by Mrs. George Spencer said, "People who live in the shacks get their food from garbage cans. The shacks are made from anything the men can pick up in our neighborhood. Our children at times come across these men." Besides, Mrs. Spencer said, the city has already promised to do something about this problem and has failed to follow through. The response was delivered by then mayor of Hooverville George Parish. Parish said, "I live in a shack. I try to keep my shack as clean as possible. I don't love living in a place like that. But what am I going to do when I can't get any other place? They tell me I'm too old [at 62] when I ask for work. I'd leave my shack if I could get another place. And I don't live out of a garbage can, and many of us who live in shacks do not." After further debate, the Public Safety Committee decided to consider what they had heard and put off any action on the issue for a week.[20]

A week later the Public Safety Committee reconvened. The civility that marked their earlier meeting was gone. Three hundred angry residents from various shacktowns attended. A newspaper reported, "Boos and cat-calls went up from the squatters as Beacon Hill residents described the shack residents as a menace to children and a health problem. Lusty cheers rent the air as the shacktowners applauded their spokesmen who appealed for a 'live and let live' policy." A couple of defenders from outside their shacktown community even spoke up in their favor. One, John Stanley, said "[Y]ou are virtually signing the death warrant of these poor men if you turn them out of their little homes." William Kinloch, a shacktown resident of the Sears Tract, said, "I am a seafaring man. The law of the sea is to help those in distress. Don't take the plank away from the sailor who has helped you into the boat and taken only a plank for himself." Norton and the committee, having listened to both sides, decided the best solution was to get the two parties to work together. As a result, a subcommittee made up of shack residents and community club members was formed.[21]

The committee of three community members and three shacktown representatives met the following day. Shacktown resident Byrd Kelso, who described himself as an "unemployed union organizer," had just finished a survey of the various shantyvilles in Seattle and reported to the subcommittee. According to Kelso's count there were 22,204 shacks located in the city, almost certainly an exaggeration. He said that 64% of those living in the shacks were single men and added disingenuously that 63% were voters. The primary problem according to Kelso was that relief was simply too difficult to get.

The new subcommittee also listened to Fire Chief William Fitzgerald who complained about the number of fires his department was forced to respond to from these areas. Finally,

Police Chief William Sears said that the illegal towns were responsible for five or six murders in the last few weeks alone along with a rash of assaults recently. Councilman Samuel Humes moved that the City Council create another special committee comprised of city, county and federal officials to determine how to get better housing and relief for the inhabitants.[22]

D. C. Conover, new president of the Consolidated Clubs after Barrett's resignation, made it clear that club members saw the problem of shacktowns getting worse rather than better. A few years before there had only been a couple thousand shacks, but referring to Kelso's new numbers, Conover made it clear that Seattle was being overrun. Further, several leaders of the South District Consolidated Commercial club claimed they were being targeted for harassment. Windows were broken by slingshots and sinister phone calls were made telling the members to "lay off."

County Clerk Carroll Carter addressed the committee offering a possible compromise. A federal act had been passed to help clean up areas such as Hooverville. Like many of Roosevelt's policies, it required states to chip in part of the funding. But if the state's 1939 legislature approved an enabling act, money could be found to implement a slum clearance program through the federal government. This would satisfy both sides by providing money to help the homeless find better housing while clearing away the unsanitary conditions to which the community clubs objected.[23]

Norton, at the meeting of December 7, suggested an alternate solution to the problem. The city could adopt the Swedish model for homelessness. Using that model, Seattle would open a new area for the homeless away from residential centers. Money could be found using state and federal resources and a regular community could be built for the men. This would be teamed with the destruction of any vacated premise in current shacktowns. Norton believed that this solution would meet the needs of both the squatters and the home-owners as well.[24]

In a four hour meeting on December 9, the advisory board finally struck a compromise. First, all agreed that no one would be forced out of shacks in which they currently lived. Second, the present limits of the Beacon Hill shacktown would remain and no expansion would be permitted. However, on this point Kelso insisted that the people living in the shantytowns "can't be expected to do our policing in reference to the boundaries set up," but he was assured that the city would be the policing agent. Third, new housing would be investigated once a survey was conducted to determine the type of housing shacktown residents preferred.

Charles Ernst, representing the State, attended the meeting. He had serious reservations about Seattle becoming a haven for the homeless. He believed that Seattle might just be sending out a siren call for the desperate across the nation. At the advisory board meeting, Ernst said, "If, for example, word was spread that Seattle is building houses for its shacktown residents, it would be just a 'come on' for transients all over the nation."[25]

From the proposals offered to the Advisory Committee, Councilman Norton sent two resolutions to the Seattle City Council. Number one recommended that the federal government provide "a substantial sum" to be used to subsidize the current relief to the unemployed so that shacktown residents could afford better housing as per County Clerk Carter's recommendation. Resolution number two suggested that the city prevent any new construction of shacks in "first or second residence districts."[26]

The slow progress and plethora of committees and subcommittees began to wear on the community clubs. The secretary of the Consolidated South District Commercial Clubs, H. W. Broenkow, voiced the frustration of his organization. Broenkow felt the City Council was moving much too slowly on the elimination of all shacks. He also expressed resentment at the city asking the community clubs to come up with solutions. "The city Council or any other group that asks us to present a solution has lost the entire point of the situation. We are amateurs…it is up to the professionals to solve the problem. That is what they are being paid for…," said Broenkow. He went on to accuse the officials of political cowardice saying they were too afraid of losing the votes of the shacktown residents.[27]

On Christmas Eve 1938, the Seattle Times expressed the conundrum well:

"Seattle's shacktown problem is one of several angles. A cluster of makeshift huts and shelters adds nothing to the beauty of the landscape and gives no pleasure to homeowners anywhere within range of vision. Through their community clubs and otherwise many residents are asking to be relieved of what they regard at least as an offense to the eye and a possible menace to health; meanwhile conceding as everyone must, that an occupied shacktown cannot be ruthlessly razed and its population left with no place to go. In the course of much discussion it is frequently suggested that other and better housing should be provided, but this suggestion trails vaguely away from the point of responsibility. Whose duty is it to provide such housing? Then comes the question – how?…They cannot be helped by herding together in a public barracks. We hear of low-income housing and low rent housing; but shacktown dwellers are without incomes and generally without any means of paying even low rents. Organized effort would better apply to finding work for the shacktown dwellers who wish to get out."[28]

With Seattle's urging, the Washington State Legislature cleared the way to vote on an enabling act to accepted federal money for low-cost housing and slum clearance. This gave federal grants to towns and cities that provided matching funds to help construct housing for the displaced. In order to encourage passage of the act, it was touted as an employment and money-making bill as well, since the additional housing would help the lumber and construction industries.[29] With the dual purposes of clearing shacktowns and providing jobs, the enabling act was passed February 22, 1939.[30]

Two days later, the West Seattle Commercial Club met to magnanimously support cheap housing for shacktown residents in their area. Resident Everett Fenton, however, warned, "Naturally many people wish cheap housing and will never seek anything but slum dwellings unless a firm hand is taken. This menace to public health and safety will continue to grow unless some policy is reached and action taken."[31] Clearly, the enabling act was thought a step in the right direction, but the club members were leery having seen previous promises sluggishly performed or denied outright.

Within a month, however, on March 13, 1939, the Seattle City Council unanimously voted to accept a reported $8,000,000 from the federal government to assist in slum-removal. This money was to be supplemented by state funds, and the resources were earmarked to help with rent, electricity and water for those without an income. To fill-in any gaps of funding, the State Department of Social Security had agreed to help shacktown dwellers with additional matching funds as well.

Once new housing was constructed, the old, unsanitary shacks would be destroyed. A large crowd watched the proceedings without disruption. Finally, after years of surveys, committees and debates, concrete action was being taken to help eliminate the unhealthy slum-towns that pocked Seattle.[32]

In an editorial on April 12, the Seattle Times warned its readers that simply providing additional money to shacktown residents wouldn't mean that they would immediately abandon their hovels and rent better housing. Two issues concerned the writer. First, "[h]abituated shacktown dwellers, long free from rental obligations, may prefer to remain 'as is,' rather than pay any rent at all." Second, while most shacks were occupied by single men, the families that did live in the shacktowns tended to be large, and the $8 minimum which was being provided for housing would not be nearly enough to relocate them. This meant the price to house most families would be substantially higher than predicted causing the overall cost to jump. In fact, the only way to rid the city of the shacktowns was, the article reiterated, "to bring business and industry back to a point where employment at living wages will be within reach of all who are willing to work."[33]

Unfortunately, those like the writer of the editorial who predicted that many of the poor couldn't be lured out of their shacks so easily were too often correct. Jack Taylor, County Commissioner, realized that the relief offered by the city had to be absolutely tied to the requirement that the residents move. Therefore, at a meeting at the YWCA in downtown Seattle on May 5, 1939, he suggested to the Consolidated South District Commercial Club a way to induce squatters to give up their shanties and move to better shelter. At the moment, the shacktown residents who hadn't moved were receiving $21 a month. Perhaps they could be lured into leaving their shacks if an additional $9 a month were added to their relief with the stipulation that they find improved housing. With that, Taylor said, "we should be able to eliminate more than 700 residents of the area."

Outside the YWCA, a crowd of between 75 and 100 shacktown residents gathered. A Workers' Alliance spokesman said that they weren't strictly opposed to the tearing down of the shacks, but they wanted to be sure that good quality housing was provided first. Back inside, Councilman Norton, again playing the mediator, attempted to reassure the members of the audience that no one should rush to a decision. There was plenty of time, he said, regardless of what had previously been reported, fire and police had told him that the shacktowns presented no serious problem.[34]

Throughout the following year little changed. Community clubs still feared the expansion of the remaining shacktowns. In November 1939, even the imagined threat of a new shacktown was enough to spark the Rainier Heights Commercial Club to action. Despite the lack of any evidence, they feared the infiltration of a new shacktown on an open gully between 20th Avenue and Jackson Street. The Club proposed that the city fill in the gully and turn it into a playground to prevent its misuse by transients.[35] The Consolidated South District was presented with a more legitimate concern. In May 1940, they approached the city to complain that 100 new shacks had recently been constructed in the south industrial area. They stressed that this was not an isolated incident and noted that growing shacktowns were a trend throughout the city. The Club hoped that a federal census would bolster their claim and help dictate further actions.[36]

That same month, a final investigation into the Seattle shack problem was completed. It showed that 1,686 shacks still remained, and three-fourths of those were in three locations. One of the more disconcerting issues was the percentage of families that had begun taken up residence in these unhealthy villages. Among the dwellers were 110 children under 15 years of age. The survey showed that eleven shacks held two children, seven held three or four, and three shacks housed five youngsters. Once again, the issue of destruction of abandoned houses was forefront. The most serious objection by the South District Commercial Club was that 137 shacks in their district remained vacated and had not been torn down. In what must have been a frustrating repetition for the community clubs, the city again pledged to destroy the abandoned shacks.[37]

Shacktown: Census

Wilber Engel walked into Hooverville on April 2, 1940. Thankfully, the rain was supposed to hold off until that night, but the prediction of temperatures in the mid-fifties was just about right for walking and standing on shacktown doorsteps. When Donald Roy had surveyed the shantytown six years earlier, he had left Engel a gift. Roy's map had already divided the town into sections and each shack was given a letter designating the section and a number unique to the individual building. After Roy left, other sections were created as the need arose, but Hooverites always following Roy's basic pattern. This made it easier to deliver mail, and it made Engel's job easier as well.

Wilbur Engel had been a miner for awhile, but like everyone he needed to branch out to make ends meet. Three years before, Wilbur had been arrested for picketing a grocery store that advertised in the Seattle Star newspaper during a strike.[1] He must have had other odd jobs after. Now, though, Engel would be the second person to systematically document this shacktown. His new, temporary job was that of census-taker.

Engel wrote "Hooverville" down the side of the first column of an oversized page in the book that he carried. Then he proceeded to shack 43-N and interviewed Edward Ryan, a sixty-four year old Irish fellow who owned the shack he was living in. It was worth $15, thought Ryan. No, he hadn't become a citizen, he told Engel, even though he had been living right here in Hooverville for at least the last five years. Ryan had no job, no income at all, in fact. He hadn't made a dime in the previous year, 1939. Leastwise, he hadn't made any money he wished to admit to this stranger. Engel jotted this all down carefully on the extra-long sheet of paper. That was the first recorded individual in Hooverville for the 1940 census. Engel would proceed on and transcribe the lives, in 34 lines, of each of the inhabitants of Hooverville.

The number of people living in Hooverville had shrunk some in the years between Roy's survey of 1934 and Engel's, six years later. Roy recorded 646 residents; Engel found 443. Much remained the same, though. It was still a man's world in Hooverville, even if the number of women had increased. In 1934, Roy claimed there were 7 women; by 1940 that number had grown to 19. Thirteen of the women Engel counted were married; six chose to remain single, although at least two of these lived with men, leaving just four women living alone in the entire town.

Certain stories can be discerned from Engel's rough data. Fifty-two year old Walter Crews, originally from North Carolina must have heard the cries of the Dodson's newly born son, Harvey, who lived next door. John Dodson, a white man, married Stella, an Indian. Considered a "mixed marriage" in 1940, their two sons were identified as "Indian" as well.

How John, Stella, John, Jr. and three month old Harvey ended up in shack 16 B is anyone's guess, but John wasn't the worst off in Hooverville. He had a trade as an electrician's helper and had some government work the previous year, about 11 week's worth, he figured. It brought in about $170 which surely wasn't much with four mouths to feed. Still, it was better than most living there. The rumbling of the train could be felt inside their cramped little shack, since they lived next to the railroad tracks. Stella had to make the trip across the shantytown for water at least a couple of times a day when John was working, but section B did have more space than other areas of the village in which the young ones could play.

Besides John, Jr. and Harvey, the only other children in Hooverville were Ernest and Adah Wright's two sons, Edward, 16 and Robert Lee 6. Otherwise, Hooverville remained the distinctly childless encampment it had always been.

The oldest man living in Hooverville in 1940 was Lawrence Latsky. Born before the Civil War, Latsky was 82 when Engel stopped by to visit him at shack 11 H. Unfortunately, Engel was unable to get much else from Latsky. Most of the other columns on his sheet were left blank. Two years younger but no less taciturn, Helger Helgeson from Norway camped in the M section. But just as this was no place for the young, it was also no place for the very old. Only two other men were over seventy. Hooverville remained a staunchly middle age place. Sixty-four percent were between 41 and 60 years of age. An additional 21% were over 60. That left only 15% of those living in Hooverville under 40 years of age.

Hooverville also continued to be racially mixed. It stayed a haven for those of Philippine descent, although the percentage was shrinking. In 1934, Roy had counted 120 who identified their race as Filipino. Engel in 1940 would register 64. But just as in Roy's survey, men from the Philippines tended to stick together. They were much more likely to double bunk or live next to others from their home country. The percentage of black Hooverites stayed steady as the real number declined from 29 to 21. Those identified as Mexican went from 25 to 18. Indians, never a significant percentage of shack dwellers, rose from 2 to 6, mostly on the strength of the Dodson family. The single Chilean that Roy had come across six years prior was still in Hooverville in 1940, living in shack 4-H, near the center of the village. Forty-four year old Juan Oyasso, the only person resolutely listing his race as "Chilean," was a railroad laborer still looking for work. Surprisingly, not a single Japanese, Chinese or Asian outside of the Philippines is listed.

Hooverville continued to be a refuge for people from around the United States and the world. Thirty-four states and the territories of Alaska and Hawaii were all represented in the 1940 census. There were thirteen residents from Washington State but more from Illinois (15) and Minnesota (19). Europe, too, had left many on Seattle's waterfront. Twenty-six different European nations were listed as places of birth for the Hooverites Engel interviewed. Forty-eight individuals were from Sweden, thirty-four came from Finland and thirty-one from Norway. Outside of Scandinavia, Austria had contributed fourteen, Poland thirteen and Russia twelve. Topping all, however, was the sixty-five originating from the Philippines.

Walter Schowestra had the distinction of being the only person in Hooverville not born in either a state or foreign country. Instead, Schowestra had apparently been born at sea. This caused Engel a moment of difficulty as he originally wrote something in the citizenship column only to cross it out. He ended up simply writing that Schowestra was born on a ship which was "U. S. owned."

The majority of Hooverites were not citizens. Only 165 of the 443 residing there had been born in the United States. Two hundred sixty were either listed as "alien" or "having first papers." Having first papers meant they were filing for citizenship but had only progressed to the first step. In fact, only thirty-nine of those foreign-born who were living in Hooverville had fully progressed through the naturalization process to become US citizens. The primary reason why there were so many non-citizens in the shantytown was the lack of nearby family. With nowhere else to turn, they bunched together and created their own subsistence community on the waterfront.

Education was another area that remained relatively consistent in Hooverville. Eighty-two had never darkened the schoolhouse door. Eighth grade was the key year for most the men, though. One hundred fifteen had gotten as far as the eighth grade, the last year of what was considered elementary education, before calling it quits. Only forty-seven went any further. The rest, roughly 200 dropped out sometime between first and seventh grade. Two did make it all the way through college: Fabian Vilallion from the Philippines and Willard Cheney, a mechanical engineer from Oregon. Eight others had attended some college but not graduated.

While most had been employed at one time or another, only 26 had a job when Engel came to call, but the breadth of experience these unemployed men had was impressive. There was an accountant, a baker, a barber, a blacksmith, a brick mason and a bread wrapper. There were over fifty involved in logging in one form or another. Fifty more were connected to railroad work. Another fifty plus were in the construction trades. Eleven were miners, thirty-six farm hands and nine had made their living as painters. There was a ship builder, a stage hand, a steam fitter, a teamster, a warehouseman and a waitress. It was a village full of experience and potential. The only thing they lacked was work.

Even though they remained unemployed they continued to trade goods, collect junk and beg food. Most claimed to have absolutely no income for the previous year, but the more honest admitted to limited funds. Twenty-three said they made less than a hundred dollars the previous year; ninety made between one hundred and five hundred; twenty-six between five hundred a thousand, as much or more as someone working on WPA. Nicholas Petrovich claimed to have made the most of anyone living in Hooverville. That, however, was only because

213

he was fully employed throughout the past year working every week at the Seattle Iron and Metal Corporation. He listed his yearly income in 1939 as $1,050.

Engel finished with his survey of Hooverville on April 17, with the exception of a quick stop to pick up the last four remaining houses in Hooverville on May 11. He had trudged over the dirt paths and knocked on the doors of the shack dwellers and probably knew more about them then anyone who hadn't lived there. But the job was over for Engel. He submitted the paperwork, collected his check and moved on with his life.[2]

21

Shacktown: Burns

By 1940, Jesse Jackson was living exactly where he had hoped to avoid, a flop house. The census-taker for his area found him at the King County Welfare Shelter Carcolton Flop House. By then, he had been unemployed for 429 weeks, over eight straight years. He was able to scrape a bit of money together as a WPA park foreman, but it couldn't have been much. George Parish, the current Hooverville mayor, resided at shack 7-L. The house was worth a grand total of $30, and he had been without private employment for nearly nine years.[1]

It was clear by this time that the era of the shacktown was over. The community clubs had voiced their displeasure, but the city's slow and cautious approach made it clear that that wasn't what caused the shantyvilles to surrender. In fact, the torching of the villages was more of a cremation than a burning out. Most of those left on the waterfront and in the cracks and crevices of Seattle were more obstinate than desperate. Relief was available and Roosevelt's job programs had helped provide enough money to lift the men from the unsanitary shacks to the less-unsanitary shelters. The need for this type of housing was past and most accepted it.

By September 1940, the Sears Tract was being eyed as the location for a new Veterans' Hospital. The shacks had apparently been destroyed as the men who evaluated the land "stood in the dried, uncut grass and Scotch broom...on the east slope of Beacon Hill." Not a word was mentioned of houses, homeless or the water pipeline that had been discussed four years previous.[2]

On October 1, 1940, on six acres of "sandy, wind-blown Harbor Island" the beginning of the end was announced. As part of Roosevelt's shoring up of the national defenses, the shacktown on the Duwamish was to be replaced by a dry dock for the Todd Shipyards. Not everyone had left the Duwamish, despite the original order in 1931 that sent the first "pioneers" to the Skinner and Eddy dock to clear a space for Hooverville. Instead, several had dug in, and, with time and increased poverty, the village had expanded. By 1940 there were four hundred shacks sitting on the Duwamish site. The houses were rickety to be sure, but there were a few four or five room shanties sitting on the island. Several had even constructed chicken houses or rabbit hutches to contain their livestock. That Tuesday in October, though, it would all be committed to the flame.

The residents had received warning on September 19 that they were to be out and most obeyed, but a few waited until the last moment. In truth, one man waited almost too long. After the gasoline had been poured and the match struck, some of the men who had called this their home helped spirit the fire along. One group of men started leaning old wood and junk around a shack of a friend of theirs. They had just splashed some oil to get the fire burning when one of the men decided to take one last peek in the window of his old friend's place. To his shock, he saw the owner of the shack fast asleep. He was awakened just in time and dashed out. He stood next to his buddies and watched as the shack he had lived - and almost died - in, went up in flames. Despite this, not an injury was sustained and none of the residents attempted to stand in the way of progress. They knew it was too late.

"Old Man" Fisher, who had resided on the Duwamish for five years watched as his own shack burned up. "Let her burn I say! Damn her, she's a warm house for once," he said. Fisher hung around and was even offered a job by two salvagers who were loading a truck with scrap lumber. He looked back at his shack and hollered, "I get paid for this and you get burned! I've got a job!" But his age was no match for his determination and in the end he had to ask the salvagers for help lifting the wood onto the truck. Fisher intended to follow several others up the river where they planned on rebuilding.[3]

One man, determined not to lose everything, managed to push, pull and drag his hovel to the water. From there he hoisted his entire shack onto a raft and floated downriver. The Duwamish shacktown was no more.[4]

Even with the destruction of that shacktown, there was hesitation at wholesale leveling. The idea of destroying all vacated shacks continued to be bandied about, but even as late as March 18, 1941, the razing of abandoned hovels was held up on a bureaucratic issue. Seattle City Council couldn't decide which department had the authority to clear out the vacant shacks. As a result, the Council met to determine whether the police, fire or Building Department would have the honors.[5]

The placement of the remaining residents continued to be an unresolved issue as well. City Council President in 1941, Mrs. F. F. Powell, requested that "the King County commissioners...allot some ground where the shack people who are interested in farming may be given a chance to work out their livelihood." Those not inclined to farm would have to be accommodated, but she felt this was a step toward independence for the homeless. She concluded by saying, "There will be no general destruction of shacktowns until new places are found for the people..."[6]

Two weeks later, though, the first major burn of Hooverville began. A third of the shacks were targeted and Two-Name Dave

217

Green played his "ragtime requiem" for the place, while Mayor Parish looked on. The kerosene was poured, the shacks torched and the Caterpillar tractors bulldozed the debris. Parish said that most of those who were evacuated were already settled into new digs. Some had rooms in shelters or flop houses, if they were living on relief. Others were rebuilding on West Marginal Way on county owned property. The fact was, though, the destruction was not funereal. Jobs were replacing the hovels. Defense programs would be using the space and businesses were already flooding into the area. The Seattle Times article that reported the burning said it best, "During the Great Days of Hooverville, a scheme to burn it down would have been greeted by roars of protest by some of the best soap box speakers in town and the burning would have been attended by police, crowds, and confusion. But nobody paid any attention today. Everybody was too busy."[7]

While that wasn't the end of shacktowns in Seattle, it was the acknowledged beginning of the end. A week later the North End Federated Clubs complained that many of the displaced Hooverites were moving into Interbay. The request by the club for action was really a call for the elimination of the entire Interbay shacktown.[8] More aggressive policing of abandoned shacks became a priority. A special committee recommended the destruction of Interbay, Holgate and one of the Beacon Hill shacktowns. The committee said that only the Louisville shacktown Mayor, Brosseau, was attempting to cooperate and had said he would let them know when a shack was vacated. Therefore, they recommended that that Louisville be eliminated through attrition. In order to make sure that abandoned shacks were being properly identified, the Committee suggested that a full-time guard be hired to patrol the various shantytowns. Councilmen Norton and Bob Jones, realizing that the homeless still needed someplace to live, suggested that those shacktowns near residential areas should be given priority for destruction before any others were eliminated.[9]

A guard was hired with the job of identifying the houses to be razed. A plan to grant the guard a 1929 touring car which had held the likes of President Roosevelt and Prince Olav of Norway for the endeavor was suggested. Council President Powell reiterated her concern that residents not be ousted without help and alternative quarters.[10]

On May 3, 1941, an accidental fire almost ended Hooverville a shade prematurely. At 1:30 in the morning, a fire ripped through six houses on the waterfront. The fire department reported without a trace of irony that there were no injuries and "no loss."[11] But three days later there was nothing accidental about it. "Before a mere handful of 'mourners,'" the Seattle Times reported, " the last remnants of Hooverville, depression-born waterfront shacktown today went up in the smoke of the shacks' own funeral pyres." This was the opening sentence of the Seattle Times article describing the demise of the shacktown created by Jackson and the original 20 or so on that October day in 1931. Fires could be seen from some distance away as the scrounged wood and linoleum was eaten by the flame. A handful of ex-Hooverites stood to the side with their belongings loaded on pushcarts as they watched the village of the desperate turn to smoke. One man hurried around inside his shack until the last minute. As the house next door was leveled, he shouted, "I'll be out in a minute, you son of a gun, then you can have her." As he walked out, he turned to his friends and said, "Well, that ends two and a half years here. I had a lot of fun in that shack, kept my peace, cooked my own meals and bothered no one. There goes my home! Long may she burn!" With that and a handshake or two, the most visible reminder of the Great Depression passed into history.[12]

Hooverville burning. *Courtesy of Paul Dorpat.*

Epilogue: Last Rites

There were still remnants of other shacktowns left in Seattle after the last burn at Hooverville. Even a week before the December 7, 1941 attack on Pearl Harbor, Byrd Kelso continued to fight for the preservation of the Louisville shacktown. Saying that rent in Seattle had grown too high and that those living in Louisville couldn't afford better housing, Kelso recommended that the destruction of the village, scheduled for December 20, be postponed until there was an increase in relief for the unemployed.[1] As late as April 1942, Seattle City Councilman Norton was suggesting that the fire department burn whatever left-over shacks there were for practice.[2] For the most part, though, little is known about the shantyvilles after the war began as all news was subsumed by the new crisis. It's easy to suppose that the inhabitants of the shacktowns had access to work with the onset of war, so they no longer needed relief and were able to find better housing. Perhaps it's even true. What we do know is the shacks were destroyed as the land became more valuable due to the influx of war workers.

The poor are difficult to track when they move away from the limelight. Jesse Jackson, even as an ex-mayor of Hooverville, is no exception. In 1962, as the World's Fair was opening in Seattle, a reporter was able to locate him, though. Jackson aged poorly. His sunken mouth and slightly out-of-balance eyes were crowned by wispy gray hair. Gnarled hands gripped a parking meter and his worn coat and flannel shirt would have fitted in well at Hooverville in its prime as would his three-day stubble. In contrast, the mood of the article is almost jovial as Hooverville was remembered. The writer John Reddin called it "an impromptu and expedient experiment in socialism – sort of a tarpaper Carthage that was put to the torch in 1941…" Reddin tracked down Jackson, now age 73, at a "logger-employment agency." Jackson reminisced about the men that visited him in his shack. He talked of Albert D. Rosellini and Arthur B. Langlie, both eventually governors of Washington State. He claimed to have shook hands with Daniel C. Roper, Secretary of Commerce under Roosevelt. He talked wistfully of his contacts with the Seattle police. "I knew 'em all – Ernie Yoris, when he was chief of 'dicks,' and Harlan Callahan, the sheriff." But there isn't a hint as to Jackson's life after Hooverville.[3] Jackson continued on for fourteen years after the interview, finally dying in October 1976, in Federal Way, Washington. Not even the shortest of obituaries marked his passing.

Carl Brannin, the man most responsible for creating the UCL, left Seattle reluctantly in 1933. His family needed him in Texas. Once there, though, he became active in the Dallas Unemployed Leagues and helped organized one of the first sit-ins when relief money was cut. In 1935, he was arrested for walking the picket line with the International Ladies Garment Workers' Union.

Later he planned a couple ill-fated campaigns for political office. In an attempt to become governor of Texas on the Socialist ticket, Brannin was able to garner only 962 votes and finally decided that politics might not be in his future. He broke with the Dallas Socialist Party when they advocated the nationalization of all industry, something Brannin felt was too extreme. In the 1940s, Brannin needed to work again as his oil well began to dry up. As a housing inspector, he found cheaper shelter for poor blacks in Texas. He also created his own privately owned, low-cost housing projects.

During the 1950s and 1960s, Brannin became involved in the National Association for the Advancement of Colored People and the Americans for Democratic Action. On November

22, 1963, he was among the many who waited futilely for President Kennedy to deliver a luncheon speech in Dallas. When Brannin heard that the President had been assassinated on his way to the luncheon, he didn't forget his lifelong fight for justice. Instead, he insisted the American Civil Liberties Union visit Lee Harvey Oswald in jail to make sure he was not being abused.

He traveled extensively, campaigned against the Vietnam War, and marched for civil rights into his 80s. On June 16, 1985, at the age of 96, Carl Brannin died.[4]

Hulet Wells, Carl Brannin's partner, struggled after leaving the Communist-dominated UCL. He finally did find relief work so that his eighteen year old son would be eligible for the Civilian Conservation Corp. Later, he became an aid for Marion Zioncheck, who had just won his second term as Congressman. When Zioncheck committed suicide while in office in 1936, Wells went back to the postal service in Washington, D. C. Returning to Seattle after World War II, Wells became the president of the Seattle branch of the American Federation of Labor. A lifelong socialist, he died on February 15, 1970 at the age of 91.[5]

William K. Dobbins, the UCL president who pushed the Communist agenda and was leader during the organization's collapse, died in 1967. He was 69. After his stint in the UCL, Dobbins became president of the Building Services Employees Union. Counter to the Communist agenda at the time, he sided with Franklin Roosevelt and took a WPA job. At some point his politics changed enough that he became a Democratic Precinct Committeeman and remained such for many years.[6]

King County Commissioner John C. Stevenson, radio personality and strong supporter of the UCL fiercely opposed by Mayor Dore, died on August 6, 1966 in Honolulu, Hawaii at age

73. His obituary mentions that he was "active in the Washington State Commonwealth Federation," and in 1936 he had been elected chairman of the King County Commissioners.[7] What it fails to mention, however, is that in 1933 Stevenson had been identified as "John C. Stockman" of New York. As Stockman, he had been indicted in an illegal stock scheme. A request for extradition had been filed by New York but rejected by Governor Clarence Martin on a technicality. [8]

Donald Francis Roy, the young man who wrote his Master's thesis on Hooverville, found his calling. He became a sociologist whose special skill was blending in with those he studied. After getting his Ph.D. at the University of Chicago, he wrote "Banana Time," a much respected and widely-quoted study, which detailed his experiences working in a garment factory in New York City. He described how workers carved out different times during the day to build relationships and make the workplace more tolerable. He went on to work at low level jobs in 20 different industries in order to record and analyze the experience. Roy died in 1980 at the age of 70 or 71.[9]

The second mayor of Hooverville, George Parish, is lost to history until his death on July 24, 1956, at age 79.

The president of the Dix Commission which sought to help the UCL and the homeless by providing city and county funds for their activities, Irving Fisher Dix died in 1966 at the age of 83. During World War II, Dix was appointed to oversee the War Production Board as regional manager for the Los Angeles area. He moved to Spokane in 1955 and remained active in charity work, volunteering to serve on the board of Goodwill Industries.

The murderess Mary Kelly was sent to the penitentiary where she was a model prisoner. Surprisingly, upon release she headed back to live on the Duwamish, the very place where she had killed Otto Johanson. At age 56, she received a proposal for marriage. The wedding was scheduled for October 7, 1947. The night of October 6, Mary fell ill and died the next morning before she could take her vows.[10]

Stephen Eringis, the man who sought to found a Hooverville College until his co-founder was killed in an auto accident, served in World War II as an Army intelligence officer. In 1947, he returned to Baltimore where he died in 1963 at the age of 75.[11]

Seattle City Councilman William L. Norton, who defended the shacktown residents from eviction, continued in his council position for 13 years until 1950. He was the first commander of the United States Power Squadron in Seattle. Under his command, the USPS trained civilian volunteers in water navigation and assisted the Coast Guard Auxiliary and Red Cross during World War II. Throughout his life, he was a member of many clubs and organizations including the Institute of Hypnosis and Millionair Club. Professionally, he led the Divine Science Center until ill health forced him to retire shortly before his death in 1967 at age 67.[12]

Charles Ernst, the bane of the unemployed, who ran relief efforts in Seattle and, later, throughout Washington State, died of a heart attack on July 29, 1968 in Massachusetts, his home state. He was 81 years old. During WWII Ernst was put in charge of a Japanese relocation camp named Topaz near Delta, Utah. He remained director there from September, 1942 to June, 1944. After working for the Red Cross and the American Public Welfare Association, he returned to the Boston House where he had begun his career. [13]

Final Thoughts

Time passes. A generation is buried and their stories are buried with them. What is left must be sifted out of the mounds of dusty words. Holes are left which never can be filled. Why did Jackson end up living in a flop house? Why did UCL membership turn control of the organization over to the communists even though they were in the minority? Did Ernst or Dore or Governor Martin ever have a three-in-the-morning moment in which they doubted the certainty of their positions? But the book is closed and that generation can't speak from beyond the grave. Their last words are all on the printed page. Sometimes we can gather them into a new coherency or interpret their meaning with new eyes, but any questions that weren't answered at the time can only be left to conjecture now.

There's a strong temptation by some to say that every problem has a solution if people will just work hard enough; hard work will win out. One thing the Great Depression demonstrated was the falseness of that idea. The men of the UCL believed it. But when the full cataclysm of the economic failure bore down on them, their best efforts were of no use. They limped along bravely for a brief while, but the reality of no jobs, charity stretched to the breaking point, and the political assault against their organization forced them to recognize the futility of "pulling yourself up by the bootstraps."

The men of Hooverville, likewise, weren't the failures of society. They were the ones whose resources and stamina had simply been eaten up earlier in other battles. It isn't coincidence that the majority of the men in the shacktowns were in their fifties. Most had scraped through hard times before, but now, during the worst times, they began with barely any reserve at all. The problem that they faced was what to do when the little

226

you have is taken from you? Where do you go? In a society that believed in individual responsibility, they built their own homes and scrounged their own food. Instead of becoming examples of rugged individualism, they became the despised. Those who hadn't suffered severest deprivation resented seeing the unhealthy conditions and tired of the constant need for food, medical care and other services that shack dwellers required for minimum subsistence.

There is a reason so many shacks and homes of the poor had photographs of Franklin Roosevelt tacked up inside. Both groups of unemployed, those who had never experienced it before and those who had always had a difficult time, began with the common belief that the Depression was a manageable problem. But as it wore on and as solutions were tried and failed at the private, local and state level, a new degree of fear set in. Then FDR was elected. Roosevelt finally offered something no one else was able to and the only solution all seemed to agree on: jobs on a consistent basis.

There are some conservatives who worship at the feet of Capitalism. They say Roosevelt interfered with the fine-tuned machinery of the system. Had he only left it alone, the ship would have righted itself. Instead, we went deeply in debt to pay for his programs. Certainly, those who support this ideology admit, there would have been some short-term pain, but the United States would have been better off in the long run. After all, his programs didn't end the Depression, only World War Two did that.

This critique of Roosevelt, then and today, is made by the comfortable. Those who voiced this opinion during the Depression were those who believed they were affected by the economic woes because they were forced to let servants go or move to a smaller house or even, at the extreme, get rid of their

227

telephone service. Today, the distance of time has created a new army of comfortable critics. They harp on the lack of self-reliance demonstrated by the out-of-luck. They dwell on a possible future economic collapse caused by a crushing debt, laid at the feet of an administration many decades in the past. Or they bemoan that period of history as the beginning of the crumbling of a once great nation that no longer is willing to stand on its own two feet.

The truth is that without Roosevelt's policies many more people would have died and many families would have been torn apart. That threat to family and life is easy to ignore now, but in the 1930s, it was the reality of daily life. Starvation was growing and shacktowns were not an isolated problem. Across the nation, they sprouted up by the hundreds. These people were not lazy, they were desperate to work. Fist-fights were not uncommon where day-labor was offered. Thousands showed up when a handful of jobs were advertised. Most men only gave up after months of daily rejection. Revolutions are started for less.

Roosevelt recognized this. His plan was not a well-designed, pre-ordained march to a set destination. It didn't have "socialism" as its goal. It was a patchwork of emergency measures that were drawn up to meet the challenges of the day. While he didn't have the destination in mind, he understood the role of government. First, it must protect its people, and second, it must defend itself from anarchy. These two ideas feed on each other, and during the Great Depression, the people were feeling far from protected. The men in the UCL, for the overwhelming part, were not communists. Yet, even they were willing to give communists a hearing because of the desperation of the times. If these men, who were doing everything in their power to maintain independence and not rely on charity or government aid were electing communists to lead them, one has to wonder about the tendency of those less independently-minded. Roosevelt was not subverting capitalism; he was saving it by protecting the people.

It is striking how quickly Communism as a popular organization collapsed in Seattle once the Federal Government began to offer jobs. Because the people finally felt they could rely on the government, even tentatively, the interest in radical theory evaporated. The UCL was not established as a front for a communist takeover, it was formed by men who simply wanted to help themselves and their families. Despite the political desires of the founders or later manipulations of ideologues, the backbone of the organization - the unemployed who joined - were not looking to radicalize America. They only wanted to feed their own. Once they could do that, the organization held no further allure for them. Had they not been able to help their families, had the government opted out of its responsibilities to help its citizens, communism might have appeared more attractive and a foothold might have been established.

If the collapse of the UCL demonstrated the effectiveness of the New Deal programs, Hooverville and the shacktowns reflect a possible future not taken. Speculation isn't evidence, but educated guesswork can illuminate possible pathways. Had the government forgone assistance to the poor and unemployed, two possible roads might have developed. First, it is probable that the radical ideas mentioned above could have received a more intense following. There were already, after only a couple years of deep depression, plenty of instances of marches, protests and riots. Inability to feed, house and protect family and self are the tinder, and determined radicalism is the spark that leads to the flame of serious societal discord. It is possible that with no relief in sight and little hope of governmental action, the unemployed and underemployed might have created a violent upheaval.

A second possibility is that the poor might have become increasingly complacent and defeated. More men might well have abandoned their families as many had already done. Driven by shame and necessity, they could well have gathered with others like themselves. The shacktowns and Hoovervilles might have expanded and invaded wide swaths of urban areas. Slums, crime and general disillusionment could have grabbed hold of American life. Neither of these two views presents a positive alternative to the events that transpired.

The third road not taken is that favored by those who oppose government intervention. They suppose that business, unencumbered by regulation and unburdened by additional taxes, would have been able to provide the jobs needed to pull the country out of the Depression without assistance. Certainly, according to the more educated of these theorists, the employees would have had to suffer with the employer for a short while, both receiving lower incomes for a time, but ultimately the job market would have come back and the lack of national debt and lower taxes would have made for a brighter future. The problem with this theory is that it violates the first principle of history, that is, people live in the present. It assumes that people who daily looked for work or who built tin shacks on waterfronts would have patiently waited for the capitalist system to work its magic. The very fact that the desperate created the UCL and Hoovervilles in the first place contradicts that premise. If they built these villages and formed this organization at the birth of the Depression, what might they have done had the economic deprivation continued?

Acknowledgements

I received much support writing this book. Those who contributed most materially in its construction are passed, but not forgotten - at least by me. Donald Roy wrote an immensely readable account of his time at Hooverville and anyone who wants a ground-level view should start there. Jesse Jackson's short but remarkably well-written autobiography is entertaining and leaves the reader wanting much more. The trio of Master's thesis writers, Arthur Hillman, John Hogan and T. R. Willis were excellent guides in trying to navigate the maze that is the history of the UCL. Also, the anonymous writers of the Seattle newspapers left behind an immediate overview of the Depression era in Seattle. I am especially thankful for those who didn't feel obligated to hoe the company line.

I have always enjoyed history, and can point to several points in my life that have elevated that to true passion. But a single Christmas present when I was nineteen helped me to understand the true power of the past. When I first opened the package I was disappointed to find a nearly thousand-page doorstop of a book that I assumed I would never read. In fact, I lugged it around for a couple years before I finally cracked open the book, but when I did I was hooked. William Manchester's Glory and the Dream was the first time I truly felt transported to the time. Since then I have reread the book several times but have never told my mother, Joyce Mendall, how valuable that gift was until now.

This book would never have been created if not for Lee O'Connor and his book Take Cover, Spokane. After reading this book about bomb shelters in Spokane during the 1950s, I was complaining to my wife Jamie Gravelle that there weren't enough of these "small" histories. I said that too many people were interested in writing about an entire era or a president or the most major event of a time period and as a result we have very few histories on the pieces that make up the whole, such as Mr. O'Connor's book. She told me to write my own, then. Rather disappointed with the advice I expressed the same complaint to my brother Clay Gravelle and he told me, in effect, to quit whining and do something about it. I didn't particularly care for their responses, but the result is this book. Clay even agreed to help with some of the technical issues even though I suppose I was whining about them as well.

Those who were my first readers, Jamie, John Gese, and Carl Manly have my appreciation and thanks even if I didn't always take their advice. Sorry, Carl.

While gathering research for this book, I learned that there are two types of archives and archivists: One sees its purpose as simply collecting documents and storing them safely, and one believes they have the additional responsibility to share those documents. Two of the latter were the University of Washington Special Collections and Seattle Public Library Seattle Collection. Both were patient with a novice and volunteered resources that I wouldn't otherwise have known about.

One of those serendipitous moments occurred after having completed the writing of this book. I only found one picture that illustrated the UCL and realized I would need to get permission to use it. Having seen the photo on Paul Dorpat's website, I emailed him explaining my project and the reason for contacting him. Within hours, he responded with not only permission but a copy of the photograph. Later, he was kind enough to send additional pictures that are also included in this book. Thanks Paul.

Finally, there is Jamie. She has had to listen in excruciating detail to my theories and thoughts on some of the most mind-numbing minutiae regarding Hooverville, the UCL, communists, Dore and all the other parts that made up this book. While patience isn't the first word that pops to mind when thinking of Jamie, in this instance she deserves the sobriquet. In truth, her mark is on every page since I couldn't have written this book without her.

Endnotes
Prologue

[1] The exact quote taken from the report is "Goin' be sleeping on a dock. Looka that rig a bustin' down George's house. Just like nuthin! Look at that. Sure pow'ful. Right up into the fire." Writing in dialect was a racist feature of the time. The altered quote more properly reflects what was said.

[2] Ragtime Requiem Rings Out As Tractor Levels Shacks. (1941, April 10). *The Seattle Times*, p. 8.

[3] Berner, R. C. (1992). *Seattle: 1921-1940.* Seattle: Charles Press. P.302

Chapter 1 Shacktown: Eviction

[1] Pyle, E. (1936, October 29). Pyle Finds Dictator Rule In Shack-City. *Pittsburgh Post-Gazette.*

[2] Berner. P. 302

[3] Jackson, J. "The Story of Seattle's Hooverville." Social Trends in Seattle by Calvin F. Schmid (Seattle, Washington: The University of Washington Press: 1944) Pp. 286-293.

[4] Erb, L. D. (1935). Seattle's Hooverville. 8. Seattle, Washington: Unpublished. P. 4

[5] Duwamish Waterway Evictions Impending. (1926, January 25). *Seattle Daily Times*, p. 2.

[6] Dixon Orders Squatters To Quit Tideflats. (1931, May 12). *The Seattle Daily Times*, p. 9.

Chapter 2 The City: Birth of an Idea

[1] Berner, P. 301

[2] Eigner, E. (nd). *Vanguard And Unemployed Citizen*. Retrieved from
   Labor Press Project:
   http://depts.washington.edu/labhist/laborpress/Vanguard.ht
   m

[3] Boley, J. (1997, Spring). *Rebel with a Cause: Carl Brannin and His
   Work*. Retrieved from Special Collections Division of the
   University of Texas at Arlington Libraries:
   http://dspace.uta.edu/bitstream/handle/10106/5326/1997_F
   all%20%26%20Spring.pdf?sequence=1

[4] Willis, T. R. (1997). Unemployed Citizens of Seattle, 1900-1933: Hulet
   Wells, Seattle Labor, and the Struggle for Economic Security.
   In T. R. Willis, *Unemployed Citizens of Seattle, 1900-1933:
   Hulet Wells, Seattle Labor, and the Struggle for Economic
   Security*. Seattle: Unpublished.

[5] Willis, P. 196

[6] Unemployed Neighbors Get Together! (1931, July). *The Vanguard*, p.
   3.

[7] Hogan, J. A. (1934). *The Decline of Self-Help and Growth of
   Radicalism Among Seattle's Organized Unemployed*. Seattle:
   University of Washington. Pp. 2-3

[8] Hillman, A. (1934). *The Unemployed Citizens' League of Seattle*.
   Seattle: University of Washington Press. Pp. 185-186

[9] Willis, Pp. 199-200

[10] Hogan, Pp. 4-5

[11] Tax Rich To Pay Unemployment. (1931, October). *The Vanguard*, p. 1.

[12] Hillman, Pp. 186-187

[13] Irving Dix Dies in Spokane. (1966, April 9). *Spokane Daily Chronicle*, p. 5.

[14] Hillman, Pp. 188-189

[15] Hogan, P. 8

[16] Hogan, Pp. 115-123

[17] Berner, P. 306

[18] Hogan, Pp. 115-123

[19] Hillman, Pp. 190-191

[20] Hogan, Pp. 10-15

Chapter 3 Shacktown: Relocation

[1] McClary, D. (2003, March 13). *Pier 36 -- Seattle Waterfront*. Retrieved from HistoryLink.org: http://www.historylink.org/index.cfm?DisplayPage=output.cfm&file_id=4149

[2] Crichton Promotes Health of Seattle. (1913, June 29). *Seattle Times*, p. 4.

[3] Richards, L. (1930, December 6). Morning-Noon-and Night. *Seattle Star*, p. 6.

[4] Erb, P. 5

[5] Tickets Will Provide Food and Lodgings. (1930, December 11). *Seattle Times*, p. 24.

[6] Tickets Will aid Needy Man, Spoil Charity Grafting. (1931, December 23). *Seattle Times*, p. 5.

[7] Willing Job Hunter Finds Central Registry Big Help. (1932, September 21). *Seattle Times*, p. 12.

[8] Travelers' Aid Friend Indeed Of Homeless Boy. (1932, December 25). *Seattle Times*, p. 7.

[9] Jackson, P. 286

[10] Taylor, N. (2008). *American-Made: The Enduring Legacy of the WPA*. New York: Bantam Dell. P. 247

[11] Jackson, P. 287

[12] Squatters Driven Into Rain When Police Fire Shacks. (1931, October 26). *Seattle PI*, p. 1.

[13] Shelters for Jobless Fired by Policemen. (1931, October). *Seattle Star*.

[14] Terkel, S. (1970). *Hard Times*. New York: The New Press. P. 22

[15] Police Torch Use Condoned and Condemned by Officials. (1931, October). *Seattle Star*.

[16] Must Have Shelter. (1931, October 28). *Seattle Times*, p. 6.

[17] 'Jungle Villages' Under Ban; More Shacks To Burn. (1931, October 29). *Seattle Times*, p. 10.

[18] Shack Ouster Is Under Fire. (1931, October 31). *Seattle PI*, p. 3.

[19] Jackson, P. 287

Chapter 4 The City: An Idea Grows

[1] Hogan, P. 15

[2] Hogan, P. 11

[3] Hillman, P. 191

[4] Hogan, P. 190

[5] Hillman, P. 192

Chapter 5 Shacktown: Hooverville

[1] Murray Morgan (1960). *Skid Road*. New York: Ballantine Books, p. 223.

[2] Jackson, P. 287

[3] Weiser, K. (2010, August). *Hoovervilles*. Retrieved from Legends of America: http://www.legendsofamerica.com/20th-hoovervilles.html

[4] Taylor, P. 434

[5] Roy, D. F. (1935). *Hooverville: A Study of a Community of Homeless Men in Seattle*. Seattle: Unpublished thesis, P. 27

[6] Roy, Pp. 23-32

[7] Yes, Sir, City's Pastime Haven Opens Monday. (1933, Septermber 24). *Seattle Time*, p. 7.

[8] Erb, P. 3

[9] Duncan, D. (1979, March 17). Shackled by poverty, shantytown citizens survived. *Seattle Times*, p. A 5.

[10] Kelly, P. (2010, January 20). *Hoovervilles in Seattle: Map and Photos.* Retrieved from Great Depression In Washington State: https://depts.washington.edu/depress/hooverville_map.shtml

Chapter 6 The City: An Idea Hijacked

[1] Charles F. Ernst. (1968, August 5). *Seattle Times*, p. 47.

[2] Hillman, P. 195

[3] Hogan, P. 33

[4] Hillman, P. 200

[5] Hogan, P. 20

[6] Dore Adovocates Economic Changes. (1931, October 27). *Seattle Times*, p. 4.

[7] Dore Counter Move Likely, Friends Aver. (1930 , December 29). *Seattle Times*, p. 12.

[8] Hogan, Pp. 20-22

[9] Hillman, P. 210

[10] Why Did We Vote For Dore? (1932, June 9). *Seattle Star*, p. 1.

[11] Dore Abolishes Laing's Office. (1932, July 5). *Seattle Star*, p. 1.

[12] Hillman, P. 201

[13] Kelly, J. (n.d.). *UCL Branch activities: additional notes*. Retrieved from Great Depression in Washington State:

http://depts.washington.edu/depress/UCL_branch_notes.sht
ml#georgetown

[14] Dennett, E. V. (1990). *Agitprop: The Life on an American Working-Class Radical*. Albany: State University of New York Press. P. 30

[15] Hillman, Pp. 204-205

Chapter 7 Shacktown: Mayor

[1] Jackson, Pp.289-291

[2] Taylor, P. 446

[3] Menefee, S. (1932, December 2). Studies in Rugged Individualism - I. *Unemployed Citizen*, p. 1.

[4] Menefee, S. (1932, December 9). Studies in Rugged Individualism - II. *Unemployed Citizen*, p. 1.

[5] Menefee, S. (1932, December 16). Studies in Rugged Individualism - III. *Unemployed Citizen*, p. 4.

[6] Menefee, S. (1932, December 23). Studies in Rugged Individualism - IV. *Unemployed Citizen*.

[7] Blume, Deborah, The Chemists War, Slate

[8] Frank R. Menne, M. D. (nd). *Acute Methyl Alcohol Poisoning: A report of twenty-two instances with postmortem examinations*. Portland, Oregon: unknown.

[9] Roy, Pp. 90-91

Chapter 8 Shacktown: Aid

[1] Amundson, M. (2009, December 27). *Uniion Gospel Mission (Seattle)*. Retrieved from HistoryLink.org: http://www.historylink.org/index.cfm?DisplayPage=output.cfm&file_id=9248

[2] Thousands Seek Work Vainly In This City. (1931, February). *The Vanguard*, p. 1.

[3] Meat Dealers OfCity Pledge Aid Against Hunger. (1930, November 20). *Seattle Times*, p. 10.

[4] Collection Plate and Bequests Provide Millions for Charity. (1936, August 5). *Seattle Times*, p. 8.

[5] Richards, L. (1930, December 6). Morning-Noon-and Night. *Seattle Star*, p. 6.

[6] County To Stop Relief Kitchen. (1937, October 22). *Seattle Times*, p. 3.

[7] Marshall, J. (1931, January 1). Tramp, Tramp, Tramp the Boys Are Marching! *Seattle Star*, p. 1.

[8] Sunshine Club Shows Little Increase in Line. (1931, January 1). *Seattle Star*, p. 1 and 3.

[9] 19,661 Aided By Community Fund in Feb. (1932 , March 1). *Seattle Times*, p. 7.

[10] A Sad Experience. (1932, December 20). *Seattle Times*, p. 6.

[11] Well Cared For. (1933, January 5). *Seattle Times*, p. 6.

[12] Levy, H. P. (1933, February 9). Rost Beef! Um! *Seattle Times*, p. 9.

[13] Marshall, J. (1931, January 1). Tramp, Tramp, Tramp the Boys Are Marching! *Seattle Star*, p. 1.

[14] M., U. (1934, March 6). Workers Fight Gulls on City Dump for Offal. *Voice of Action*, p. 3.

Chapter 9 The City: An Idea Under Assault

[1] Kelly, J. (n.d.). *UCL Branch activities: additional notes*. Retrieved from Great Depression in Washington State: http://depts.washington.edu/depress/UCL_branch_notes.shtml#georgetown

[2] Willis, Pp. 223-224

[3] Unknown. (1932, July 3). What Do The Unemployed of State Want? -- 2: Work. *Seattle Times*, p. 1.

[4] Press, A. (1932, July 2). Thousands Set For Olympia Relief March, Say Leaders. *Seattle Times*, p. 1.

[5] Dennett, P. 36

[6] Press, A. (1932, July 5). Hartley Not In His Office When Jobless Call. *Seattle Times*, p. 5.

[7] Dennett, P. 37

[8] Cronin Gives Star Statement on Conference. (1932, July 8). *Seattle Star*, p. 3.

[9] Dennett, P. 39

[10] Terkel, P. 84

[11] Hogan, P. 26

[12] Hogan, P. 27

[13] Willis, P. 253

[14] Police Back Evans' Move To Operate Food Depot. (1932, September 8). *Seattle Times*, p. 1.

[15] Two Charged With Stealing Food Supplies. (1932, Septemeber 9). *Seattle Times*, p. 7.

[16] Hogan, P. 69

[17] Candidate Calls City's Reception Greatest on Trip. (1932, September 20). Seattle Times, pp. 1, 8.

[18] Taxpayers Demand County Start Work Plan For Jobless. (1932, November 2). *Seattle Star*, p. 2.

[19] Paid Managers To Control All Unemployed Job. (1932, October 14). *The Vanguard*, p. 2.

[20] Evans Hogs U. C. L. Berries. (1932, October 21). *The Vanguard*, p. 1.

[21] Hoover, H. (1932, July 17). *Statement About Signing the Emergency Relief and Construction Act of 1932*. Retrieved from The American Presidency Project: http://www.presidency.ucsb.edu/ws/?pid=23170

[22] Blumell, B. D. (1984). *The Development of Public Assistance in the State of Washington During the Great Depression.* New York: Garland Publishing, Inc. P. 67

[23] Kelly, J. (n.d.). *UCL Branch activities: additional notes*. Retrieved from Great Depression in Washington State: http://depts.washington.edu/depress/UCL_branch_notes.shtml#georgetown

[24] Mayor Dore Public Enemy. (1932, October 14). *The Vanguard*, p. 1.

[25] 1,000 Jobless Marchers Gather At State Capitol. (1933, Janurary 17). *Seattle Times*, p. 2.

[26] Kamenz, A. (n.d.). *On to Olympia! The History Behind the Hunger Marches of 1932-1933*. Retrieved from Great Depression in Washington State: http://depts.washington.edu/depress/hunger_marches.shtml

[27] Police Disperse 1,000 And Arrest 3 At Food Depot. (1933, January 20). *Seattle Times*, p. 3.

[28] Hogan, Pp. 70-71

[29] Dobbins' Resignation Is Step Forward Says CP. (1934, April 3). *Voice of Action*, pp. 1,4.

[30] Commission Idea Takes Hold Of County board. (1933, January 20). *Seattle Times*, p. 26.

[31] Blumell, P. 77

[32] Morris, K. (1982, October). *Records of the Washington Emergency Relief Administration, 1919-1940*. Retrieved from Archivegrid: http://beta.worldcat.org/archivegrid/record.php?id=1546902 57

[33] Blumell, P. 90

[34] Unknown. (unknown). *Essay: The Federal Emergency Relief Administration*. Retrieved from University of Washington Digital Collections: http://content.lib.washington.edu/feraweb/essay.html

[35] Federal Relief Funds Aid State's Transient Indigent. (1933, December 10). *Seattle Times*, p. 13.

Chapter 10 Shacktown: Roy

[1] Roy, Pp. 1-23

[2] Three-Fourth Of Fund-Aided Men Are Seattleites. (1933, January 22). *Seattle Times*, p. 8.

[3] Roy, Pp. 36-75

[4] Roy, Pp. 96-97

Chapter 11 The City: An Idea Suffocates

[1] How to Get Food: Stores to Supplant Commissaries. (1933, February 14). *Seattle Times*, p. 1.

[2] Levy, H. P. (1985). There Were Days Like That. In H. P. Levy, *There Were Days Like That* (p. 103). Glendale, California: Blue Whale Press.

[3] Jobless Will Visit Martin To Ask New County Aid Group. (1933, February 15). *Seattle*, p. 5.

[4] Stevenson Orders Demonstrators to Leave Courthouse. (1933, February 16). *Seattle Times*, p. 5.

[5] Dennett, Pp. 42-43

[6] Ejection From City Hall Ends Relief Protest. (1933, February 17). *Seattle Times*, pp. 1,2.

[7] U. C. L. Demands Dobbins Resign Post As Leader. (1933, February 18). *Seattle Times*, p. 12.

Chapter 12 The City: Ghost of an Idea

[1] Kamenz

[2] Hogan, P 82

[3] Hogan, Pp. 82-85

[4] Dennett, Pp. 39-41

[5] Dennett, P. 221

[6] Dennett, P. 41

[7] Demonstrators At Olympia Call Off Parade. (1933, March 2). *Seattle Times*, p. 11.

[8] Action, E. B. (1933, March 25). The Truth About the March to Olympia. *A New Weekly Paper*, p. 3.

[9] Blumell, Pp. 100-101

[10] Hogan, Pp. 88-89

[11] Blumell, Pp. 103-104

[12] Workers Save Blonder Home. (1933, April 3). *A New Weekly Paper*, pp. 1, 3.

[13] Victory in Ballard Eviction; Get New Home, Furniture. (1933, April 10). *Voice of Action*, p. 1.

[14] Blonder Convicted. (1933, April 10). *Voice of Action*, p. 2.

[15] Blonder Family Is Evicted. (1933, April 17). *Voice of Action*, p. 1

[16] Berner, P. 320

[17] Last Witnesses In Riot Trial Testify Today. (1933, July 1). *Seattle Times*, p. 3.

[18] Deputy's Threat To Shoot Is Told At Rioting Trial. (1933, June 27). *Seattle Times*, p. 2.

[19] Hogan, Pp. 90-91

[20] Defense Blames Sheriff's Men For Home Riot. (1933, June 20). *Seattle Times*, p. 4.

[21] 7 Convicted In Frandsen Riot Give Selves Up. (1934, April 16). *Seattle Times*, p. 20.

Chapter 13 The City: A New Idea

[22] Berner, P. 325

Chapter 14 Shacktown: Crime

[1] 'Hooverville's Mayor' Discovers Stolen Groceries. (1935, December 26). *Seattle Times*, p. 2
[2] Doughnut Truck Disappears; Shacktown Dwellers Feast. (1934, February 17). *Seattle Times*, p. 12.

[3] Thief Shot By Grocer. (1936, October 1). *Seattle Times*, p. 5
[4] Burglar Takes Two Child's Banks, $35. (1936, December 4). *Seattle Times*, p. 10.
[5] 14 Dogs Howl At Hooverville, Master Jailed. (1936, February 23). *Seattle Times*, p. 2.
[6] Two Seattle men Slain In Fights. (1935, May 27). *Seattle Times*, p. 4.
[7] Victim of Stabbing Dies; 3 Are Held. (1940, October 24). *Seattle Times*, p. 36.
[8] Victim of Stabbing Dies; 3 Are Held. (1940, October 24). *Seattle Times,* p. 36.
[9] Man Is Slain In 'Shacktown' Brawl. (1938, August 16). *Seattle Times*, p. 2.
[10] Slayer given Year In Jail. (1938, October 11). *Seattle Times*, p. 30.
[11] Death Suspect Is Bound Over. (1937, March 19). *Seattle Times*, p. 15.
[12] 'Shacktown' Slayer Gets 20 Year Term. (1937, August 24). *Seattle Times,* p. 2.

[13] Man Admits Slaying Over 25 Cent Debt. (1938, June 28). *Seattle Times*, p. 13.

[14] Woman War Veteran In Murder Quiz. (1935, January 16). *Seattle Times*, p. 1 and 14.

[15] Russian Mary's Trial Completed. (1935, March 6). *Seattle Times*, p. 1 and 5.

[16] Scates, S. (2012). *Warren G. Magnuson and the Shaping of Twentieth-Century America*. Seattle: University of Washington Press.

[17] Roy, p.79.

[18] Annoyer Stabs Women's Escort. (1935, October 11). *Seattle Times*, p. 13.

[19] Pair Stabbed At 'House Party' In Shacktown. (1934, June 22). *Seattle Times*, p. 3.

[20] 2 Stabbed In Night Attacks. (1938, November 5). *Seattle Times*, p. 2.

[21] Traffic Victim Was Suicide, Says Death Report. (1933, April 12). *Seattle Times*, p. 4.

[22] Neighbors Identify Victim of Drowning. (1938, May 11). *Seattle Times*, p. 7.

[23] Body Found in Bay Identified. (1938, September 11). *Seattle Times*, p. 8.

[24] Man Found Dead In Waterway. (1938, December 5). *Seattle Times*, p. 3.

[25] Man Killed In Bridge Plunge. (1939, December 1). *Seattle Times*, p. 2.

[26] Molthan, J. (1933, January 13). Jump In Suicide Due To Crisis. *Unemployed Citizen*, p. 1.

[27] Christmas Card Found in Dead Man's Pocket. (1933, May 5). *Seattle Times*, p. 13.

[28] Daily Statistics. (1934, September 1). *Seattle Times*, p. 5

[29] Daily Statistics. (1934, December 28). *Seattle Times*, p. 17.

[30] Vital Statistics. (1935, July 10). *Seattle Times*, p. 20.

[31] Beer Is Seized In Hooverville Raid. (1940, August 23). *Seattle Times*, p. 32.

[32] Fifth Shackown Raid Yields Beer and Mash. (1940, September 18). *Seattle Times*.

[33] 4 Men Taken In Home Brew Raids. (1940, October 27). *Seattle Times*, p. 15.

[34] Home Brewing Still Keeping Federals Busy. (1940, November 2). *Seattle Times*, p. 18.

[35] Suspect In Church Fire Under Quiz. (1935, May 4). *Seattle Times*, p. 1.

[36] Church 'Firebug'. (1935, May 6). *Seattle Times*, p. 5.

[37] $300,000 Damage Laid To Firebug. (1935, May 7). *Seattle Times*, p. 3.

[38] $15,000 Fire Hits Brace Lumber Co. (1935, May 10). *Seattle Times*, p. 8.

[39] 75 years Ago: Fire Bug in Seattle. (2010, Winter). *Archives Gazette*, 3.

[40] Firebug Given Prison Sentence. (1935, May 28). *Seattle Times*, p. 7.

[41] His Destructive Operations? (1957, April 28). *Seattle Times.*

[42] Special Fire Sleuths Run Down Arsonists. (1940, May 25). *Seattle Times*, p. 16.

Chapter 15 The Idea Haunts Still

[1] Splitters Try to Disrupt Citizens League. (1933, September 4). *Voice of Action*, p. 3.

[2] More about the Re-organizing. (1933, September 18). *Voice of Action*, p. 3.

[3] Marching Forward. (1933, September 25). *Voice of Action*, p. 2.

[4] Uncover Plot to Smash citizens' League. (1933, October 2). *Voice of Action*, p. 1.

[5] Fakers Federation Holds First Meeting. (1933, October 9). *Voice of Action*, p. 3.

[6] Jail Term Given Man ForTrying To Incite Strike. (1933, November 2). *Seattle Times*, p. 11.

[7] Police Are Called To Jobless Gathering. (1933, November 5). *Seattle Times*, p. 11.

[8] Who's Vanguard? (1933, December 11). *Voice of Action*, p. 4.

[9] Fight for Relief. (1934, March 20). *Voice of Action*, p. 3.

[10] Child Welfare. (1934, February 12). *Voice of Action*, p. 4.

[11] Dobbins' Resignation Is Step Forward Says CP. (1934, April 3). *Voice of Action*, pp. 1,4.

[12] Capital Hill UCL, Frank Leader Win $2 Prizes for Stories. (1934, August 10). *Voice of Action*, p. 4.

[13] U. C. L. Starts New Program Of Expansion. (1935, February 22). *Voice of Action*, p. 1.

[14] Commonwealth Group Spurns U. C.L. Members. (1936, April 5). *Seattle Times*, p. 12.

[15] Board Reverse Previous Vote. (1936, May 23). *Seattle Times*, p. 2.

[16] Murray's Radio Speech Draws Bristol Retort. (1936, November 1). *Seattle Times*, p. 13.

Chapter 16 Shacktown: Events

[1] Suffia, D. (1974, May 30). The rise and fall fo Seattle's Hooverville. *Seattle Times*, p. A 13.

[2] Hooverville College Head Fears Political Control. (1934, July 15). *Seattle Times*, p. 30.

[3] Teacher Killed When Struck By Rebounding Car. (1934, August 17). *Seattle Times*, p. 4.

[4] 'Hooverville' Leader's Widow Asks Death Cash. (1934, September 22). *Seattle Times*.

[5] Roper's First View of Seattle is Hooverville. (1934, June 25). *Seattle*, p. 1.

[6] Pyle, E. (1936, October 29). Pyle Finds Dictator Rule In Shack-City. *Pittsburgh Post-Gazette*.

[7] Hooverville council cites Noisy Dweller. (1939, October 29). *Seattle Times*, p. 2.

Chapter 17 The City: A New Idea Strives

[1] Phillips, C. (1969). *From the Crash to the Blitz: 1929-1939.* Toronto: The Macmillan Company. P. 268

[2] Taylor, loc 1842

[3] *Civil Works Administration Photographs.* (n.d.). Retrieved from University Libraries University of Washington Digital Collections: http://digitalcollections.lib.washington.edu/cdm/singleitem/c ollection/civilworks/id/101/rec/5

[4] Taylor, loc. 1924

[5] Berner, P. 324

Chapter 18 The City: A Revolutionary Idea

[1] C. W. A. Men May Get Transfer To New Relief Group. (1934, March 18). *Seattle Sunday Times*, p. 10.

[2] Taylor, loc 2117

[3] Phillips, P. 277

[4] Phillips, P. 256

[5] Hopkins, H. L. (1936). Report of Works Progress Administration, June 22, 1936. *CF 151547. Comptroller Files 1802-01.* Seattle Municipal Archives.

[6] W. P. A. Jobs For those On Relief. (1935, November 3). *Seattle Sunday times*, p. 9.

[7] Gannon, G. (2014, August 11). *United States. Works Progress Administration (Wash.). [Press releases, AG-PR 1 & 2, PR 16-100].* Retrieved from Legacy Washington: http://www.sos.wa.gov/legacy/publications_detail.aspx?p=105 P. 40

[8] Gannon, P. 28 and 46

[9] Gannon, P. 63

[10] Gannon, P. 92

[11] Gannon, P. 94

[12] Gannon, P. 102

[13] Gannon, P. 107

[14] W. P. A. $375,000 for Street Work. (1936, March 16). *Seattle Times*, p. 2.

[15] Abel, D. G. (1937). *Letter, January 9, 1937 "WPA," Box 36, Folder 11 Department of Engineering Unrecorded Subject Files, 2602-02.* Seattle Municipal Archives.

[16] 125 Again Sit Down To Wait. (1936, November 18). *Seattle Times*.

[17] 700 Workers Report On Jobs; Police Keep Peace. (1937, February 8). *Seattle Times*, pp. 1, 3.

[18] Spread of 'Sit' Strikes Feared. (1937, January 27). *Seattle Times*, p. 15.

[19] Police End Battle On W. Seattle W. P. A. Job. (1937, February 11). *Seattle Times*, pp. 1,3.

[20] Laborers On W. P. A. Jobs Are Guarded By Officers. (1937 , February 11). *Seattle Times*, pp. 1,9.

[21] Bell Delays Sit-Strike Trial; Frees Defendents. (1937, February 13). *Seattle Times*, pp. 1, 3.

[22] Bell Frees And Warns 42 in W. P. A. Sit-Strike. (1937, February 20). *Seattle Times*, pp. 1, 3.

[23] W. P. A. Pickets Bolster 'Lines'. (1937, February 15). *Seattle Times*, p. 4.

[24] Congress' Aid Asked in W. P. A. Strike Crisis. (1937, February 18). *Seattle Times*, pp. 1,2.

[25] Workers To Take Poll At Projects Tomorrow. (1937, February 21). *Seattle Times*, pp. 1,3

[26] Peace Plan is Heavily Supported By Workers. (1937, February 24). *Seattle Times*, p. 1.

[27] W. P. A. Strikers Return To Jobs. (1937, February 25). *Seattle Times*, p. 2.

[28] Taylor, loc 5328

[29] Martin Works on Relief Plan. (1938, April 1). *Seattle Daily Times*, p. 8.

[30] Jobless in City Hall Refuse To Get Out and Go to Camp. (1938, April 2). *Seattle Daily Times*, pp. 1,2.

[31] County Reopens Blue Ox Lodge. (1938, April 3). *Seattle Daily Times*, p. 9.

[32] Homeless Eat; Dish Shortage. (1938, April 4). *Seattle Daily Times*, p. 13.

[33] John F. Dore. (1938, April 19). *Seattle Times*, p. 4.

[34] State Jobless Trek To Olympia. (1938, April 5). *Seattle Daily Times*, p. 10.

[35] County Seeks to Restrict Relief. (1938, April 6). *Seattle Times*, p. 2.

[36] Phillips, P. 277

[37] Men, Told to Quit Shelter, Sue Hegland. (1939, April 1). *Seattle Times*, p. 1.

[38] Tents Removed;Jobless Remain. (1939, April 7). *Seattle Times*, p. 18.

[39] Jobless Hear Relief Criticism. (1939, April 10). *Seattle Times*, p. 2.

[40] County May Not Oust Jobless. (1939, April 11). *Seattle Times*, p. 7.

[41] W. P. A. Prepares To Revise Wage. (1939, July 7). *Seattle Times*, p. 13.

[42] Washington's W. P. A. Strikers Are Returning. (1939, July 13). *Seattle Times*, p. 4.

[43] President Assails Aid-Bill Walkout. (1939, July 14). *Seattle Times*, p. 1.

[44] Taylor, loc 7116

[45] Taylor, loc 7196

[46] Taylor, loc 7660

[47] Taylor, loc 7767

Chapter 19 Shacktown: Clubs

[1] City Water To Be Supplied Hill Squatters. (1936, August 2). *Seattle Times*, p. 2.

[2] Squatter Colony On Beacon Hill May Lose Homes. (1936, August 20). *Seattle Times*, p. 3.

[3] City's 'Tenants' Ask Bigger Water Pipe. (1936, October 13). *Seattle Times*, p. 24.

[4] Club Asks Clean-Up Of Garbage Dump. (1937, March 14). *Seattle Times*, p. 13.

[5] Garbage Fill Protest Filed. (1937, November 2). *Seattle Times*, p. 10.

[6] Shack Razing Delayed By City. (1938, February 24). *Seattle Times*, p. 9.

[7] Clubs Pressing Fight On Shacks. (1938, March 25). *Seattle Times*, p. 13.

[8] Beacon Group Seeks Courts. (1938, April 1). *Seattle Time*

[9] Beacon Hill Club May Aid 'Shacks' Fight. (1938, April 4). *Seattle Times*, p. 13.

[10] Shacks Draw New Protests. (1938, April 21). *Seattle Times*, p. 12.

[11] Shack 'War' To Be Redoubled. (1938, April 23). *Seattle Times*, p. 13.

[12] Angel Studies Drive On Shacks. (1938, April 12). *Seattle Times*, p. 2.

[13] Shacktown Plaints To Be Investigated. (1938, October 12). *Seattle Times*, p. 5.

[14] Group Protests Shack Razing. (1938, October 18). *Seattle Times*, p. 4.

[15] March 9 Election Aspirants Presented to Readers. (1937, February 28). *Seattle Times*, p. 14.

[16] Harlin Seeks Phone Rate Cut. (1938, October 21). *Seattle Times*, p. 27.

[17] South District Clubs Ask Ban on Shacks. (1938, October 25). *Seattle Times*, p. 7.

[18] Council Saves Homes For Shacktowners. (1938, October 26). *Seattle Times*, p. 21.

[19] Police Would Raze Shacks. (1938, November 9). *Seattle Times*, p. 13.

[20] Council Hears Both Sides Of Shack Dispute. (1938, November 22). *Seattle Times*, p. 2

[21] Boos Punctuate Shack Hearing. (1938, November 29). *Seattle Times*, p. 3.

[22] 22,204 Shacks Counted In City. (1938, November 30). *Seattle Times*, p. 8.

[23] Shacktown Hits Back At Foes. (1938, December 2). *Seattle Times*, p. 24.

[24] New Shacks For Old Suggested. (1938, December 7). *Seattle Times*, p. 3.

[25] Board Reverse Previous Vote. (1936, May 23). *Seattle Times*, p. 2.

[26] 2 Resolutions Framed In War On Shacktowns. (1938, December 11). *Seattle Times*, p. 2.

[27] Clubs Continue Fight On Shacks. (1938, December 16). *Seattle Times*.

[28] Wood, J. A. (1938, December 24). Speaking for The Times. *Seattle Times.*

[29] Boom Foreseen If Housing Bill Passes. (1939, January 24). *Seattle Times*, p. 8.

[30] Bills Passed By The House. (1939, February 23). *Seattle Times*, p. 8.

[31] Club Considers Shacks, Sewers. (1939, February 24). *Seattle Times*, p. 30.

[32] Council O.K's Housing Plan. (1939, March 14). *Seattle Times*, p. 18.

[33] Wood, J. A. (1939, April 12). Speaking for The Times. *Seattle Times.*

[34] 3-Way Drive On Shacks Is Urged. (1939, May 5). *Seattle Times*, p. 23.

[35] Club Will Ask Park To Keep Out Squatters. (1939, November 12). *Seattle Times*, p. 21.

[36] Club To Study Shack Problem. (1940, May 22). *Seattle Times*, p. 28.

[37] Seattle 'Shack' Situation Told. (1940, May 24). *Seattle Times*, p. 19.

Chapter 20 Shacktown: Census

[1] *Spokane Daily Chronicle.* (1937, October 5). Retrieved from google.com/newspapers: http://news.google.com/newspapers?nid=1338&dat=1937100 5&id=E7wzAAAAIBAJ&sjid=GfUDAAAAIBAJ&pg=6070,2063496

[2] US Census. (2014, July 28). *1940 United States Federal Census.* Retrieved from ancestry.com: http://interactive.ancestry.com/2442/m-t0627-04381-

00996/66334792?backurl=http%3a%2f%2fsearch.ancestry.co
m%2fcgi-
bin%2fsse.dll%3fnew%3d1%26gsfn%3dgeorge%2b%26gsln%3
dparish%26rank%3d1%26gss%3dangs-
g%26msbdy%3d1877%26pcat%3dROOT_CATEGORY%26h%3d
66334792%26db

Chapter 21 Shacktown: Burns

[1] US Census. (2014, July 28). *1940 United States Federal Census*.
Retrieved from ancestry.com:
http://interactive.ancestry.com/2442/m-t0627-04381-
00996/66334792?backurl=http%3a%2f%2fsearch.ancestry.co
m%2fcgi-
bin%2fsse.dll%3fnew%3d1%26gsfn%3dgeorge%2b%26gsln%3
dparish%26rank%3d1%26gss%3dangs-
g%26msbdy%3d1877%26pcat%3dROOT_CATEGORY%26h%3d
66334792%26db

[2] Vets' Heads View Site Of Hospital . (1940, September 8). *Seattle Times*, p. 8.

[3] 'Old Man Fisher' Gets Job---Tearing Down His Own Shack. (1940, October 2). *Seattle Times*, p. 14.

[4] Island Shacktown Bows Out to Make Way for Ship Slips. (1940, October 1). *Seattle Times*, pp. 1,5.

[5] Councilmen Delay Shacktown Action. (1941, March 18). *Seattle Times*, p. 8.

[6] Shack Dwellers May Get Farms. (1941, March 31). *Seattle Times*, p. 2.

[7] Ragtime Requiem Rings Out As Tractor Levels Shacks. (1941, April 10). *The Seattle Times*, p. 8.

---

[8] Clubs Ask End of Shacktown. (1941, March 18). *Seattle Times*, p. 17.

[9] Guard Proposed For Shacktowns. (1941, April 22). *Seattle Times*, p. 2.

[10] Auto Patrol Of Shacks Urged. (1941, April 29). *Seattle Times*, p. 5.

[11] Shacktown Houses Burn With 'No Loss'. (1941, May 3). *Seattle Times*, p. 17.

[12] Bulldozer, Flames Make Hooverville Just Memory. (1941, May 6). *Seattle Times*, p. 5.

Epilogue: Last Rites

[1] More Welfare Funds Sought. (1941, December 1). *Seattle Times*, p. 4.

[2] Norton, W. (1942, April 13). *Request from Commissioner of Health regarding destruction of shacks, April 13, 1942. CF 173660. Comptroller Files, 1802-01, Seattele Municipal Archieves.* Retrieved from Seattle Municipal Archives: http://www.seattle.gov/cityarchives/exhibits-and-education/digital-document-libraries/hoovervilles-in-seattle

[3] Ex-Mayor Of Hooverville Recalls '30's. (1962, July 4). *Seattle Times*, p. A.

[4] Boley, J. (1997, Spring). *Rebel with a Cause: Carl Brannin and His Work.* Retrieved from The Compass Rose: http://libraries.uta.edu/speccoll/crose97/brannin.htm

[5] Willis, Pp. 275-276

[6] William K. Dobbins, 69. (1967, December 13). *Seattle Times*, p. 28.

[7] John C. Stevenson, 'Radio Speaker' of 30's, 40's Dies. (1966, August 6). Seattle Times, p. 2.

8 N. Y. Officials To Reopen Fight For Stevenson. (1933, November 10). Seattle Times, p. 9.

9 *Don Roy Papers, Duke University Archives.* (n.d.). Retrieved from
        Duke University Libraries:
        http://library.duke.edu/rubenstein/findingaids/uaroy/

10 Stanley Swanson. (1948, May 16). Murder in the Houseboat. *Seattle Times*.

11 Rites in East For Stephen Eringis. (1963, February 12). *Seattle Times*, p. 35.

12 Rev. William L. Norton, 67. (1967, July 25). *Seattle Times*, p. 26.

13 Charles F. Ernst (1968, August 5). *Seattle Times*, p. 47.

Bibliography

$15,000 Fire Hits Brace Lumber Co. (1935, May 10). *Seattle Times*, p. 8.

$300,000 Damage Laid To Firebug. (1935, May 7). *Seattle Times*, p. 3.

1,000 Jobless Marchers Gather At State Capitol. (1933, Janurary 17). *Seattle Times*, p. 2.

1,500 Leave On March To Olympia. (1933, March 1). *Seattle Times*, p. 3.

125 Again Sit Down To Wait. (1936, November 18). *Seattle Times*.

14 Dogs Howl At Hooverville, Master Jailed. (1936, February 23). *Seattle Times*, p. 2.

19,661 Aided By Community Fund in Feb. (1932 , March 1). *Seattle Times*, p. 7.

1940 census. (1940, April 8). Retrieved from ancestry.com: http://interactive.ancestry.com/2442/m-t0627-04381-00996/66334792?backurl=http%3a%2f%2fsearch.ancestry.com%2fcgi-bin%2fsse.dll%3fdb%3d1940usfedcen%26so%3d2%26pcat%3dROOT_CATEGORY%26MS_AdvCB%3d1%26rank%3d1%26new%3d1%26MSAV%3d2%26msT%3d1%26gss%3dangs-g%26gs

2 Resolutions Framed In War On Shacktowns. (1938, December 11). *Seattle Times*, p. 2.

2 Stabbed In Night Attacks. (1938, November 5). *Seattle Times*, p. 2.

22,204 Shacks Counted In City. (1938, November 30). *Seattle Times*, p. 8.

3-Way Drive On Shacks Is Urged. (1939, May 5). *Seattle Times*, p. 23.

4 Men Taken In Home Brew Raids. (1940, October 27). *Seattle Times*, p. 15.

7 Convicted In Frandsen Riot Give Selves Up. (1934, April 16). *Seattle Times*, p. 20.

700 Workers Report On Jobs; Police Keep Peace. (1937, February 8). *Seattle Times*, pp. 1, 3.

75 years Ago: Fire Bug in Seattle. (2010, Winter). *Archives Gazette*, 3.

A Sad Experience. (1932, December 20). *Seattle Times*, p. 6.

Abel, D. G. (1937). *Letter, January 9, 1937 "WPA," Box 36, Folder 11 Department of Engineering Unrecorded Subject Files, 2602-02.* Seattle Municipal Archives.

Action, E. B. (1933, March 25). The Truth About the March to Olympia. *A New Weekly Paper*, p. 3.

Amundson, M. (2009, December 27). *Uniion Gospel Mission (Seattle)*. Retrieved from HistoryLink.org: http://www.historylink.org/index.cfm?DisplayPage=output.cfm&file_id=9248

Angel Studies Drive On Shacks. (1938, April 12). *Seattle Times*, p. 2.

Annoyer Stabs Women's Escort. (1935, October 11). *Seattle Times*, p. 13.

Auto Patrol Of Shacks Urged. (1941, April 29). *Seattle Times*, p. 5.

Beacon Group Seeks Courts. (1938, April 1). *Seattle Times*, p. 28.

Beacon Hill Club May Aid 'Shacks' Fight. (1938, April 4). *Seattle Times*, p. 13.

Beer Is Seized In Hooverville Raid. (1940, August 23). *Seattle Times*, p. 32.

Bell Delays Sit-Strike Trial; Frees Defendents. (1937, February 13). *Seattle Times*, pp. 1, 3.

Bell Frees And Warns 42 in W. P. A. Sit-Strike. (1937, February 20). *Seattle Times*, pp. 1, 3.

Berner, R. C. (1992). *Seattle: 1921-1940.* Seattle: Charles Press.

Bills Passed By The House. (1939, February 23). *Seattle Times*, p. 8.

Blonder Convicted. (1933, April 10). *Voice of Action*, p. 2.

Blonder Family Is Evicted. (1933, April 17). *Voice of Action*, p. 1.

Blum, D. (nd, nd nd). *The Chemist's War*. Retrieved from Slate: http://www.slate.com/articles/health_and_science/medical_examiner/2010/02/the_chemists_war.3.html

Blumell, B. D. (1984). *The Development of Public Assistance in the State of Washington During the Great Depression.* New York: Garland Publishing, Inc.

Board Approves Shack Program. (1938, December 9). *Seattle Times*, p. 20.

Board Reverse Previous Vote. (1936, May 23). *Seattle Times*, p. 2.

Body Found in Bay Identified. (1938, September 11). *Seattle Times*, p. 8.

Boley, J. (1997, Spring). *Rebel with a Cause: Carl Brannin and His Work*. Retrieved from The Compass Rose: http://libraries.uta.edu/speccoll/crose97/brannin.htm

Boley, J. (1997, Spring). *Rebel with a Cause: Carl Brannin and His Work*. Retrieved from Special Collections Division of the University of Texas at Arlington Libraries: http://dspace.uta.edu/bitstream/handle/10106/5326/1997_Fall%20%26%20Spring.pdf?sequence=1

Boom Foreseen If Housing Bill Passes. (1939, January 24). *Seattle Times*, p. 8.

Boos Punctuate Shack Hearing. (1938, November 29). *Seattle Times*, p. 3.

Bulldozer, Flames Make Hooverville Just Memory. (1941, May 6). *Seattle Times*, p. 5.

Burglar Takes Two Child's Banks, $35. (1936, December 4). *Seattle Times*, p. 10.

C. W. A. Men May Get Transfer To New Relief Group. (1934, March 18). *Seattle Sunday Times*, p. 10.

Capital Hill UCL, Frank Leader Win $2 Prizes for Stories. (1934, August 10). *Voice of Action*, p. 4.

Charles F. Ernst. (1968, August 5). *Seattle Times*, p. 47.

Child Welfare. (1934, February 12). *Voice of Action*, p. 4.

Christmas Card Found in Dead Man's Pocket. (1933, May 5). *Seattle Times*, p. 13.

Church 'Firebug'. (1935, May 6). *Seattle Times*, p. 5.

City Water To Be Supplied Hill Squatters. (1936, August 2). *Seattle Times*, p. 2.

City's 'Tenants' Ask Bigger Water Pipe. (1936, October 13). *Seattle Times*, p. 24.

Civil Works Administration Photographs. (n.d.). Retrieved from University Libraries University of Washington Digital Collections: http://digitalcollections.lib.washington.edu/cdm/singlei tem/collection/civilworks/id/101/rec/5

Club Asks Clean-Up Of Garbage Dump. (1937, March 14). *Seattle Times*, p. 13.

Club Considers Shacks, Sewers. (1939, February 24). *Seattle Times*, p. 30.

Club To Study Shack Problem. (1940, May 22). *Seattle Times*, p. 28.

Club Will Ask Park To Keep Out Squatters. (1939, November 12). *Seattle Times*, p. 21.

Clubs Ask End of Shacktown. (1941, March 18). *Seattle Times*, p. 17.

Clubs Continue Fight On Shacks. (1938, December 16). *Seattle Times*.

Clubs Pressing Fight On Shacks. (1938, March 25). *Seattle Times*, p. 13.

Collection Plate and Bequests Provide Millions for Charity. (1936, August 5). *Seattle*, p. 8.

Commission Idea Takes Hold Of County board. (1933, January 20). *Seattle Times*, p. 26.

Commonwealth Group Spurns U. C.L. Members. (1936, April 5). *Seattle Times*, p. 12.

Congress' Aid Asked in W. P. A. Strike Crisis. (1937, February 18). *Seattle Times*, pp. 1,2.

Council Hears Both Sides Of Shack Dispute. (1938, November 22). *Seattle Times*, p. 2.

Council O.K's Housing Plan. (1939, March 14). *Seattle Times*, p. 18.

Council Saves Homes For Shacktowners. (1938, October 26). *Seattle Times*, p. 21.

Councilmen Delay Shacktown Action. (1941, March 18). *Seattle Times*, p. 8.

County May Not Oust Jobless. (1939, April 11). *Seattle Times*, p. 7.

County Reopens Blue Ox Lodge. (1938, April 3). *Seattle Daily Times*, p. 9.

County Seeks to Restrict Relief. (1938, April 6). *Seattle Times*, p. 2.

County To Stop Relief Kitchen. (1937, October 22). *Seattle*, p. 3.

Crichton Promotes Health of Seattle. (1913, June 29). *Seattle Times*, p. 4.

Cronin Gives Star Statement on Conference. (1932, July 8). *Seattle Star*, p. 3.

Daily Statistics. (1934, September 1). *Seattle Times*, p. 5.

Daily Statistics. (1934, December 28). *Seattle Times*, p. 17.

Death Suspect Is Bound Over. (1937, March 19). *Seattle Times*, p. 15.

Defense Blames Sheriff's Men For Home Riot. (1933, June 20). *Seattle Times*, p. 4.

Demonstrators At Olympia Call Off Parade. (1933, March 2). *Seattle Times*, p. 11.

Dennett, E. V. (1990). *Agitprop: The Life on an American Working-Class Radical.* Albany: State University of New York Press.

Deputy's Threat To Shoot Is Told At Rioting Trial. (1933, June 27). *Seattle Times*, p. 2.

Dixon Orders Squatters To Quit Tideflats. (1931, May 12). *The Seattle Daily Times*, p. 9.

Dobbins' Resignation Is Step Forward Says CP. (1934, April 3). *Voice of Action*, pp. 1,4.

Don Roy Papers, Duke University Archives. (n.d.). Retrieved from Duke University Libraries: http://library.duke.edu/rubenstein/findingaids/uaroy/

Dore Abolishes Laing's Office. (1932, July 5). *Seattle Star*, p. 1.

Dore Adovocates Economic Changes. (1931, October 27). *Seattle Times*, p. 4.

Dore Counter Move Likely, Friends Aver. (1930 , December 29). *Seattle Times*, p. 12.

Doughnut Truck Disappears; Shacktown Dwellers Feast. (1934, February 17). *Seattle Times*, p. 12.

Duncan, D. (1979, March 17). Shackled by poverty, shantytown citizens survived. *Seattle Times*, p. A 5.

Duwamish Waterway Evictions Impending. (1926, January 25). *Seattle Daily Times*, p. 2.

Eigner, E. (nd). *Vanguard And Unemployed Citizen*. Retrieved from Labor Press Project: http://depts.washington.edu/labhist/laborpress/Vanguard.htm

Ejection From City Hall Ends Relief Protest. (1933, February 17). *Seattle Times*, pp. 1,2.

Erb, L. D. (1935). Seattle's Hooverville. 8. Seattle, Washington: Unpublished.

Evans Hogs U. C. L. Berries. (1932, October 21). *The Vanguard*, p. 1.

Ex-Mayor Of Hooverville Recalls '30's. (1962, July 4). *Seattle Times*, p. A.

Fakers Federation Holds First Meeting. (1933, October 9). *Voice of Action*, p. 3.

Federal Relief Funds Aid State's Transient Indigent. (1933, December 10). *Seattle Times*, p. 13.

Fifth Shackown Raid Yields Beer and Mash. (1940, September 18). *Seattle Times*.

Fight for Relief. (1934, March 20). *Voice of Action*, p. 3.

Firebug Given Prison Sentence. (1935, May 28). *Seattle Times*, p. 7.

Frank R. Menne, M. D. (nd). *Acute Methyl Alcohol Poisoning: A report of twenty-two instances with postmortem examinations.* Portland, Oregon: unknown.

Gannon, G. (2014, August 11). *United States. Works Progress Administration (Wash.). [Press releases, AG-PR 1 & 2, PR 16-100].* Retrieved from Legacy Washington: http://www.sos.wa.gov/legacy/publications_detail.aspx?p=105

Garbage Fill Protest Filed. (1937, November 2). *Seattle Times*, p. 10.

Group Protests Shack Razing. (1938, October 18). *Seattle Times*, p. 4.

Guard Proposed For Shacktowns. (1941, April 22). *Seattle Times*, p. 2.

Harburg, Y. (n.d.). Brother, Can You Spare a Dime. *1931*.

Harlin Seeks Phone Rate Cut. (1938, October 21). *Seattle Times*, p. 27.

Hillman, A. (1934). *The Unemployed Citizens' League of Seattle.* Seattle: University of Washington Press.

His Destructive Operations? (1957, April 28). *Seattle Times*.

Hogan, J. A. (1934). The Decline of Self-Help and Growth of Radicalism Among Seattle's Organized Unemployed. Seattle: University of Washington.

Home Brewing Still Keeping Federals Busy. (1940, November 2). *Seattle Times*, p. 18.

Homeless Eat; Dish Shortage. (1938, April 4). *Seattle Daily Times*, p. 13.

Hoover, H. (1932, July 17). *Statement About Signing the Emergency Relief and Construction Act of 1932*. Retrieved from The American Presidency Project: http://www.presidency.ucsb.edu/ws/?pid=23170

Hooverville College Head Fears Political Control. (1934, July 15). *Seattle Times*, p. 30.

Hooverville council cites Noisy Dweller. (1939, October 29). *Seattle Times*, p. 2.

'Hooverville' Leader's Widow Asks Death Cash. (1934, September 22). *Seattle Times*.

'Hooverville's Mayor' Discovers Stolen Groceries. (1935, December 26). *Seattle Times*, p. 2.

Hopkins, H. L. (1936). Report of Works Progress Administration, June 22, 1936. *CF 151547. Comptroller Files 1802-01.* Seattle Municipal Archives.

How to Get Food: Stores to Supplant Commissaries. (1933, February 14). *Seattle Times*, p. 1.

Irving Dix Dies in Spokane. (1966, April 9). *Spokane Daily Chronicle*, p. 5.

Island Shacktown Bows Out to Make Way for Ship Slips. (1940, October 1). *Seattle Times*, pp. 1,5.

Jackson, J. (n.d.). The Story of Seattle's Hooverville.

Jail Term Given Man ForTrying To Incite Strike. (1933, November 2). *Seattle Times*, p. 11.

Jobless Hear Relief Criticism. (1939, April 10). *Seattle Times*, p. 2.

Jobless in City Hall Refuse To Get Out and Go to Camp. (1938, April 2). *Seattle Daily Times*, pp. 1,2.

Jobless Will Visit Martin To Ask New County Aid Group. (1933, February 15). *Seattle*, p. 5.

John F. Dore. (1938, April 19). *Seattle Times*, p. 4.

'Jungle Villages' Under Ban; More Shacks To Burn. (1931, October 29). *Seattle Times*, p. 10.

Kamenz, A. (n.d.). *On to Olympia! The History Behind the Hunger Marches of 1932-1933.* Retrieved from Great Depression in Washington State:

http://depts.washington.edu/depress/hunger_marches.
shtml

Kelly, J. (n.d.). *UCL Branch activities: additional notes*. Retrieved
from Great Depression in Washington State:
http://depts.washington.edu/depress/UCL_branch_not
es.shtml#georgetown

Kelly, P. (2010, January 20). *Hoovervilles in Seattle: Map and
Photos*. Retrieved from Great Depression In Washington
State:
https://depts.washington.edu/depress/hooverville_ma
p.shtml

Laborer Admits He Hit Man With Stick. (1940, October 29).
Seattle Times, p. 3.

Lwq

Laborers On W. P. A. Jobs Are Guarded By Officers. (1937 ,
February 11). *Seattle Times*, pp. 1,9.

Last Witnesses In Riot Trial Testify Today. (1933, July 1). *Seattle
Times*, p. 3.

Levy, H. P. (1933, February 9). Rost Beef! Um! *Seattle Times*, p.
9.

Levy, H. P. (1985). There Were Days Like That. In H. P. Levy,
There Were Days Like That (p. 103). Glendale, California:
Blue Whale Press.

listed, N. (1933, 2 28). *Seattle Times*.

M., U. (1934, March 6). Workers Fight Gulls on City Dump for Offal. *Voice of Action*, p. 3.

Man Admits Slaying Over 25 Cent Debt. (1938, June 28). *Seattle Times*, p. 13.

Man Charged With Murder. (1937, August 3). *Seattle Times*, p. 22.

Man Found Dead In Waterway. (1938, December 5). *Seattle Times*, p. 3.

Man In 'Shack Murder' Guilty. (1937, June 13). *Seattle Times*, p. 5.

Man Is Slain In 'Shacktown' Brawl. (1938, August 16). *Seattle Times*, p. 2.

Man Killed In Bridge Plunge. (1939, December 1). *Seattle Times*, p. 2.

Man Slugged, Stripped; Two Suspects Held. (1940, October 14). *Seattle Times*, p. 5.

Man Stabbed When He Visits Shacktown. (1941, January 12). *Seattle Times*, p. 9.

Man, Stabbed Twice, Found in Shacktown. (1940, November 17). *Seattle Times*, p. 2.

March 9 Election Aspirants Presented to Readers. (1937, February 28). *Seattle Times*, p. 14.

Marching Forward. (1933, September 25). *Voice of Action*, p. 2.

Marshall, J. (1931, January 1). Tramp, Tramp, Tramp the Boys Are Marching! *Seattle Star*, p. 1.

Martin Works on Relief Plan. (1938, April 1). *Seattle Daily Times*, p. 8.

Mayor Dore Public Enemy. (1932, October 14). *The Vanguard*, p. 1.

McClary, D. (2003, March 13). *Pier 36 -- Seattle Waterfront.* Retrieved from HistoryLink.org: http://www.historylink.org/index.cfm?DisplayPage=output.cfm&file_id=4149

Meat Dealers OfCity Pledge Aid Against Hunger. (1930, November 20). *Seattle Times*, p. 10.

Men, Told to Quit Shelter, Sue Hegland. (1939, April 1). *Seattle Times*, p. 1.

Menefee, S. (1932, December 2). Studies in Rugged Individualism - I. *Unemployed Citizen*, p. 1.

Menefee, S. (1932, December 9). Studies in Rugged Individualism - II. *Unemployed Citizen*, p. 1.

Menefee, S. (1932, December 16). Studies in Rugged Individualism - III. *Unemployed Citizen*, p. 4.

Menefee, S. (1932, December 23). Studies in Rugged Individualism - IV. *Unemployed Citizen*.

Menefee, S. (1933, January 6). Studies in Rugged Indivdualism - VI. *Unemployed Citizen*, p. 3.

Molthan, J. (1933, January 13). Jump In Suicide Due To Crisis. *Unemployed Citizen*, p. 1.

More about the Re-organizing. (1933, September 18). *Voice of Action*, p. 3.

More Welfare Funds Sought. (1941, December 1). *Seattle Times*, p. 4.

Morris, K. (1982, October). *Records of the Washington Emergency Relief Administration, 1919-1940*. Retrieved from Archivegrid: http://beta.worldcat.org/archivegrid/record.php?id=154690257

Murray's Radio Speech Draws Bristol Retort. (1936, November 1). *Seattle Times*, p. 13.

Must Have Shelter. (1931, October 28). *Seattle Times*, p. 6.

Neighbors Identify Victim of Drowning. (1938, May 11). *Seattle Times*, p. 7.

New Shacks For Old Suggested. (1938, December 7). *Seattle Times*, p. 3.

Norton, W. (1942, April 13). *Request from Commissioner of Health regarding destruction of shacks, April 13, 1942. CF 173660. Comptroller Files, 1802-01, Seattele Municipal Archieves*. Retrieved from Seattle Municipal Archives: http://www.seattle.gov/cityarchives/exhibits-and-education/digital-document-libraries/hoovervilles-in-seattle

'Old Man Fisher' Gets Job---Tearing Down His Own Shack. (1940, October 2). *Seattle Times*, p. 14.

Paid Managers To Control All Unemployed Job. (1932, October 14). *The Vanguard*, p. 2.

Pair Stabbed At 'House Party' In Shacktwon. (1934, June 22). *Seattle Times*, p. 3.

Peace Plan is Heavily Supported By Workers. (1937, February 24). *Seattle Times*, p. 1.

Phillips, C. (1969). *From the Crash to the Blitz: 1929-1939*. Toronto: The Macmillan Company.

Police Are Called To Jobless Gathering. (1933, November 5). *Seattle Times*, p. 11.

Police Back Evans' Move To Operate Food Depot. (1932, September 8). *Seattle Times*, p. 1.

Police Disperse 1,000 And Arrest 3 At Food Depot. (1933, January 20). *Seattle Times*, p. 3.

Police End Battle On W. Seattle W. P. A. Job. (1937, February 11). *Seattle Times*, pp. 1,3.

Police Probing Death of Man In 'Shacktown'. (1933, July 27). *Seattle Times*, p. 8.

Police Torch Use Condoned and Condemned by Officials. (1931, October). *Seattle Star*.

Police Would Raze Shacks. (1938, November 9). *Seattle Times*, p. 13.

President Assails Aid-Bill Walkout. (1939, July 14). *Seattle Times*, p. 1.

Press, A. (1932, July 5). Hartley Not In His Office When Jobless Call. *Seattle Times*, p. 5.

Press, A. (1932, July 2). Thousands Set For Olympia Relief March, Say Leaders. *Seattle Times*, p. 1.

Pyle, E. (1936, October 29). Pyle Finds Dictator Rule In Shack-City. *Pittsburgh Post-Gazette*.

Ragtime Requiem Rings Out As Tractor Levels Shacks. (1941, April 10). *The Seattle Times*, p. 8.

Rev. William L. Norton, 67. (1967, July 25). *Seattle Times*, p. 26.

Richards, L. (1930, December 6). Morning-Noon-and Night. *Seattle Star*, p. 6.

Rites in East For Stephen Eringis. (1963, February 12). *Seattle Times*, p. 35.

Roper's First View of Seattle is Hooverville. (1934, June 25). *Seattle*, p. 1.

Roy, D. F. (1935). *Hooverville: A Study of a Community of Homeless Men in Seattle*. Seattle: Unpublished thesis.

Russian Mary's Trial Completed. (1935, March 6). *Seattle Times*, p. 1 and 5.

Scates, S. (2012). *Warren G. Magnuson and the Shaping of Twentieth-Century America*. Seattle: University of Washington Press.

Seattle 'Shack' Situation Told. (1940, May 24). *Seattle Times*, p. 19.

Shack Dwellers May Get Farms. (1941, March 31). *Seattle Times*, p. 2.

Shack Murder Trial Is Opened. (1937, October 4). *Seattle Times*, p. 3.

Shack Ouster Is Under Fire. (1931, October 31). *Seattle PI*, p. 3.

Shack Razing Delayed By City. (1938, February 24). *Seattle Times*, p. 9.

Shack 'War' To Be Redoubled. (1938, April 23). *Seattle Times*, p. 13.

Shacks Draw New Protests. (1938, April 21). *Seattle Times*, p. 12.

Shacktown Hits Back At Foes. (1938, December 2). *Seattle Times*, p. 24.

Shacktown Houses Burn With 'No Loss'. (1941, May 3). *Seattle Times*, p. 17.

Shacktown Plaints To Be Investigated. (1938, October 12). *Seattle Times*, p. 5.

'Shacktown' Slayer Gets 20 Year Term. (1937, August 24). *Seattle Times*, p. 2.

Shacktown Slaying Trial Is Opened. (1938, October 3). *Seattle Times*, p. 4.

Shelters for Jobless Fired by Policemen. (1931, October). *Seattle Star*.

Slayer given Year In Jail. (1938, October 11). *Seattle Times*, p. 30.

South District Clubs Ask Ban on Shacks. (1938, October 25). *Seattle Times*, p. 7.

Special Fire Sleuths Run Down Arsonists. (1940, May 25). *Seattle Times*, p. 16.

Splitters Try to Disrupt Citizens League. (1933, September 4). *Voice of Action*, p. 3.

Spokane Daily Chronicle. (1937, October 5). Retrieved from google.com/newspapers: http://news.google.com/newspapers?nid=1338&dat=1 9371005&id=E7wzAAAAIBAJ&sjid=GfUDAAAAIBAJ&pg= 6070,2063496

Spread of 'Sit' Strikes Feared. (1937, January 27). *Seattle Times*, p. 15.

Squatter Colony On Beacon Hill May Lose Homes. (1936, August 20). *Seattle Times*, p. 3.

Squatters Driven Into Rain When Police Fire Shacks. (1931, October 26). *Seattle PI*, p. 1.

Stabbing Suspect Held in California. (1940, April 18). *Seattle Times*, p. 2.

Stanley Swanson. (1948, May 16). Murder in the Houseboat. *Seattle Times*.

State Jobless Trek To Olympia. (1938, April 5). *Seattle Daily Times*, p. 10.

Stevenson Orders Demonstrators to Leave Courthouse. (1933, February 16). *Seattle Times*, p. 5.

Suffia, D. (1974, May 30). The rise and fall fo Seattle's Hooverville. *Seattle Times*, p. A 13.

Sunshine Club Shows Little Increase in Line. (1931, January 1). *Seattle Star*, p. 1 and 3.

Suspect In Church Fire Under Quiz. (1935, May 4). *Seattle Times*, p. 1.

Tax Rich To Pay Unemployment. (1931, October). *The Vanguard*, p. 1.

Taxpayers Demand County Start Work Plan For Jobless. (1932, November 2). *Seattle Star*, p. 2.

Taylor, N. (2008). *American-Made: The Enduring Legacy of the WPA.* New York: Bantam Dell.

Teacher Killed When Struck By Rebounding Car. (1934, August 17). *Seattle Times*, p. 4.

Tents Removed;Jobless Remain. (1939, April 7). *Seattle Times*, p. 18.

Terkel, S. (1970). *Hard Times.* New York: The New Press.

Thief Shot By Grocer. (1936, October 1). *Seattle Times*, p. 5.

Thousands Seek Work Vainly In This City. (1931, February). *The Vanguard*, p. 1.

Three-Fourth Of Fund-Aided Men Are Seattleites. (1933, January 22). *Seattle Times*, p. 8.

Tickets Will aid Needy Man, Spoil Charity Grafting. (1931, December 23). *Seattle Times*, p. 5.

Tickets Will Provide Food and Lodgings. (1930, December 11). *Seattle Times*, p. 24.

Traffic Victim Was Suicide, Says Death Report. (1933, April 12). *Seattle Times*, p. 4.

Travelers' Aid Friend Indeed Of Homeless Boy. (1932, December 25). *Seattle Times*, p. 7.

Two Charged With Stealing Food Supplies. (1932, Septemeber 9). *Seattle Times*, p. 7.

Two Seattle men Slain In Fights. (1935, May 27). *Seattle Times*, p. 4.

U. C. L. Demands Dobbins Resign Post As Leader. (1933, February 18). *Seattle Times*, p. 12.

U. C. L. Starts New Program Of Expansion. (1935, February 22). *Voice of Action*, p. 1.

Uncover Plot to Smash citizens' League. (1933, October 2). *Voice of Action*, p. 1.

Unemployed Neighbors Get Together! (1931, July). *The Vanguard*, p. 3.

Unknown. (1932, July 3). What Do The Unemployed of State Want? -- 2: Work. *Seattle Times*, p. 1.

Unknown. (unknown). *Essay: The Federal Emergency Relief Administration*. Retrieved from University of

Washington Digital Collections:
http://content.lib.washington.edu/feraweb/essay.html

US Census. (2014, July 28). *1940 United States Federal Census*.
Retrieved from ancestry.com:
http://interactive.ancestry.com/2442/m-t0627-04381-
00996/66334792?backurl=http%3a%2f%2fsearch.ances
try.com%2fcgi-
bin%2fsse.dll%3fnew%3d1%26gsfn%3dgeorge%2b%26g
sln%3dparish%26rank%3d1%26gss%3dangs-
g%26msbdy%3d1877%26pcat%3dROOT_CATEGORY%26
h%3d66334792%26db

Vets' Heads View Site Of Hospital . (1940, September 8). *Seattle Times*, p. 8.

Victim of Stabbing Dies; 3 Are Held. (1940, October 24). *Seattle Times*, p. 36.

Victory in Ballard Eviction; Get New Home, Furniture. (1933, April 10). *Voice of Action*, p. 1.

Vital Statistics. (1935, July 10). *Seattle Times*, p. 20.

W. P. A. $375,000 for Street Work. (1936, March 16). *Seattle Times*, p. 2.

W. P. A. Jobs For those On Relief. (1935, November 3). *Seattle Sunday times*, p. 9.

W. P. A. Pickets Bolster 'Lines'. (1937, February 15). *Seattle Times*, p. 4.

W. P. A. Prepares To Revise Wage. (1939, July 7). *Seattle Times*, p. 13.

W. P. A. Strikers Return To Jobs. (1937, February 25). *Seattle Times*, p. 2.

Washington's W. P. A. Strikers Are Returning. (1939, July 13). *Seattle Times*, p. 4.

Weiser, K. (2010, August). *Hoovervilles*. Retrieved from Legends of America: http://www.legendsofamerica.com/20th-hoovervilles.html

Well Cared For. (1933, January 5). *Seattle Times*, p. 6.

Who's Vanguard? (1933, December 11). *Voice of Action*, p. 4.

Why Did We Vote For Dore? (1932, June 9). *Seattle Star*, p. 1.

William K. Dobbins, 69. (1967, December 13). *Seattle Times*, p. 28.

Willing Job Hunter Finds Central Registry Big Help. (1932, September 21). *Seattle Times*, p. 12.

Willis, T. R. (1997). Unemployed Citizens of Seattle, 1900-1933: Hulet Wells, Seattle Labor, and the Struggle for Economic Security. In T. R. Willis, *Unemployed Citizens of Seattle, 1900-1933: Hulet Wells, Seattle Labor, and the Struggle for Economic Security.* Seattle: Unpublished.

Woman War Veteran In Murder Quiz. (1935, January 16). *Seattle Times*, p. 1 and 14.

Wood, J. A. (1938, December 24). Speaking for The Times. *Seattle Times*.

Wood, J. A. (1939, April 12). Speaking for The Times. *Seattle Times*.

Workers Save Blonder Home. (1933, April 3). *A New Weekly Paper*, pp. 1, 3.

Workers To Take Poll At Projects Tomorrow. (1937, February 21). *Seattle Times*, pp. 1,3.

Yes, Sir, City's Pastime Haven Opens Monday. (1933, Septermber 24). *Seattle Time*, p. 7.

Made in United States
North Haven, CT
17 November 2022

26880340R00157